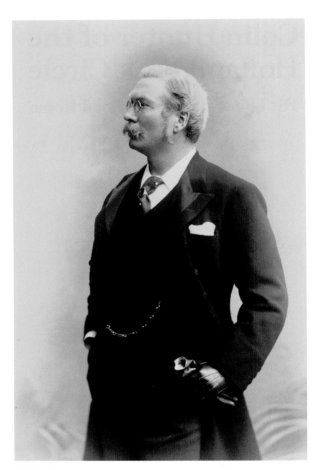

**Colin Hunter**
Photo taken in London
Courtesy of his great granddaughter Marcia Rider (USA)

# Colin Hunter of the Holland Park Circle

His Life and Melbury Road Home

**Godfrey Bell**

UNICORN

*Dedicated to Leigh*

Published in 2018 by
Unicorn, an imprint of Unicorn Publishing Group LLP
5 Newburgh Street
London
W1F 7RG
www.unicornpublishing.org

Text © Godfrey Bell

ISBN 978-1-911604-54-9

10 9 8 7 6 5 4 3 2 1

Designed by Nick Newton Design

Printed in Slovenia

**Notes to the reader**

Dimensions of images are always quoted height × width.

Unless precise dimensions are known, they should be considered only as approximate.

Several paintings are sold through auctioneers as attributed to Colin Hunter. Sometimes attributed is intended to mean "in the style of" but it is definitely not the named artist. In those cases the work has not been included in this book. Sometimes, however, some auctioneers use the term "attributed to" as meaning, "it might be a genuine Hunter but it is not certain". In this case the painting may have been included here – leaving the reader to form their own opinion on its authenticity.

aka = also known as

LL lower left; LR lower right

**Acknowledgements**

The author thanks sincerely the following people for their support in completing this book:

Marie Collett (research)

Leigh Glover (photos and sketches)

David Henderson (photos)

Scott Kuster (great great grandson of Colin Hunter)

Andrew Potter (Royal Academy library)

David Reese (photos)

Kate Rider (great great granddaughter of Colin Hunter)

Marcia Rider (great granddaughter of Colin Hunter)

Cover illustration: detail of **Harbour Scene**, undated (see page 139)

# CONTENTS

# PREFACE

This book does not pretend or aspire to offer a current professional art critic's view of Colin Hunter's works or talent. An in-depth analysis and critique of Colin Hunter's style and achievements is deliberately avoided as the author is neither an artist nor art critic himself and has not sought a present-day art critic's opinion on any of Hunter's works illustrated here. However, historic reviews of his works have been included.

The author is merely an interested amateur who has enjoyed researching Colin Hunter. The book offers an extensive collection of the artist's works that range from his early painting days (1860s) to the last months of his life (1904). Many of his paintings were highly acclaimed and Hunter exhibited regularly in the Royal Academy in London. Several works were purchased by public or national galleries as far afield as Australia and South Africa. One is in Tate Britain. Undoubtedly, Hunter had some less successful paintings which may not be as highly acclaimed as others, but the astute observer will surely spot his finest – and highly acclaimed – art amongst a life time of works collated here.

Predominantly Hunter painted seascapes and scenes of fisher folk at work in Scotland's west coast villages. But he also did landscapes, particularly in his younger years, and the occasional portrait.

Periodically Hunter's art is still offered for sale around the world – many works through the prestigious auction houses such as Sotheby's, Christie's, Bonhams or Lyon & Turnbull.

Hunter was a prolific painter. This book has included works for which the author has been able to source good images suitable for publication. There are hundreds of others around the world, but despite efforts to track down their owners or locations, or to obtain decent photos of the works or permission to reproduce them, it falls sadly short of showing off all Hunter's output. This was a disappointment for the author. If you know of a work that is not included here or is not accompanied with a good image, please let the author know if you can help. Please contact him via the publishe, whose details may be found in the frontmatter, with the subject line "Colin Hunter works".

All the collected images are reproduced here to reflect the works of the artist over his life time – but without any attempt to filter them by artistic merit. The reader must form their own opinion as to the rightful place Colin Hunter deserves to hold in the school of Scottish artists and in the larger school of Victorian artists – or indeed in the Holland Park Circle.

Alongside the collection of Hunter's paintings illustrated here, runs the story of Colin Hunter himself and of his family and life at 14 Melbury Road in Kensington, London.

# REVIEWS

## The pathos of toilful lives ...

Aesthetic charm is an indefinite quality and a large number of people found it in Colin Hunter's pictures. The story he portrays in each picture deals chiefly with the life of fisher-folk. It is always graphic, convincing and charged with deep feeling. Even such trivial events as mussel-gathering become interesting because no pictures are so pleasing to the majority of people as those which illustrate some view of nature with which they like to consider themselves familiar, and in many of his pictures Colin Hunter sought to express the universal struggle for existence.

Hunter revealed and epitomised some phase of the arduous lives led by those who gain their living from the sea. The pathos of toilful lives as realised in Hunter's pictures is all the more poignant for the very restraint and dignity with which it is expressed, even in those pictures which make the most direct appeal to the sympathies of the onlooker.

R C Trafford, The Art of Colin Hunter ARA,
*The Windsor Magazine*, 1912

## A glamour seemed to lie upon the land ...

... Hunter possessed a quality of his own in which he was without a rival. This was a perception not so much of the tragic sorrow – as of the immemorial sadness of the sea which washes the Celtic fringes and sunset shores of these islands. His west coast pictures, painted in Scotland or Ireland, are instinct, as perhaps no others have ever been, with that brooding melancholy, half in love with sadness and wholly resigned to fate, which is frequently spoken of as characteristic of Celtic sentiment; a melancholy deeper and more poignant than one finds in the [seascape works of other painters].

It is in pictures such as **Trawlers waiting for darkness** (1873), **Their only harvest** (1879),[1] and **Signs of herring** (1899), where the sentiment of dying light is associated with some incident of sea-toil with its perils and uncertainties, that this pathetic quality is most marked. But in other pictures of the western sea-lochs, seen under conditions of daylight and atmosphere which appealed to the most sensitive side of his nature, it is present also in rich measure.

When Hunter painted a hillside of grey rock and green brae and purple peak, lying under a quiet but rather sullen grey sky, reflected in deeper tones in the still loch across whose unrippled surface sheep were being ferried in a clumsy boat,[2] or a load of bracken,[3] which cast a long quivering shadow of tarnished gold, was being slowly rowed home, a glamour seemed to lie upon the land. One felt the air pregnant with a suggestion of mystery and knew that the silences were unbroken save by the bleat of sheep, the crying of sea birds, or the rare pulsation of distant oars.

From *Scottish Painting, Past and Present, 1620–1908*,
James Lewis Caw, 1908

---

1 If this date is correct it must refer to the second painting entitled Their Only Harvest. The first was painted and exhibited in the Royal Academy in 1878.

2 Probably referring to 'Changing pastures' 1898 (see page 225)

3 Probably referring to 'Bringing home the bracken' 1898 (see page 223)

Hunter's seascapes possess a quality of brooding melancholy, of romantic nostalgia. Rather than choosing sparkling sunlight, he preferred to paint sunsets, evenings or approaching storms.

*The Dictionary of Scottish Painters 1600–1960,*
Paul Harris & Julian Halsby, pub. Canongate

From the first, Hunter's work was vigorous and, for its period, strong and rich in tone.

*Dictionary of National Biography,* 1912

Those who care for Mr Colin Hunter's work, will easily recognise his characteristic sea piece,[4] in which the sea is painted with his masterful knowledge of its ever-varying moods.

From R de Cordova, 'The Panels in Sir Lawrence Alma-Tadema's Hall', Strand Magazine, vol XXIV no. 144, December 1902 p 623, illustrated as A seascape.

Mr Colin Hunter is a powerful and complete painter, by which I mean that he employs all the resources of texture, colour, tone, and handling ...

One of the greatest qualities of Colin Hunter's marines is his ability to render the mood of the sea. In **Lobster Fishers**,[5] for example, the artist superbly defines wind and wave with bold lines and tonal values. Few etchers of Colin Hunter's time could create such a fine composition with such masterful simplicity.

Paul Gilbert Hamerton 'Landscape', 1885

... the sea pictures of Colin Hunter ... who uses the palette-knife to load the lights of the waves till the impasto actually defines the line of the water as if with a solid crest. This tells with tremendous effect while the light falls from above, but with a low or side light falsifies instead of intensifying the truth. But it cannot be denied that this method gives irresistible force to such a picture as Colin Hunter's **Harvest of the Sea** (1872)[6] and to his other pictures **The Leeshore** and **The Village of Aroch** (1878), when seen at the distance and under the light for which they are calculated.

*The Times,* 26th May 1879

At the present moment the most vigorous painter of [the Scottish school of landscape painters] is Mr Colin Hunter.

*The Art Journal,* April 1885

Colin Hunter is one of our painters exceptionally endowed with the precious power of giving life to landscape, and thus quickening even slow imaginations.

*The Times,* 18th May, 1880

An artist's opinion of the work of a fellow artist is always of value. Thus, it was Sir Hubert von Herkomer RA who observed Hunter's power as an etcher. He said of **Shaking the nets**:[7]

"We are not at all surprised to learn that Mr Hunter has already, after but little practice, acquired a strong liking for the etching needle. The artist is already well known as a painter and is one of the strong and vigorous members of the young Scottish school – a school which is not only full of rich promise for the future, but well established now on the only sound principle in art, the combination of hard study from nature with artistic freedom in the use of knowledge and in the disposal of natural materials. It is evident at a glance that Mr Hunter and his most able companions, have observed much and know much whilst, at the same time, they work without any painful slavery to minute detail.

The difference between any one of Mr Hunter's pictures and a photograph is enormous; yet the picture though broad in manner and neglectful of detail except when it is really significant, conveys to us more of the general impression of nature than the photograph. Mr Hunter's knowledge has been acquired in great part out of doors, where he works for six months every year, taking his canvas with him."

Sir Hubert von Herkomer RA, *c.*1888

In Colin Hunter's **Salmon Fishers, Loch Fyne**, ... certainly there is in the whole [Melbourne International Exhibition 1880] no finer specimen of vigorous brushwork, nor any more masterly interpretation of nature.

The Pamphlet Collection of Sir Robert Stout, Vol 41, published Victoria University of Wellington Library, New Zealand

---

4  Probably referring to the 'A sea piece' panel of Alma-Tadema's, aka 'A seascape' or 'Fishing boat off the coast' (see page 179)

5  See page 149

6  See page 94

---

7  See page 240

# INTRODUCTION

## Colin Hunter's works have come home

I had never heard of Colin Hunter when I moved into my flat at 14 Melbury Road in Kensington, London – just across the road from the south-west corner of Holland Park.

The small block of flats was built in 1955 and could not hold a candle to some of its neighbouring fine Victorian homes in Melbury Road. This road, is a lovely tree-lined avenue that sweeps up from Kensington High Street and bends left before joining Abbotsbury Road and Addison Road. It seemed that nearly every house in it boasted a blue plaque announcing who lived there in the later nineteenth-century. Most of the blue plaques named artists.

I was intrigued. Why was our building not of the same grandeur of many of its neighbours? And why did all these artists, several of them famous, live around here? Almost touching our boundary to the south were the gardens of Leighton House, the home (and now a museum) of Lord Leighton who was the President of the Royal Academy of Arts from 1878–96.

And several buildings in the neighbourhood had vast north facing windows – clearly the grand homes and studios of artists. All built, it appeared, in the 1870s and 1880s. All sumptuous. All magnificent.

But not number 14.

My curiosity took me to the library at the town hall of the Royal Borough of Kensington and Chelsea and I discovered that there was once another grand artist's home and studio where I lived. But in the London Blitz in October 1940 a bomb hit it directly. The beautiful building that was destroyed eminently complemented the splendid neighbouring homes that still stand today and are adorned with blue plaques.

Number 14 was the home and studio of Colin Hunter, a Scottish artist who was born in 1841 and died at the age of 63 in 1904. He exhibited almost one hundred works at the Royal Academy every successive year bar one (1869), from 1868–1903 – the year before he died – and he painted many, many more[8] that were not exhibited there.

I wanted to know more about this artist. I started an almost irrational urge to collect his works that periodically came up for auction. Many times, of course, I was outbid. It reached the point that I did not really mind if I liked the painting or not: I just wanted to bring it back to 14 Melbury Road where it had been painted or had been completed in Colin's studio and where it had most certainly been hung before being exhibited or sold.

More than a hundred and twenty years after they had been painted or hung here, these works of Colin Hunter's had come home.

*Godfrey Bell, 14 Melbury Road, 2016*

---

8  The exact number of works that Hunter completed has never been established with any credible reliability.

## Colin Hunter – unfairly faded into obscurity

Colin Hunter was a hugely successful Victorian artist – a painter in oils, water-colourist and engraver/etcher.

He regularly achieved art sales worth more than £100,000 a year (at today's value) and in 1881, a particularly successful year for Hunter, he earned more than £150,000 from his art sales.

He lived in one of the finest homes and studios in the prestigious artists' enclave of Melbury Road and was both neighbour and friend of renowned artists such as Frederick Leighton, G F Watts, Luke Fildes and Marcus Stone.

His paintings were exhibited at the Royal Academy throughout his career with his last works shown in 1903 when he was a sick man and just a year before he died. Moreover, although all art works exhibited at the RA were listed in index catalogues (sometimes more than 2,000 a year particularly in the later Victorian era), anything from only four percent to about ten percent were selected for the illustrated catalogue – *The Royal Academy Pictures*.[9] That being so, Hunter was extremely lucky (or deservedly recognised for his talent) to have three or four paintings regularly selected each year for the *Royal Academy Pictures* book. Many artists did not ever have any of their works illustrated in this esteemed publication.

Hunter's pictures were bought by wealthy art lovers and by galleries, museums and public bodies such as city councils, around the world including South Africa, USA, Australia and of course England and Scotland.

Around one hundred and fifty art works were exhibited in the Royal Academy and Royal Scottish Academy alone. Unsurprisingly as many art works again, were not exhibited publicly at all. The index of art works in this book is long, and even at the risk of one painting having been entitled differently over the years, it cannot be certain that the index is exhaustive as new titles keep cropping up in auction houses – most frequently in the UK, Europe and the USA.

Hunter was well regarded by art book publishers who frequently asked him if they could publish his paintings or etchings. One of his most admired works **The Baiters**, was published in the coveted frontispiece position in *The British Seas*.[10] His sales and purchases by public collections together

---

9  Acknowledgement, Andrew Potter, Royal Academy Library
10  *The British Seas*, W Clark Russell, pub Seeley, London, 1892

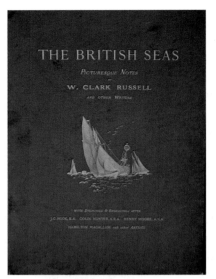

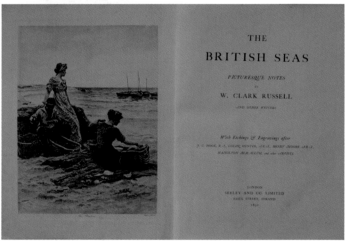

A Hunter was selected for the coveted frontispiece position with **The Baiters** in *The British Seas*.

with the contribution he made to the art world, particularly in relation to his genre of marine and coastal fishing village life in Scotland, were frequently and carefully observed and noted by the national and international press.

Despite Hunter being recognised world-wide as a successful artist, there were some curious contradictions. Not all artists liked his work.

Artists are elected to the Royal Academy based on their perceived ability by a group of their peers. Age is not a factor but even when Hunter was elected an Associate member (ARA) in 1884 at the age of 42, his success caused resentment among some. And elevation to full membership of the Academy eluded him – although it must be observed that he died relatively young at the age of 63. It must have been a disappointment for Hunter not to get the RA credential, but he could still hold his head high in the ranks of Royal Academicians. He was by no means "a minor Associate" or passed over with any implication of indifference. Of course some outstanding artists were extremely young when they were elected ARA. Turner, Landseer and Millais were all 24. Frederick Leighton was ARA at 34 and the Academy's President at 48. But some equally eminent artists were older than Hunter when they were recognised by the Academy with Associate status – Constable was 43 and Henry Moore was 54. And age was no barrier to being awarded full membership. William Mark Fisher who was born in the same year as Hunter, was 78 when he was elected RA.[11] Had Hunter lived longer, he may have yet been elected RA.

RA or not, ARA was a coveted honour in the art world. It won Hunter almost automatic inclusion in artist dictionaries and encyclopaedias, invitations to publish his works – and column inches in newspaper reviews and comment. In light of this it is surprising that there has been no published biography on Colin Hunter until now.

One hundred and fifty years ago Hunter had his first painting accepted in the Royal Academy exhibition and this launched his enormously successful career. Sadly and somewhat puzzlingly, since his death he has faded into obscurity – but only relatively so. He is far from a household name and his paintings can sell in auction houses from very little to a lot. Some at a few hundred pounds and some at many thousands. But none command the mouth-watering sums that a Hunter would fetch in his own heady Melbury Road days.

This is unfair and unjustified. Not even the harshest critic can deny that some of his paintings are quite brilliant. Some are not. But that can be said of any artist.

Colin Hunter is long overdue a revival.

11  Acknowledgement: Andrew Potter, Royal Academy Library

*Chapter 1*

# Colin Hunter is Dead

## Colin Hunter is Dead

So read headlines of newspapers around the world.

For an artist I had never heard of I was surprised to find that when he died in 1904, news of his death was transmitted by electric telegraph across the globe.

In the *New York Times* on 26th September 1904, the headline read "DEATH OF COLIN HUNTER. Well-known painter of sea subjects." It went on to say Colin Hunter was one of the best known English[12] painters of sea subjects of the latter part of the nineteenth century.

In New Zealand in *The Star* on 30 September 1904 the headline read "Colin Hunter, artist, is dead, aged sixty-three."

The *Wanganui Chronicle* (New Zealand) on 1st October 1904: "A London cable announces the death of Colin Hunter, the artist. Deceased was born in 1841. Among his principal pictures were: **Trawler Waiting for Darkness** (RA 1873), **Salmon Stake Nets** (RA 1874), **Their Only Harvest** (RA 1878) [sic], **Waiting for the Homeward Bound** (RA 1883) and **Herring Market at Sea** (RA 1884).

*The Press*, Christchurch, New Zealand 1st October 1904: "The death is announced of Mr Colin Hunter, artist. Colin Hunter, ARA, was born in Glasgow on July 16th 1841 ... He visited Niagara, which he painted from a tiny rock in the middle of the foaming current."

In the *Sydney Evening News* 30th September 1904, the announcement of his death added: **Salmon stake nets** exhibited at the Royal Academy in 1874 and **Drifting** also exhibited at the RA,[13] are now in the Sydney Art Gallery,[14] and **Waiting for the Homeward Bound** exhibited at the Royal Academy in 1882, is in the Adelaide collection.

---

12  That should have read British or Scottish

13  Despite this reference in the *Sydney Evening News*, no painting called 'Drifting' has been found in the Royal Academy records. Unless the painting was re-named at some point. However, it was offered for sale under this name in Australia by auctioneers W A Little in Sydney in 1920. (see page 104)

14  Salmon stake nets (also known as Salmon fishers, Loch Fyne) is no longer in the Sydney Art Gallery. It has since been sold.

Every national and regional paper in the United Kingdom covered the news. And of the international newspapers I searched, it was unusual to find one that did not announce the death of Colin Hunter.

Hunter rubbed shoulders with Frederick Leighton and Luke Fildes, George Frederic Watts, Marcus Stone, Valentine Prinsep, William Burges, Hamo Thornycroft – all of whom were famous Victorian artists, architects or sculptors. They all lived in the elite Holland Park district of west London, many in Melbury Road itself and were Colin Hunter's neighbours and friends.

There is no doubt that Colin Hunter was an eminent Victorian artist but his eminence seems to have diminished over the century since his death. Even so it is worth reflecting that in Hunter's day he sold his works for between £300 and £700. This was a staggering sum in the 1880s. The equivalent today would be between £25,000 and £58,000. And it explains how, despite his "leg up" by marrying well, Colin Hunter became a very successful artist – and a wealthy one – in his own right.

Nearly forty years after he died, his magnificent home and artist's studio at 14 Melbury Road, which was called Lugar Lodge (sometimes Lugar House), was bombed and destroyed in World War II. Had it not been, undoubtedly English Heritage would have ensured his home bore a blue plaque today, as his neighbours' houses do, to mark permanently what was once the home of another great artist of the Melbury Road set. Disappointingly, English Heritage has a strict policy of marking only homes of celebrities that still stand. But the freeholders of 14 Melbury Road came to the rescue and erected a private plaque to rightly indicate the address where the distinguished artist lived and painted and died.

*Chapter 2*

# His family and descendants

## Colin Hunter ARA RI RSW RE
## 1841–1904

Colin Hunter was born in Glasgow, Scotland, on 16th July 1841, son of John Hunter and Ann McArthur. He was the youngest of a family of seven children, with one known brother Alan (or Allan) and three known sisters, Elisabeth, Janet and Catherine. Two other children, one believed to be another son, have not been traced, but the church baptism register clearly records Colin as "the 7th child". When Colin was a boy, the family lived in Helensburgh, Dumbarton, Scotland, where his father was a bookseller and general merchant and sub-postmaster and then postmaster. In later years his father was a factor (estate agent).

In 1873 in Glasgow, at the age of thirty-two, Colin married twenty-one year old Isabella Rattray Young, a descendant of the Dundonald clan which carried something of an aristocratic pedigree.[15] She came from a moneyed family, the second daughter of John Hamilton Young, a surgeon dentist. Isabella was an accomplished pianist.

### Four children

Colin and Isabella had four children but only one child produced a line of descendants although the Hunter family name has not endured through the generations.

All their children were born in Scotland. John Young Hunter[16] was the first son and he became an artist like his father.

Colin and Isabella's second son, Alan (named after his father's brother), died a bachelor at the age of thirty-four. He studied at Cambridge where he was a great athlete picking up a Cambridge "Blue" for the mile. Alan became a rice merchant and died of tuberculosis which he may have contracted in Burma.

Their third child and first daughter was Colina Isabella Hunter. Colina was engaged to be married to a soldier who was killed in the Great War. She died a spinster at the age of ninety-one in Tonbridge, Kent, England.

Colin and Isabella's fourth child and second daughter was Annie Agnes Hunter. She married Charles Alfred Wase but they had no children.

### John Young Hunter

The only living direct-line descendants of Colin Hunter are the descendants of his first son, John Hunter. John married a New Zealander Mary Yerberry Towgood, also an artist, in 1899. They married in the St Barnabas Church in Addison Road – just around the corner from where John lived with his parents in Melbury Road. In 1905 they had a daughter Gabrielle Young Hunter who was born in Newmarket in Suffolk. Colin had died just the year before and so he never met his first and only grandchild. John travelled frequently to the USA where he met a New Yorker, Eve (often recorded as Eva) Hatfield Renz, a woman sixteen years younger than his wife Mary and twelve years younger than John. John's first marriage broke up and he married Eve in America in 1921.

John and Eve settled in Taos, New Mexico, where he lived and painted until he died there in 1955 at the age of eighty. Eve died in 1967 in Albuquerque.

But it was John and his first wife, Mary, who provided Colin Hunter with his only line of descendants still living today.

John and Mary's only child Gabrielle married Edward Kuster, an American impresario, in 1928 in Germany.

They had two children, Colin Edward Kuster and Marcia Gabrielle Kuster. Both Colin and Marcia married and had children and grandchildren all of whom today live in California or New Mexico. Marcia married Frederick Rider and so it is these American family names of Kuster and Rider that can be traced to their Scottish artist ancestor.

---

15  Ref: Edwardian pre-Raphaelites, The Art of John and Mary Young-Hunter, Pyms Gallery 2000

16  To family and friends John was known as Jack.

There are, of course, other family names that can be connected to Colin Hunter (for example by marriage and through great nephew and niece lines). But the Colin Hunter family name has vanished.

## John Young-Hunter, the hyphenated name

At some point, for reasons unknown but probably to identify himself more clearly from his artist father, John hyphenated his middle and family name and became known as John Young-Hunter. However, it must have been after 1903. By then father and son were frequently exhibiting their art works in the Royal Academy together (along with John's first wife, Mary). Annual exhibitions at the Royal Academy became a bit of a family affair. In 1896 John exhibited with his father and the index in the catalogue listed him as Hunter, J Y. But when he exhibited again in the RA the following year he had switched his index entry to read Hunter, J Young. Perhaps this heralded John's intention to change his family name one day to Young-Hunter. It was still Hunter, J Young in 1903, but some time after this you could not find him under H, only under Y for Young-Hunter.

## Hunter's failing health over three years: the death of "the famous Scottish painter"

Colin Hunter died at his home at 14 Melbury Road on 24th September 1904 but apparently he had been ill for some time. According to his death certificate he died of "cerebral softening for some years". Although the term is not used today, the cause of this is usually a stroke. His funeral was held in Helensburgh on 29th September 1904 and he is buried there in his childhood home town.

That the press gave somewhat surprising headlines and detailed coverage of Hunter's illness and death can only be a reflection of the celebrity status the "famous artist" held.

In an extraordinary ("startling statement") article first made in the *Daily News* and then covered by the *Evening Telegraph*, Hunter's care made equally startling headlines.

## Late Colin Hunter's Last Illness Startling Statement

The *Daily News* makes the startling statement regarding the illness and death of Mr Colin Hunter ARA, the famous Scottish painter, that for close upon three years Mr Hunter had suffered from grave internal maladies as well as brain trouble and throughout that long time, while he was slowly and surely dying, he was in the hands of Christian Scientist healers who were absolutely ignorant of all medical science.

When Mr Hunter fell ill so great was the faith of his poor wife in the powers of these people that she at once sent for a healer. Six or seven were tried in succession. Then there came to this country from India a new miracle worker, Charles A. Wase,[17] a young man of thirty years. Mr Wase rapidly acquired the position of principal healer among the Christian Scientists. He was sent for by the family to attend Mr Colin Hunter, and for nearly two years he has been in attendance upon the unhappy and dying artist. Whenever Mr Hunter felt a little better it was believed that he was cured. Only last month Mr Hunter was almost persuaded to move from his own home to the rooms in Bryanston Street in order that he might be nearer to the fount of faith. Mr Wase was in attendance on Friday night beside the death bed.

During the early part of the illness one of the healers happened to be a Christian Scientist who had previously been a medical practitioner. Some three or four months or so ago another medical man was called in. This was Dr John H Clarke of 8 Bolton Street Piccadilly a homeopathic practitioner.

Seen by a representative of the *Daily News* yesterday, Dr Clarke stated: "I am an old friend of the family. I was called in, and I had no objection to the presence of the healer – in fact, I believe he did Mr Hunter good. The last time I saw Mr Hunter was on Thursday last, within thirty-six hours of his death. I am sure I need not say that every care was given him which mortal man can give."

From *The Evening Telegraph*, Thursday September 29, 1904.

## Christian Science An Aristocratic Craze

The pathetic circumstances surrounding the illness and death of Mr Colin Hunter ARA have once again directed public attention to that strange American craze which, says the *Daily News*, incredible as the fact may appear, has become the religion of a large and increasing section of London's aristocracy. And at the same time those circumstances gravely suggest that the pertinent question: Is not this nonsense, impudently-misnamed "Christian Science", becoming a grave public danger?

From *Sheffield Daily Telegraph*, Friday September 30, 1904.

17 Later, in 1913, this Mr Wase married Colin Hunter's youngest child and second daughter, Annie Agnes Hunter.

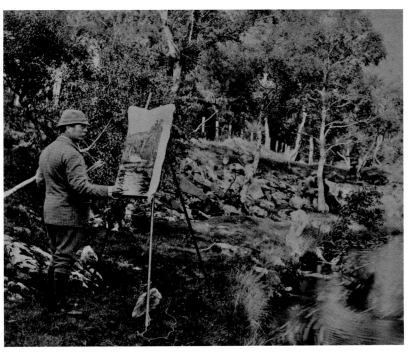

**Colin at his easel** (possibly in the Trossachs, Scotland)
Family photo, courtesy Marcia Rider

# Colin Hunter's descendants

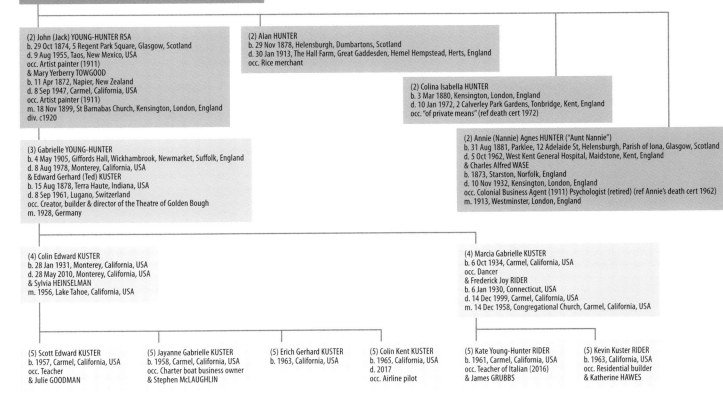

(1) Colin HUNTER ARA RSW RI RE
b. 16 Jul 1841, Glasgow, Scotland
d. 14 Sep 1904, 14 Melbury Road, Kensington, London, England
occ. Artist landscape painter (1861, 1871; Artist painter sculptor (1891 census)
& Isabella Rattray ("Bella") YOUNG
b. 16 May 1852, Glasgow, Scotland
d. 27 Apr 1940, 17 Fairmount Rd, Bexhill, Surrey, England
m. 20 Nov 1873, 5 Regent Park Square, Parish of Govan, Glasgow, Scotland

(2) John (Jack) YOUNG-HUNTER RSA
b. 29 Oct 1874, 5 Regent Park Square, Glasgow, Scotland
d. 9 Aug 1955, Taos, New Mexico, USA
occ. Artist painter (1911)
& Mary Yerberry TOWGOOD
b. 11 Apr 1872, Napier, New Zealand
d. 8 Sep 1947, Carmel, California, USA
occ. Artist painter (1911)
m. 18 Nov 1899, St Barnabas Church, Kensington, London, England
div. c1920

(2) Alan HUNTER
b. 29 Nov 1878, Helensburgh, Dumbartons, Scotland
d. 30 Jan 1913, The Hall Farm, Great Gaddesden, Hemel Hempstead, Herts, England
occ. Rice merchant

(2) Colina Isabella HUNTER
b. 3 Mar 1880, Kensington, London, England
d. 10 Jan 1972, 2 Calverley Park Gardens, Tonbridge, Kent, England
occ. "of private means" (ref death cert 1972)

(3) Gabrielle YOUNG-HUNTER
b. 4 May 1905, Giffords Hall, Wickhambrook, Newmarket, Suffolk, England
d. 8 Aug 1978, Monterey, California, USA
& Edward Gerhard (Ted) KUSTER
b. 15 Aug 1878, Terra Haute, Indiana, USA
d. 8 Sep 1961, Lugano, Switzerland
occ. Creator, builder & director of the Theatre of Golden Bough
m. 1928, Germany

(2) Annie (Nannie) Agnes HUNTER ("Aunt Nannie")
b. 31 Aug 1881, Parklee, 12 Adelaide St, Helensburgh, Parish of Iona, Glasgow, Scotland
d. 5 Oct 1962, West Kent General Hospital, Maidstone, Kent, England
& Charles Alfred WASE
b. 1873, Starston, Norfolk, England
d. 10 Nov 1932, Kensington, London, England
occ. Colonial Business Agent (1911) Psychologist (retired) (ref Annie's death cert 1962)
m. 1913, Westminster, London, England

(4) Colin Edward KUSTER
b. 28 Jan 1931, Monterey, California, USA
d. 28 May 2010, Monterey, California, USA
& Sylvia HEINSELMAN
m. 1956, Lake Tahoe, California, USA

(4) Marcia Gabrielle KUSTER
b. 6 Oct 1934, Carmel, California, USA
occ. Dancer
& Frederick Joy RIDER
b. 6 Jan 1930, Connecticut, USA
d. 14 Dec 1999, Carmel, California, USA
m. 14 Dec 1958, Congregational Church, Carmel, California, USA

(5) Scott Edward KUSTER
b. 1957, Carmel, California, USA
occ. Teacher
& Julie GOODMAN

(5) Jayanne Gabrielle KUSTER
b. 1958, Carmel, California, USA
occ. Charter boat business owner
& Stephen McLAUGHLIN

(5) Erich Gerhard KUSTER
b. 1963, California, USA

(5) Colin Kent KUSTER
b. 1965, California, USA
d. 2017
occ. Airline pilot

(5) Kate Young-Hunter RIDER
b. 1961, Carmel, California, USA
occ. Teacher of Italian (2016)
& James GRUBBS

(5) Kevin Kuster RIDER
b. 1963, California, USA
occ. Residential builder
& Katherine HAWES

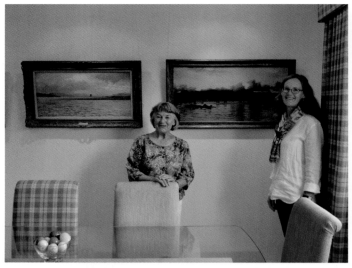

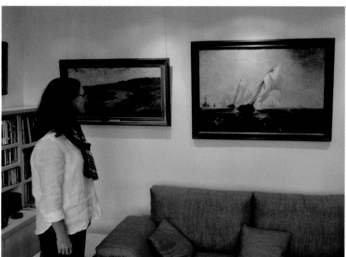

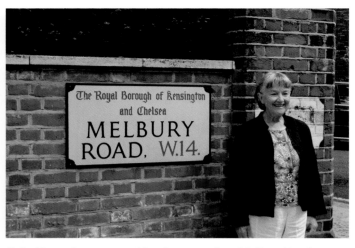

Colin Hunter's great granddaughter, stands in Melbury Road directly opposite her ancestor's home, and outside the home (then) of another Melbury Road Royal Academician artist, Sir Luke Fildes. Hunter and Fildes frequently exhibited works in the RA together.

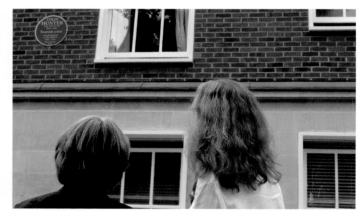

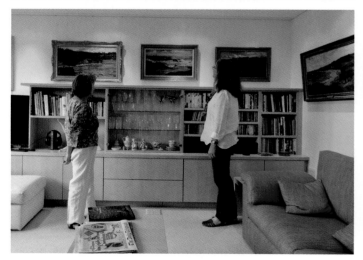

Colin Hunter's great granddaughter Marcia Rider and his great great granddaughter Kate Young-Hunter Rider, both from California, USA, visit 14 Melbury Road and view some of their ancestor's paintings that have "come home". August 2016

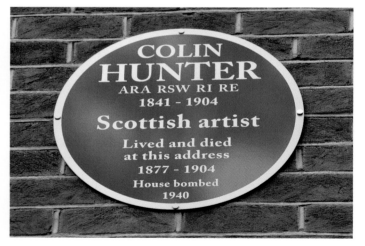

Colin Hunter's descendants stand outside the block of flats at 14 Melbury Road that replaced their ancestor's home that was destroyed in the London Blitz in 1940, 36 years after his death. They are looking at the blue plaque on the building that indicates that Colin Hunter lived, worked and died at this address.

# Photos and Portraits of Colin Hunter

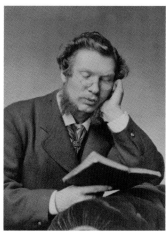

**Colin Hunter early 1870s**
© National Portrait Gallery, London
Photo by Valentine Blanchard
Taken in photographer's studio, 48 Piccadilly, London

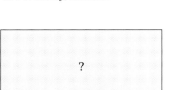

**Pettie Portrait of Hunter**
Another portrait of Colin Hunter was painted by John Pettie RA. It was exhibited in the Royal Academy in 1878. After Colin's death in 1904, his wife Isabella had the portrait (probably at 14 Melbury Road). Despite exhaustive research, an image of this portrait has never been found and Colin's living descendants have no knowledge of it.

> Mr Pettie's chief triumphs this year are, once more, in costumed portraiture; a head of Colin Hunter with a Flemish flat cap and black doublet, giving admirable effect to his ruddy complexion and reddish hair and suggesting a painter of Antwerp who might have known Rubens.
> *The Times*, May 4 1878

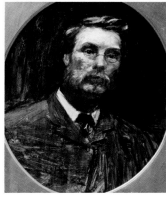

**Colin Hunter self portrait**
1882, oil on canvas, 34.5 × 29.7 cm, 13.6" × 11.7"
Aberdeen Art Gallery & Museums Collections
**Provenance**
Bequeathed to Aberdeen Art Gallery by Alexander Macdonald, 1901 (Interestingly, this was while Colin was still alive, so Hunter must have sold or gifted his self portrait to Macdonald before then).

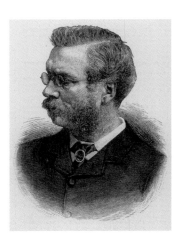

**Colin Hunter ARA 1884**
Engraving. Illustration for *The Illustrated London News*, May 1884
© Private collection / Bridgeman Images

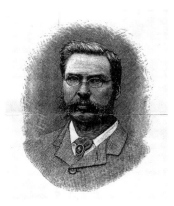

**Colin Hunter before 1885**
Engraved by C Dietrich
Published in *The Art Journal*, April 1885
Courtesy Kate Rider

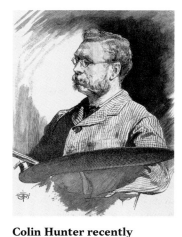

**Colin Hunter recently elected ARA**
from *The Graphic*, 3rd May 1884
Portrait is from a sketch taken from life by Walter Wilson.
Courtesy British Library

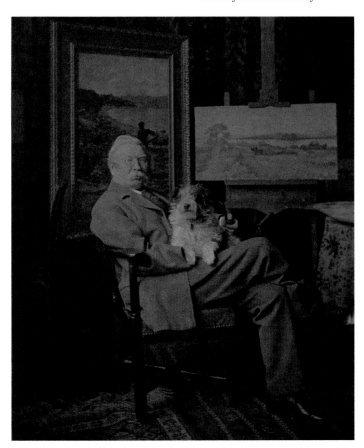

**Colin Hunter at 14 Melbury Road after 1895**
Halftone postcard print
© National Portrait Gallery, London
Published by Richard Williams Thomas; Charles William Faulkner & Co ('C.W.F. & co')
Directly behind Hunter is one of his paintings which was exhibited in the New Gallery in 1895. **Digging Potatoes**. See page 205

*Chapter 3*
# Chronology

## A Scottish, Victorian oil painter, water-colourist and engraver/etcher

### Time line

| | | |
|---|---|---|
| 1841 16th July | | Born in Glasgow, Scotland |
| 1841 22nd Aug | | Baptised in Glasgow ("7th child of John and Ann") |
| 1844 | c.3yo | Moved to Helensburgh due to father's failing health |
| 1851 census | 9yo | Clyde Street, Kidston's Land, Helensburgh, Dumbarton |
| 1861 census | 19yo | Princes Street, Helensburgh, Dumbarton |
| 1863 | 22yo | 28 Barony Street, Edinburgh |
| 1866 | 25yo | 59 St Vincent Street, Glasgow |
| 1868 | 27yo | 12 St Andrew's Square, Edinburgh |
| 1868 | 27y | First picture hung in the RA – **Taking in the nets** |
| 1871 census | 29yo | 54 George Square, Glasgow |
| c.1871 | 30yo | 2 Langham Place, Chiswick, London |
| 1873 | 32yo | First major success **Trawlers Waiting for Darkness** |
| 1873 | 32yo | Parklee, Helensburgh, (ref: his marriage certificate) |
| 1873 20th Nov | 32yo | Married Isabella Young, in Glasgow |
| 1874 | 33yo | 22 Park Village East, London |
| 1874 29th Oct | 33yo | 61 Carlton Hill, St John's Wood, London |
| 1876–1904 | 36–63yo | 14 Melbury Road, Kensington, London |
| 1878 29th Nov | 37yo | His son Alan was born at 12 Adelaide Street, Helensburgh |
| 1878 13th Dec | 37yo | His father died at 12 Adelaide Street, Helensburgh |
| 1879 | 37yo | **Their Only Harvest** purchased by Chantrey Bequest |
| 1879 | 38yo | Elected RSW |
| 1881 | 40yo | Elected RE |
| 1882 | 43yo | Elected RI |
| 1883 | 42yo | Elected ROI |
| 1884 | 43yo | Elected ARA |
| 1887 | 46yo | Resigned RE |
| 1891 census | 49yo | 14 Melbury Road, London |
| 1901 census | 59yo | 14 Melbury Road, London |
| 1904 24th Sep | 63yo | Died at 14 Melbury Road, buried in Helensburgh |

## Memberships

RSW (Royal Scottish Society of Painters in Water Colours)

RE (Royal Society of Painter-Etchers and Engravers)(today called Royal Society of Painter-Printmakers)

RI (Royal Institute of Painters in Water Colours)

ROI (Royal Institute of Oil Painters)

ARA (Associate of the Royal Academy)

*Membership notes:*

**RSA (Royal Scottish Academy)**

Hunter was not elected as RSA even though he exhibited a large number of works in the RSA Annual Exhibitions. But when he moved to London about 1871 he was only about thirty years old – too young to be considered for RSA membership. Also, at that time, artists were not eligible for nomination if they were not practicing in Scotland.[18]

**RE**

The Royal Society of Painter-Etchers and Engravers (RE) was established in London in 1880 and given a Royal Charter in 1888. Colin Hunter was therefore one of its earliest members.

**RI**

The Royal Institute of Painters in Water Colours was founded in 1831.

**ROI**

The Royal Institute of Oil Painters (ROI) was founded in 1882 and was granted royal status by King Edward VII in 1909. Its membership is restricted to about 65 who are elected into the society by existing members.

---

18  Acknowledgement: Sandy Woods, Collections Curator RSA

## First exhibition

The first picture Hunter ever sent to London was "a large landscape" (never identified) exhibited with the British Artists in 1866.

## Exhibited at the Royal Academy

Hunter's career was long and successful. He showed ninety-seven pictures at the Royal Academy. Many were acquired for public collections.

The address shown in brackets is where Hunter lived when he painted the work.

1868   **Taking in the nets** (12 St Andrew's Square, Edinburgh)

1869   *Hunter submitted nothing*

1870   **Taking shelter from a squall**. *A small painting and hung rather high*[19]

1871   **Becalmed** (2 Langham Place, London) *A small painting and hung rather high*[20]

1872   *First works to attract the attention of both artists and the general public:*[21]
  **Herring trawlers** (See page 94)
  **Sailing free**

1873   **Trawlers waiting for darkness** (Burlington House)
  **Three fishers**
  **After a gale**

1874   **Coming ashore**
  **Salmon stake nets** (seemingly later re-named **The salmon fishers, Loch Fyne**
  **With wind and tide** (61 Carlton Hill)

1875   **Hours of rest**[22]
  **Give way**

1876   **Daybreak, digging for bait**[23]
  **Kelp burning** (Lugar House, 14 Melbury Road)

1877   **A stitch in time**
  **Daily bread**

1878   **Ebbing tide** painted 1877
  **Store for the cabin** (14 Melbury Road)

1879   **The lee shore**
  **Their only harvest** (Tate Britain)
  **The village of Aroch**

1880   **Silver of the sea** (Iziko Museum of South Africa)
  **Iona shore**

1881   **In the gloaming**
  **Mussel gatherers**

1882   **The sea-gull's toilette**
  **Low tide**
  **Waiting for the homeward bound**

1883   **A pebbled shore**

1884   (Elected ARA)
  **Summer twilight**
  **"As they roar on the shore"**
  **The first arrivals**
  **The herring market at sea** (Manchester Art Gallery)

1885   **The rapids of Niagara above the Falls** (aka **The Horse Shoe Falls**)
  **In search of sea drift**[24]
  **Salmon fishers**
  **The girl who baits the line**[25] (Dundee Art Gallery)

1886   **Summer fishing**
  **The woman's part**
  **"Caller Haddies"**[26]
  **"When the boats come in"**[27]
  **Miss Alice Lyall**

1887   **Their share of the toil**
  **The luck of the creel**
  **Beneath blue skies**

1888   **The meeting of the waters**
  **Fishers of the North Sea**
  **Lac du Bourget, Savoie**
  **Drying fish**

1889   **Baiters**
  **Oscar Leslie Stephen** (1819–98)
  **The morning breeze**
  **The little haven**

1890   **The hills of Morven**
  **Master Gordon Ness**

---

19   *The Art Journal*, April 1885

20   *The Art Journal*, April 1885

21   *The Art Journal*, April 1885

22   Hunter sold both of these paintings (Give Way and Hours of Rest) in the same year they were exhibited, to the same buyer, E F White, for £800 (today's value £64,500)

23   Sold same year (1876) to E F White again

24   Hunter sold this in the same year to Ian Laing for £500 (today's value £45,000)

25   Subsequently renamed, probably by Dundee City Council, to whom it was later gifted, as *The lass that baits the line*

26   Hunter sold this in same year to Ian (?) Reid for £200 (today's value £18,000). "Caller Haddies" was Scots dialect for a street seller calling out "Fresh haddock" or "Fresh herring".

27   Hunter sold this in the same year for £350 (today's value £31,800)

1891    **Iona**
**Iona crofters**
**Oban regatta 1890**
**By the deep sea**

1892    **The burial of the MacDonalds of Glencoe on St Munda Island, Loch Leven 1692**
**Scourie Bay**

1893    **Waiting for low tide**
**Lobster fishers**
**Ireland**
**Reflections**

1894    **Scalloway Castle, Shetland**
**Wet sands**
**Wintry weather**
**The gleanings of the herring harvest**

1895    **Good night to Skye** (Glasgow Art Gallery)
**Tanning the herring nets**
**Salmon fishing on the Dee, Kirkcudbright – the shoulder net**

1896    **A natural harbour**
**Haddock boats beating to windward**
**A load of peat**
**The haunts of the Solan goose**

1897    **The day of rest** aka **The Little Ferry**
**Helmsdale**
**The Pool in the Wood, Helmsdale** (Liverpool Gallery)
**Miss Isobel Donaldson**

1898    **Changing pasture**
**The hills of Skye from Loch Duich**
**Bringing home the bracken**
**Still evening**

1899    **Signs of herring**
**Kyles of Skye**

1900    **Anchored to the nets**
**London from the Tower Bridge**

1901    **Herring fishers off Kildonan Castle, Isle of Arran**

1902    **Voices of the sea**
**Landing haddock**
**The sands of Bettyhill, Sutherlandshire**

1903    **Salmon fishers**
**Garth, Perthshire**
**The "Victory" off Walmer Castle**

## Exhibited at the Royal Scottish Academy (RSA)

It is interesting to note that despite the long list of paintings that were exhibited at the RA, very few of them were also exhibited at the RSA. The RA and the RSA between them exhibited about one hundred and fifty Hunters.

The address where Hunter lived when he painted these works precedes the list of titles.

*Helensburgh*

1861    **The bridge near Ballaggan**
**In Campsie Glen**

1862    **Sea-shore, Cardross**
**Glen Messan**
**A winter bower**
**On the Echaig, near Kilmun**
**White Spout – Tain, Glen Campsie**

1863    **The Clyde near Milton Lockhart**
**"The Tornan Jerk" in Arran**

*28 Barony St, Edinburgh*

1864    **Waiting for a nibble**
**The wood cutter's hut**
**Summer day on Loch Eck**
**Early spring**
**On the Gareloch**

1865    **Ben Venue**
**The Brig o'Michael**
**An Arran burn**
**A sheep track – autumn**
**Hawthorn blossom**
**Harvest Ben Venue**
**Gathering nuts**

1866    **Near the Trossachs**
**Achray River, the Trossachs**
**Loch Achray**
**In from the fishing**
**Benan, Loch Katrine**

*59 St Vincent Street, Glasgow*

1867    **The prison windows**
**In the summer time**
**Afternoon**
**The mountain stream**

1868    **Gathering bracken**
**Cloud and sunshine**
**L'Isle de Paris**
**Midday on Larbert Loch**

*12 St Andrew's Square, Edinburgh*

1869    **Taking in the nets**
        **Glen Falloch**
        **The watch disturbed**
        **A moorland loch**
        **Autumn in Glen Falloch**

1870    **Leaving a lee shore**
        **On Loch Fyne**
        **Fern gatherers returning home**
        **Trawlers waiting for darkness**
        **Mending the nets**
        **"Birkie"** (lent by T A Hill Esq)

1871    **Midday on Loch Gare**
        **Shaking the herring nets**

1872    **A shelter from the weather**
        **The end of autumn**
        **Becalmed**
        **Boys fishing**
        **"There is a rapture on the lonely shore There is society where none intrudes"** (Byron)

*22 Park Village East, London*

1874    **Trawlers waiting for darkness**

*Helensburgh*

1878    **Fisher life**

*14 Melbury Road, Kensington, London*

1881    **Silver of the sea** (lent by Donald Currie, MP)
1882    **In the gloaming** (lent by Alex Dennistoun of Golfhill, Glasgow)

*After his death*

1905    **Fishers of the North Sea** (lent by F C Stop, Surrey)
1926    **Lobster fishers** (lent by S E Thompson, Belfast) (catalogue number 209)

## Exhibitions and art galleries[28]

(number of works exhibited indicated where known)

Hunter exhibited widely in the UK but also in France, Austria, Germany, USA and Australia

Agnew & Sons Gallery (1) 1881

Arthur Tooth & Sons Gallery (2)

Berlin Universal Exhibitions 1886, 1891

Birmingham Municipal Art Gallery (1) (Exhibition of living British marine painters 1894) (*Lobster Fishers* 1883)

Dowdeswell Galleries (4)

Dundee Exhibition 1889

Fine Art Exhibition, Victoria Art Galleries,[29] Dundee 1892

Fine Art Society (1) 1894

Glasgow Institute of Fine Arts (31) (Royal Glasgow Institute of Fine Arts)

Grosvenor Gallery (1)

Guildhall, Bath (1) (*The mouth of the Helmsdale* 1898)

Hanover Gallery, First exhibition Society of Painter-Etchers, 1881

London Exhibitions Ltd, Victorian Era Exhibition, Earls Court, London 1897 (*The lass that baits the net* 1885)

London Franco-British Exhibition 1908

Manchester City Art Gallery (10)

Melbourne Exhibition 1880 (*The salmon fishers, Loch Fyne*)

New Gallery (12)

Nottingham City Art Gallery 1909 (*Herring fishers off Kildonan Castle, Isle of Arran*)

Paris 1878, 1889 (silver medal) and 1900 (honourable mention)

Philadelphia, Pennsylvania 1876

Royal Academy (RA) (97)

Royal Institute of Oil Painters (ROI) (3)

Royal Institute of Painters in Water Colours (RI) (1)

Royal Scottish Academy (RSA) (58)

Royal Scottish Society of Painters in Water Colours (RSW) (2)

Royal Society of Artists in Birmingham (4)

---

28   Contributing source: *Benezit Dictionary of British Artists*, Oxford University Press, USA 2012
29   Renamed McManus in 1984 in honour of Maurice McManus, Dundee's Lord Provost 1960-67.

Royal Society of British Artists in London[30] (6)

Royal Society of Painter-Etchers and Engraves (RE) (4)

St Louis, Missouri 1904 (*Voices of the Sea* 1902)

Stirling Fine Art Exhibition 1921

Victoria Art Gallery, Bath 1908, 1909

Vienna 1888

Walker Art Gallery Liverpool (15)

## Public collections (Museum and gallery holdings)[31]

Aberdeen Art Gallery & Museums (*William Leiper 1869, Loch scene, Fishing port, Seascape with a castle, Colin Hunter self portrait*)

Adelaide, National Gallery of South Australia (*Waiting for the Homeward Bound 1882*)

Bath, Victoria Art Gallery (*The mouth of the Helmsdale 1898* on loan to the Guildhall)

Bideford, Devon, Burton Art Gallery and Museum (*Kelp (Mussel?) Gatherers 1881, Summer fishing, Skye 1881*)

Bristol (*London View from Tower Bridge*)[32]

Cape Town, South Africa (*The Silvery Sea*)

Dundee, The Orchar Collection, Dundee Art Galleries and Museums (*Breakers 1870, On the east coast of Scotland 1888, The sands of White Hills 1889, The lass that baits the line 1895*)

Exeter, Royal Albert Memorial Museum (*Beer, Devon*)

Glasgow Gallery (*Good night to Skye 1895, Niagara Rapids 1901, A sea piece: Dawn, Low Tide; Ebbing Tide; Wet day on the Clyde; J Milne Donald; Falls of Niagara*)

Hamburg (*Collecting Shells*)

Leicester, New Walk Museum & Art Gallery, Leicester Arts and Museums Service (*Three fishers 1873*)

Liverpool (*The Pool in the Wood 1897*)

London, City of London Corporation, Guildhall Art Gallery (*A Sea View 1879*)

London, National Army Museum (*Surgeon John Henry Sylvester 1885*)

London, Tate Britain (*Their Only Harvest 1878*)

Manchester Art Gallery (*The Herring Market at Sea 1884*)

Melbourne, National Gallery of Victoria (*Young Woman Baiting the Line*)

Montreal, Canada (*Preparing the Nets*)

Preston (*Signs of Herring 1899*)

San Francisco, Achenbach Foundation, Fine Arts Museums of San Francisco (*Banffshire Harbour, Running Ashore 1880, The Morning Breeze 1890*)

Sydney, Gallery of New South Wales (*Waiting for the tide 1872, The salmon fishers Loch Fyne* (aka *Salmon stake nets*) – sold in 1959, *Drifting*)

## Where did Hunter paint? And his travels …

Hunter's early paintings were naturally of locations near his childhood home of Helensburgh, a popular watering-place of Dumbartonshire, at the mouth of the Gareloch (or Gare Loch), a branch of the Clyde, across which Greenock is about four miles away. It was here that Hunter learned his love of the landscape and of the sea and of his country. Even after he moved to London he spent every summer and autumn back in Scotland – to walk, to sail and to paint. Before he gave up clerical work when he worked in Glasgow from the age of sixteen to twenty with a shipping company, he was occasionally sent on board the firm's ships. He never forgot his attraction to the sea. During these teen years he still longed to paint and every weekend when he went home to his parents, he spent his time at a canvas. Frequently he walked the twenty-four miles from Glasgow to Helensburgh and at some point on the journey he would stop to draw or sketch.

When he was twenty years old in 1861 he gave up clerical work to become an artist, much against the advice of his parents who feared the precariousness of art as a profession. His complete lack of formal art training which his parents could not afford to give him, added to their dismay, but Hunter was determined to prove he could survive. Armed with easel and paint-box, he wandered amid the lochs and hills of the Western Highlands and the Trossachs. He was not unrealistic in his goals and was content to sell his landscapes where he could for a few sovereigns each. But by the end of a year he had made a hundred pounds and even though he had had to live frugally, he justified his ambition to be ranked as a painter.

---

30  1886 James Whistler, openly hostile to Hunter as a rival, voted president of RBA

31  Primary source of list compilation, *Benezit Dictionary of British Artists*, Oxford University Press USA 2012

32  Despite this record, the painting has not been traced in Bristol

The appeal of Hunter's pictures was universal. In general the tales of toil of the fisher-folk which he loved to portray are applicable to any coast or sea, although with an inherent love of his native land, he found them chiefly in Skye, Sutherlandshire, Ross-shire, Arran, The Hebrides, Helmsdale, Scalloway or on his dearly-loved shores of the Clyde. Occasionally he went elsewhere. For example, one of his most famous paintings, now at Tate Britain, **Their only harvest**, was painted in Connemara on the west coast of Ireland.

Many of Hunter's works were undated and untitled – and have been given descriptive and various (and varying) names since he died. But where both the location and date of his paintings are known, these have suggested how widely he travelled. Nevertheless, some guess work and assumptions have still been made.

| | |
|---|---|
| 1861 | Helensburgh |
| 1863 | Gare Loch, Trossachs National Park |
| 1873 | West coast of Scotland |
| 1874 | Loch Fyne, Firth of Clyde; Carradale, east side of Kintyre overlooking Isle of Arran |
| 1876 | New York; Wick, north east Scotland; West coast of Scotland |
| 1877 | Connemara, Ireland[33] |
| 1878 | The Clyde |
| 1879 | West coast of Scotland; Coldingham, Berwickshire; Devon; Iona |
| 1880 | Loch Fyne, Firth of Clyde; The Clyde; Greenock (on the banks of the Clyde River) |
| 1881 | Eastern Mediterranean;[34] Skye; Isle of Man (Port St Mary) |
| 1882 | The Clyde; Lamlash, Isle of Arran |
| 1883 | Cornwall |
| 1884 | Niagara Falls USA & Canada[35] (in the autumn); Cornwall; Loch Fyne, Firth of Clyde |
| 1885 | Coldingham |
| 1887 | Coldingham; Switzerland |
| 1888 | East coast of Scotland; White Hills, Aberdeenshire; France |
| 1889 | White Hills, Aberdeenshire; Oban |
| 1890 | Niagara Falls, USA;[36] Oban; Western Isles |
| 1891 | Oban; Iona |
| 1891 and/or 1894 | Devon |
| 1892 | Sutherland; Helmsdale |
| 1893 | Ireland |
| 1894 | Connemara Bay, Ireland; Shetland |
| 1895 | Skye; The Dee, Kirkcudbright |
| 1896 | The Firth of Forth |
| 1897 | Helmsdale, north east coast; Isle of Arran |
| 1898 | Helmsdale; Loch Duich, north west Highlands, overlooking Skye; Kyleakin Skye |
| 1899 | Skye; Pittenweem, Fifeshire |
| 1900 | London |
| 1902 | Sutherland |
| 1903 | Garth, Perthshire |

## Hunter's stomping ground ...

Despite Hunter's travels around Scotland, south west England, Ireland, Europe and the USA, it was the west coast of Scotland where he painted mostly.

In *The British Seas*, 1892, a short description of one of Hunter's favourite areas, mentions several of the locations of Hunter's works. (Below, such places are in bold.)

> ... we sail almost due south till **Arran** and then turn in a westerly direction ... so we reach in due time the 'Mull', or headland, which terminates the remarkable **peninsula of Cantyre**. As we round this we experience the full force of the **Atlantic** waves ... for there is nothing here between us and the Labrador coast [of Canada] ... and some dozen miles to the south-west, [we can see] the dim outlines of the **Irish coast**.
>
> No other land is in view, for it is only on the clearest day that we can possibly catch a glimpse of **Islay** and this hardly from **the Mull** itself. But if we land and climb the Knockmoss (the

---

33  *The Art Journal*, April 1885

34  *The Art Journal*, London, July 1881 refers to Hunter's "recent visit" to the Eastern Mediterranean

35  It was announced in the *Derby Mercury*, 18 June 1884: "Mr Hunter is about to go to America, some of whose fearful and wonderful sights, including Niagara, he intends to bring back with him in sketch book or on canvas."

36  It is uncertain whether Hunter visited Niagara Falls again, or painted or enlarged an earlier study of the Falls which he did in 1884.

Hill of the Plain), we can see to the west and north **Islay** and **Jura**, and sometimes even, but this is very rare, the distant **mountains of Mull**, while the **hills of Arran** rise to the east and **Ailsa Craig** is dimly seen on the horizon.

## What did Hunter paint?

### The titles say it all

Always Hunter had loved the sea. He was a skilled yachtsman and angler and the lochs and waterways of his beloved west coast of Scotland were to him as familiar and as convenient as roads. Even though he started painting inland landscapes (particularly in the Trossachs National Park) it was not long before his true interest in the lochs (the Gare Loch was on his doorstep) and the shorelines of the west coast with the working fisher-folk absorbed him completely.

So many of the titles of Hunter's paintings reveal not only his love of the sea, but also his intimate knowledge of fishing, fish, nets and the livelihoods – so often meagre – of the folk he admired and respected.

**Hunter knew his nets:**
Anchored to the nets
Barking the nets[37]
Emptying nets
Hauling in the nets at sunset
Mending the nets
Poling the nets
Salmon stake nets
Shaking the nets
Taking in the nets
Tanning the herring nets
Tarring the nets
The shoulder net (Salmon fishing on the Dee)

**And he knew his fish and understood the waters in which they lived and moved:**
Haddock boats heading to windward
Herring fishing off Kildonan Castle
Herring trawlers
Landing haddock
Lobster fishers
Mussel gatherers
Salmon fishing on the Dee

Salmon stake nets
Signs of herring
The gleanings of the herring market
The herring market at sea
Unloading herring

**And he portrayed a profound understanding and appreciation of the livelihoods of fisher-folk at sea and on the shore:**
A load of peat
After the gale
Atlantic Islands
Baiters
Bringing home the bracken
Caller haddies
Caller herrin'
Carting seaweed
Changing pastures
Daybreak: digging for bait
Drying fish
Early morning fishing fleet leaving port
Fishers of the North Sea
Harvest of the sea
Hauling in the nets at sunset
In search of sea drift
Iona crofters
Ireland
Island harvest
Kelp burning
Landing the catch
Lowering sail
Mending the lobster pot
Mussel gatherers
Normandy mussel gatherers
Reflections
The gleanings of the herring market
The lass that baits the line
The storm
The woman's part
Their only harvest
Their share of the toil
Three fishers
Trawlers waiting for darkness
Waiting for the tide
Wet sands

37 Barking was done by immersing the nets in a hot preservative substance made principally from the bark of the native oak and birch trees.

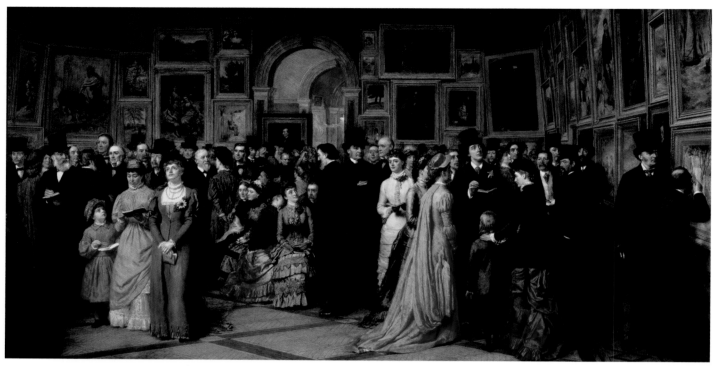

### A Private View at the Royal Academy

1881, oil on canvas, 102 × 192 cm, 40.2" × 75.6"
William Powell Frith (1819–1909)
© Pope Family Trust/Bridgeman Images

As this painting testifies the Royal Academy Exhibitions every year were grand affairs giving credence to the adage that "anybody who was anybody" would have been invited. Invitations to private views included royalty, aristocracy, prime ministers, politicians, writers, poets, clergy, artists, actors, and any prestigious and successful patrons of the arts.

In the painting above are (titles may have been awarded subsequently): Oscar Wilde (playwright and novelist), Baroness Angela Budett-Coutts (philanthropist), Anthony Trollope (novelist), Dame Ellen Terry (stage actress), Lord Frederick Leighton PRA (painter and sculptor), George du Maurier (cartoonist and author), Henry Irving (actor-manager), Sir Henry Thompson 1st Baronet (surgeon and polymath), John Coleridge 1st Baron (lawyer, judge and politician), Sir John Everett Millais 1st Baronet PRA (painter and illustrator), Sir John Tenniel (illustrator, graphic humourist and political cartoonist), Sir Julius Benedict (composer and conductor), Lillie Langtry (actress), Mary Elizabeth Braddon (novelist), Phillip Calderon RA (painter), Robert Browning (poet), Sir Stafford Northcote (Conservative politician), Thomas Huxley (biologist), William Gladstone (the British Prime Minister at this time), William Harcourt (lawyer and journalist).

And as it was a private view with the exhibiting artists in attendance, Colin Hunter is likely to be in the picture somewhere too. In that year, two of his paintings were on the walls.

The exhibition usually opened to the public on the first Monday of May and ran for twelve weeks.

To mark the opening an Annual Dinner was held for the Royal Academicians plus invited guests representing the great and good of the land. In 1868, Hunter's first showing, honoured guests included the Prince of Wales, The Prince of Teck, Prince Edward of Saxe Weimar and the Duke of d'Aumale. However, Hunter would not have been at the dinner that year as he was not yet an elected member.

Typically, visitor numbers to the RA Exhibition were enormous, sometimes exceeding 300,000 in twelve weeks.[38]

38  Acknowledgement Andrew Potter Royal Academy Library

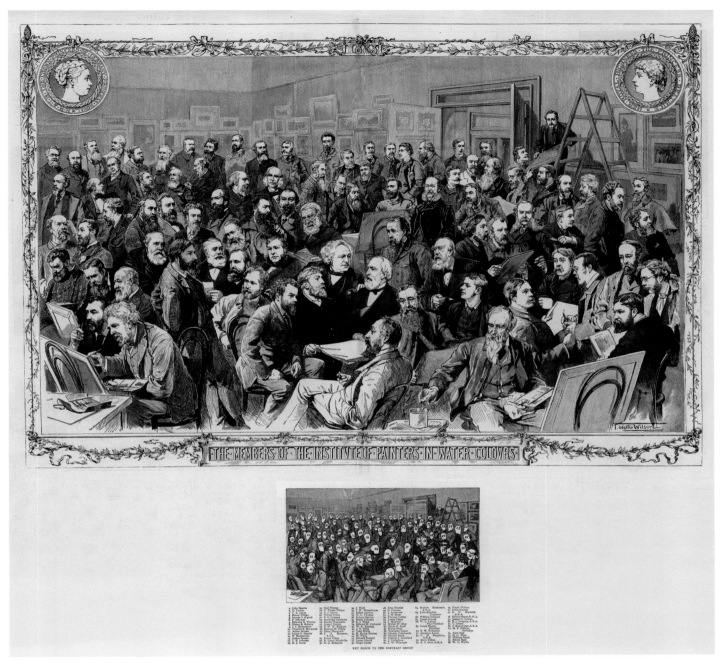

## The Members of the Institute of Painters in Water Colours

Engraving by Thomas Walter Wilson (1851–1903)
Illustration for *The Graphic* 28 April 1883.
© Private Collection. Look and Learn. Illustrated Papers Collection.
Bridgeman Images.

Colin Hunter is on the far right of the picture, second from bottom.
An enlarged cropped image of him is shown here.

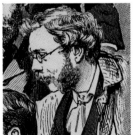

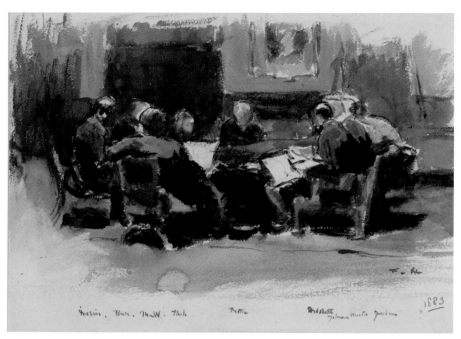

## The Sketch Club

1883, drawing by Frank Holl (1845–81), watercolour, 23 × 32 cm,
9" × 12.5"

© The Trustees of the British Museum

Reproduced with permission

Room interior with nine figures sitting at a table, portrait hanging
on wall beyond.

Portraits of:
1. Philip Richard Morris (English painter) ARA 1836–1902
2. John Burr (Scottish oil and watercolour painter) 1831–93
3. John MacWhirter (Scottish landscape painter) 1839–1911
4. James Clarke Hook (English landscape painter) later RA
   1819–1907
5. John Pettie (Scottish painter) later RA 1839–93
6. Robert Walker Macbeth (Scottish artist) later RA 1848–1910
7. Charles Edward Johnson (English artist) 1832–1913
8. Colin Hunter (Scottish artist) later ARA 1841–1904
9. Peter Graham (Scottish landscape painter) later RA 1836–1921

Inscribed with names of sitters and signed and dated F.H. 1883.

It is interesting that Colin is sharing the table here with John Pettie,
who earlier had painted a portrait of Hunter which was exhibited in
the Royal Academy in 1878. No image of that portrait has ever been
found. See page 19.

This drawing is the result of a Sketch Club evening meeting. The
Sketch Club originally started in Edinburgh in 1855 but many of
its founding members gradually moved south, including Hunter
who introduced the club to London. It was a weekly affair and
each member took their turn to host a dinner followed by two
hours or more in the studio during which they illustrated an agreed
subject. The sketches were then discussed and the evening moved
on to become a more relaxed and sociable event. It was customary
to leave the evening's sketches with the host. Some were later

developed on a larger scale: one was Holl's *Child's Funeral* (1872,
Leeds City Art Gallery).

All the artists of the Sketch Club, most of whom were Royal
Academicians, were good friends of Colin Hunter's and frequently
came to his home at 14 Melbury Road. The evenings were taken
very seriously but with Edwin Abbey (see below) amongst them an
element of jollity and humour was likely to prevail.[39]

Holl was secretary of the club for many years, but after his death in
1888, the club gradually dissolved.

Apart from those in the drawing above and Frank Holl himself,
other members and visitors to 14 Melbury Road included:
Edwin Abbey (1852–1911) American muralist, illustrator and painter
Robert Walker MacBeth RA (1848–1910) Scottish painter, etcher
and watercolourist
Thomas Alexander Graham (1840–1906) Scottish artist
Alfred Parsons RA (1847–1920) English artist, landscape painter
and garden designer
Edwin John Gregory RA (1851–1909) English painter
George Anderson Lawson HRSA (1832–1904) Scottish sculptor
Sir William Quiller Orchardson RA (1832–1910) Scottish portraitist

Clearly Hunter liked to surround himself with Scottish friends and
artists – there were many of them. Some bought his works, some sat
for him, some he sat for.

### Artistic sweeps

Although there is no evidence that the Sketch Club was one of
them, it is a fact that "artistic clubs" of one sort or another held
lotteries before each Royal Academy election. The "sweeps" were
illegal, but private sweeps were growing more popular than ever in
Hunter's day. It would not be surprising if this sketching club held
a sweep.

---

39 *Reviewing the Years*, John Young-Hunter

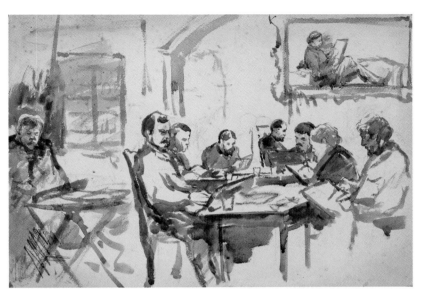

**The Sketchers at 14 Melbury Road**
40.6 × 50.8 cm, 16" × 20"
Image courtesy Marcia Rider

The group is probably sitting in Colin's studio (compare the arch above with the same in the water colour on the right). Possibly Colin Hunter himself in the foreground on far right.

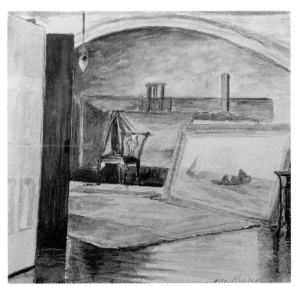

**Colin Hunter's studio at 14 Melbury Road**
By John Young Hunter
After 1888, watercolour on paper
Signed J Y Hunter LR
© Colin Hunter family estate

Resting on the floor, propped against an easel is Colin Hunter's **Fishers of the North Sea** (exhibited at the Royal Academy 1888).

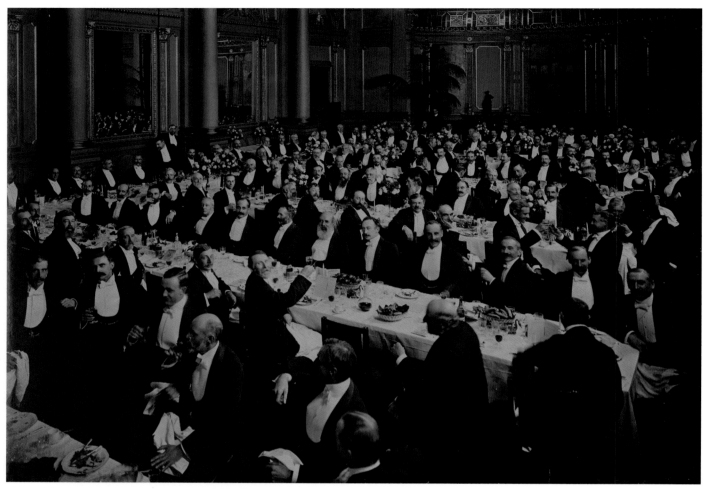

**The Alma-Tadema banquet 4th November 1899**
Photo by Fradelle & Young
© National Portrait Gallery, London

Colin Hunter attended this banquet and is in the photograph.
Also present were Francis Davis Milet (1846–1912), John Singer
Sargent (1856–1925) and Hunter's Melbury Road neighbour Hamo
Thornycroft (1850–1925).

In 1899, Sir Lawrence Alma-Tadema's contribution to the British art
world was acknowledged with a knighthood. This was a celebratory
banquet held in his honour at the Whitehall Rooms, Hotel
Metropole, London. Alma-Tadema is pictured here standing at the
top table to the left. With about 180 guests, almost every significant
late nineteenth-century artist was present. Alma-Tadema remarked
that "without the approval of the brethren the honour would lose
nearly all its attraction", exemplifying the emphasis he placed on his
personal relationships. He was awarded the Order of Merit in 1905.

Alma-Tadema commissioned Hunter to paint one of the panels for
the hall in his home, **A fishing boat off the coast** or **A sea-piece**.
See page 179

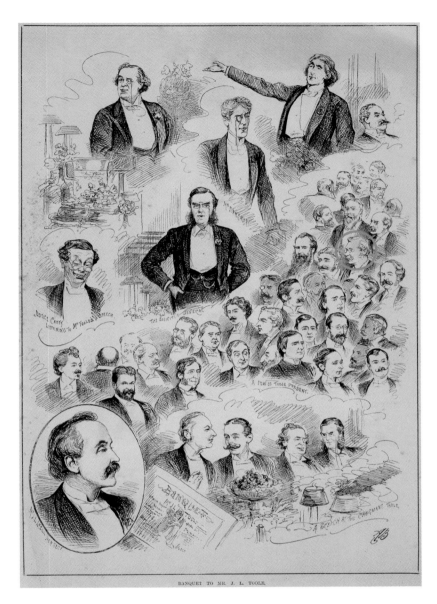

BANQUET TO MR. J. L. TOOLE.

## A banquet for Mr J L Toole

1890

Courtesy of Marcia Rider

John Lawrence Toole (1832–1906) was an eminent English actor, comedian and theatrical producer. He was particularly acclaimed for his roles in farce. He was so famous in his day that he was the first actor to have a West End theatre named after him (Toole's Theatre, formerly The Folly theatre in the Strand, but since demolished).

Toole was invited to act in Melbourne in 1890. Prior to his departure a banquet was given for him.

The event was recorded by this drawing above (artist unknown).

In the right centre is a group of faces under which is written "A few of those present."

Among them is Colin Hunter (circled) and a cropped close-up of him is shown below.

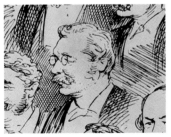

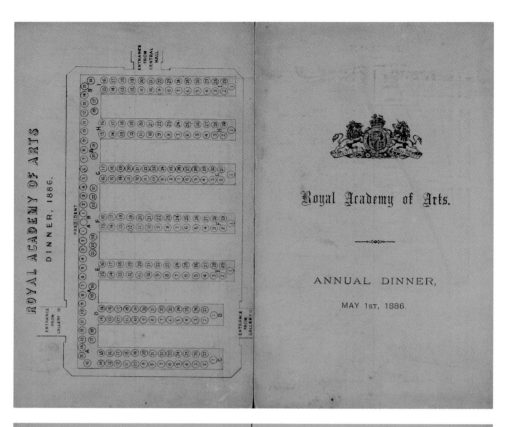

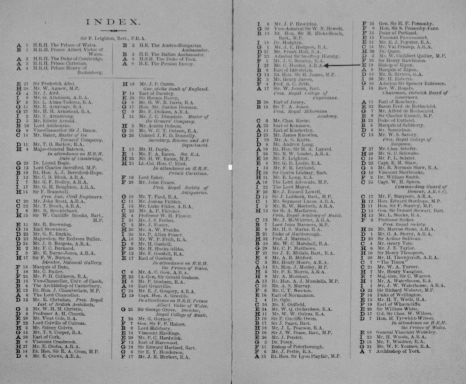

## The Royal Academy of Arts Annual Dinner 1886

Images courtesy Marcia Rider

The RA Annual Dinners were always stately and splendid affairs. Typically they were attended by royalty and here in 1886, was the Prince of Wales together with several other princes and dukes. Then, again typically, there were marquises, major-generals, lords, professors, sirs, colonels, vice-chancellors, right honourables, captains, viscounts, earls, reverends, doctors and archbishops.

And amongst the august company were Colin Hunter (arrowed) and nearly all his friends and neighbours from Melbury Road.

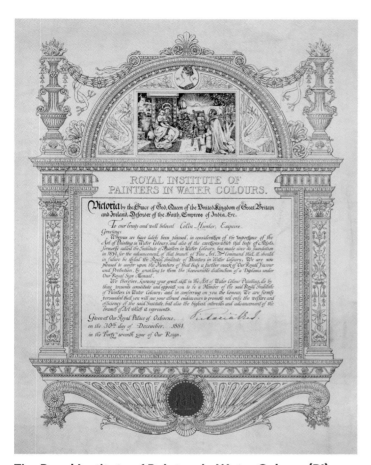

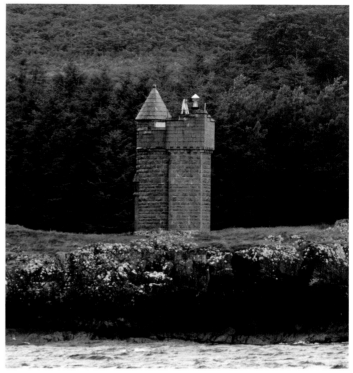

**Sir William Black Memorial Lighthouse, Duart Point Sound, Island of Mull ("Black's Tower")**

Image: William Arthur/Alamy Stock Photo

Sir William Black (1841–98) was a famous Scottish novelist and a good friend of Colin Hunter's. Black made Hunter an executor of his will. He bought three of Hunter's works which he bequeathed to his sister Mrs Morton. He also bequeathed his manuscript of *Sunrise* to Colin. All this was evidence of their close friendship.

When Black died the lighthouse was built as a memorial to him, placed on his favourite spot on Duart Point in the Island of Mull, by a group of his friends.

A Canadian newspaper, *The Ottawa Journal*, on October 23, 1899, reported that "The Highland memorial of the late William Black is, appropriately enough, to be designed by a very old friend of the novelist, in the person of Colin Hunter ARA."

However, this is contradicted by the Mull Historical & Archaeological Society who say it was designed by the Edinburgh architect, Sir William Leiper.

Interestingly, Leiper was also a friend of Hunter's and Hunter painted him (see page 88). Leiper's childhood home town was the same as Hunter's, Helensburgh.

**The Royal Institute of Painters in Water Colours (RI)**

Presented to Colin Hunter at the Royal Palace of Osborne, 30th December 1884

Hunter was elected as a member of the RI in 1882, making his debut as a full member at the opening by His Royal Highness The Prince of Wales at their new gallery in Piccadilly in 1883. Hunter exhibited one painting that year, **Iona Shore**, which was sold to a Mr Lewis Jarvis for £130.[40]

40  Acknowledgement: Rosa Sepple, President RI

*Chapter 4*

# The man and the artist

Colin Hunter's first son and eldest child was John Young Hunter (later to be known as John Young-Hunter) who also became an artist. In John's autobiography, he described his father as "reticent, uncommunicative, forceful in his opinions, caustic and critical of wrong-doing" to such an extent that he magnified his father's condemnations into criminal proportions.[41] Hunter was slow to praise. "Not so bad," from Colin, came to be recognised in the Hunter family as a generous compliment – which one should be immensely grateful to receive.

Perhaps it was not surprising that, to his son at least, it would appear that Hunter would not stand for much nonsense. Hunter was a hard-working man, strong-willed and a focussed, prolific painter. Clearly he had little patience with anyone who did not share his values, ambitions and work ethic.

Colin Hunter was truly a Victorian British artist. He was born just four years after Victoria became Queen and he died just three years after she died. Although he lived amidst many artists of the pre-Raphaelite movement particularly in his later years (his next door neighbour at 16 Melbury Road was William Holman Hunt, acknowledged to be one of the founder members of the Pre-Raphaelites) Hunter's work did not seem to be significantly influenced by it.

He was born in Glasgow on the 16th July 1841, the youngest child in a large family of six or seven children (records vary). His father, John, had different jobs throughout his life, maybe because he was not altogether a well man. At different times John was a bookseller, a general merchant, a sub postmaster and then postmaster, and a factor (Scottish term for estate agent).

Colin's mother was Anne McArthur and she and John married in 1827 in Glasgow.

The family moved to live in the seaside town of Helensburgh, less than an hour's drive (today) northwest of Glasgow, when Colin was still a little boy. Helensburgh lies on the north shore of the Firth of Clyde and the eastern shore of the entrance to the Gareloch (see page 82). This seaside town made a huge impact on Colin. He loved the sea, fishing villages, small fishing boats and fisher folk (see page 91). So much so, that the seashore is what inspired most of Colin's paintings. He rarely painted the open sea. One exception was **The America's Cup** (see page 120) which he painted in New York harbour and the yacht alone was the focus of his work with not a seashore, or any fisher folk, in sight.

On leaving school Colin Hunter began a four year apprenticeship in a shipping office in Glasgow, but he spent his leisure time sketching from nature and in 1861, at the age of twenty, he gave up office work to devote himself to art.

Hunter began his artistic career as a landscape painter. It was only later that his reputation as a seascape painter became truly established. He often painted out of doors with his Scottish artist friend and mentor John Milne Donald (1819–66) (see page 85) and his early work was largely influenced by him with many landscapes of the Trossachs and Loch Lomond areas, not far from where Hunter lived.

Donald died young and throughout the late 1860s Hunter sketched with another Scottish artist friend William McTaggart (1835–1910) in the picturesque fishing village of Tarbert on Loch Fyne on Scotland's west coast. Hunter did several paintings of Loch Fyne (see page 102) including one called **Tarbert Harbour** which, according to his accounts, he sold in 1876 to E.F. White (one of Hunter's enthusiastic collectors). Unfortunately no image of Tarbert Harbour has been found, but frustratingly it may have since been given another name and perhaps we already have it without realising it. However, **Tarbert, Loch Fyne** an etching has been found and it is actually an etching from the original painting called **Wet day on the Clyde** (see page 70).

McTaggart was not only a landscape painter as Donald was, but also a marine painter and this was an enormous catalyst for Hunter's already burgeoning passion for seascapes. Although Hunter moved to Edinburgh twice in the 1860s for brief periods, it is possible that McTaggart

41 *Reviewing the Years*, John Young-Hunter, 1963

and Hunter became firm painting buddies and continued to work together for the next ten or so years.

For a short time, only a few months between 1867 and 1868, Hunter studied in Paris where he worked in the studio of the noted French portrait painter Leon Bonnat (1833–1922). Bonnat went on to become a professor at the Ecole des Beaux Arts and taught several well-known artists. While in Paris, Hunter painted **L'Isle de Paris** which was exhibited in the RSA in 1868. Some observers do not think Hunter was especially influenced by his time with Bonnat, but it is interesting to note that after his return to Scotland in 1868 Hunter submitted his first painting to the Royal Academy – **Taking in the nets**.[42] It was accepted. Perhaps Hunter had indeed learned something of value under Bonnat – whether that was observation, composition, technique or colour or all of them. Having said that, Hunter remained highly individual in his style throughout his life and did not seek to conform to any particular school of art.

Hunter's time under Bonnat was his only formal art training, but he had a natural ability for correct drawing and an instinctive sense of beautiful colour. Composition, too, was a matter of careful consideration to him.[43] Before he began painting the picture was spontaneously right in Hunter's mind. It was rarely lost in translation from mind to brush.

1868 (when he was twenty-seven years old) was a significant year for Hunter with his first submission to the Royal Academy being accepted. Although the Glasgow Institute of Fine Arts already held many pictures of his, this was the first work that attracted the attention of the public and heralded the true launch of his career as a successful and notable artist. From this painting on, people began looking for his works. One reason for his pictures' popularity was that they appealed instantly to the public, needing no presupposed knowledge – all could identify with human endeavour and hard work, all would be touched, even humbled, by the toils of struggling fisher-folk which Colin Hunter alone expressed so poetically in his painting.

Most of Hunter's early work depicts the coastal landscape around Helensburgh, but soon he ventured further afield and painted scenes all around the Scottish coastline – on Iona, Skye (see page 174) and the Shetland Islands. He also painted in Cornwall (see pages 149–152) south west England, and Connemara on the west coast of Ireland (see page 124). He sailed to America at least once where he painted the America's Cup sailing race in New York Harbour (see page 120) and the Niagara Falls (see page 116).

By 1871 he had moved to London where he lived at 2 Langham Place in Chiswick. By 1874 he had moved again to 61 Carlton Hill in St John's Wood. Two years later he had moved into his magnificent, brand new purpose-built artist's home and studio at 14 Melbury Road. He lived here until he died.

**Taking in the nets** had raised the bar for Hunter. He soon became known as one of the leading marine painters of his day and this was confirmed with the huge success of his painting **Trawlers Waiting for Darkness** 1873 (RSA 1874) (see page 103).

Although he lived in London, every summer Hunter returned to Scotland to paint, usually with his family. Sometimes he went to Cornwall – but always to the coast. In the Hebrides, Hunter had a cutter (similar to a sloop) called *Carissima*, in which he cruised up and down the west coast of Scotland. Colin would sail for days on end assisted by a crew of four men including the cook, who handled the boat leaving Colin free to paint. Sometimes Colin was joined by his son John who also painted. The meals were of fresh fish, and occasionally very young lamb provided by the crofters en route. John said he loved the potatoes boiled in sea water.

Colin Hunter had an unceasing affection for Scotland's west coast with its many lochs and islands and it is little wonder that he sailed up and down the coast in his yacht every summer and painted ardently. Inland, too, he found an affinity with its solemn, lonely and bleak landscapes that surrounded the desolate grandeur of the mountains with rocks and heather at their base.

But it was the sea that he loved the most. It was in his blood and it is unsurprising he was a marine painter above everything else. He dabbled with portraits and landscapes. In his life time he produced hundreds of works of art but the vast majority were of the sea, the sea shore or fishing villages and fisher folk. If Colin was not planning to spend his whole summer on the yacht, the family would rent a house on some loch or other, where Colin would still

42  Disappointingly, no image of this first important painting has been found

43  *Reviewing the Years*, John Young-Hunter, 1963

immerse himself in painting every day from early morning to late evening – on the sea shore or on the yacht which he took across the lochs whenever he could. This was no holiday for Hunter. Wherever he went, time away, rather than a holiday, was only used for painting, his work, his love – his passion.

In 1882 he chartered a small steamer and for two months painted on the waves in order to be in direct contact with nature and his subject. It was in the same year he painted **Homeward Bound** (see page 142) and when he painted his first **The rapids of Niagara above the Falls** (see page 118) in 1884 (exhibited in the RA 1885), he was not content with looking at the rapids from a distance, but placed himself and easel on a rock amidst them. Undoubtedly he would have felt the spray of the water on his face as he worked. But being *in* his picture demonstrated the zeal with which Hunter enjoyed his work. There was always a fervour in Hunter's painting and even a quite daunting enthusiasm in the artist's tireless motivation and inspiration for rising to challenges of some of the most difficult subjects, compositions and locations.

Clearly Hunter was an extraordinarily dedicated artist. He would never be dissuaded from painting outdoors by squally weather or difficult terrain or heavy seas. Most artists who paint *en plein air* would naturally prefer a fine day to do so! But Hunter was an austere, serious, even dour Scot with a rigorous self-discipline. With steely resolve when he had an over-powering incentive to create a picture, physical difficulties never interfered. He would stand on a rock by the edge of the sea, his easel and canvas roped down with a seaman's knowledge of how to keep it somewhat stationary in a gale, the canvas folded inwards from both sides, an invention of his own, so that when closed, a shower of rain could not wet the surface. His palette too had to be kept dry so that it also was hinged and could be doubled over – an invention still called the Colin Hunter "dipper".

Bad weather could make painting out-of-doors an anxious and trying experience but Hunter had trained himself to endure hardships. The integrity of his purpose, the overwhelming urge to paint the beauty of his conception, made the discomfort seem of little consequence.[44]

Many of Hunter's paintings depict poor people struggling to make a living on the seashore or in their small boats – fishing for lobsters (see page 150), salmon and herring (see page 153), gathering mussels (see page 166), or baiting lines (see page 162).

In 1883 James Whistler (USA 1834–1903 London), an American artist, feared Colin Hunter as competition in Whistler's ambition to be awarded the *Chevalier de la Legion d'Honneur*. Whistler wanted Hunter eliminated from the running. He wrote to Thomas Waldo Story (Rome 1855–1915 New York), an English/American sculptor and art critic, in Rome. Whistler wrote *"... each year the government intends to give the Croix to one of the foreign exhibitors ... Waldino, you must move everything in heaven and earth to show them that Colin Hunter exists not – and that the amazing one alone should have the bit of red ribbon he requires! Don't dare come away from Paris without it in your trunk for me!"*[45]

In 1884 Hunter was elected an Associate of the Royal Academy. Full membership eluded him but it was never easy to achieve. There had to be a vacancy to start with. When he was 43 years old, a vacancy occurred and there was considerable excitement and speculation as to who would be elected. This was a momentous occasion and all RA members voted. The Arts Club was the rendezvous nearby to which they flocked after the elections and it was crowded in anticipation of the result. Edwin Abbey, writing to his brother in 1884, added this postscript: *"They elected Hunter, who dispersed magnums of fizz all evening to an admiring circle of the Arts Club. I took him home in a hansom."*[46]

However, Hunter's election as an associate member of the Royal Academy on January 31st 1884 was not welcomed by some in London artistic circles who considered others deserved the honour more. For some, Hunter's election aroused jealousy at best or dismay at worst.[47]

*Primary source: The Oxford Dictionary of National Biography*

44  *Reviewing the Years*, John Young-Hunter, 1963

45  (extract edited): The Correspondence of James McNeil Whistler, University of Glasgow
46  *Reviewing the Years*, John Young-Hunter, 1963
47  The Morning News, Belfast 1st Feb 1884

## Who did he sell his art to?

In a page of his accounts, Colin Hunter wrote a "List of owners of pictures in London".

In an extract reproduced here there are some interesting and noteworthy names and addresses including the London Stock Exchange.

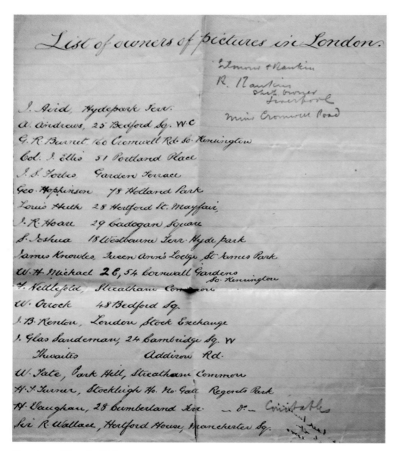

Courtesy Marcia Rider

## Hunter's personal accounts & records of some of the paintings he sold

(Some years missing. Not all account records were found.)
(See Appendix II for record of etchings and prints sold.)

*NIF: No image found*
*TV: Today's value*

| Year | Title (Hunter's own title or abbreviation) | £ | Note |
|------|---------------------------------------------|------|------|
| 1875 | Give Way | £400 | Exhib RA 1875 Sold to EF White |
| | Hours of Rest | £400 | Exhib RA 1875 NIF Sold to EF White |
| | Evening | £200 | NIF Sold to EF White |
| | **1875 sales** | **£1,045** | **TV £84,300** |
| 1876 | Earned Repose | £250 | NIF Sold to EF White |
| | Gathering mussels | £250 | NIF Sold to EF White; (similar title Mussel Gatherers painted 1881) |
| | Tarbert Harbour | £250 | NIF Sold to EF White |
| | Digging bait | £250 | NIF Exhib RA 1876 as Daybreak, Digging for bait Sold to EF White |
| | Setting sail | £120 | NIF |
| | Venice | £60 | NIF |
| | **1876 sales** | **£1,180** | **TV £95,100** |
| 78–79 | In search of sea drift | £150 | Exhib RA 1885 (unusually exhib several years after painted) |
| | The village of Aroch | £300 | Exhib RA 1879 Sold to James Fletcher; NIF |
| | Their Only Harvest | £735 | Sold to the Royal Academy |
| | The Naturalist | £150 | |
| | Chiswick | £150 | Hunter lived in Chiswick in 1871 |
| | **1878–79 Sales** | **£1,370** | **TV £119,000** |
| 79–80 | Tarbert Quay | £75 | (likely to be a print of an etching) |
| | Iona | £150 | |
| | Silver of the Sea | £750 | Exhib RA 1880 Sold to Donald Currie MP |
| | Iona shore | £525 | Exhib RA 1880 NIF |
| | Bowling | £60 | |
| | **1879–80 Sales** | **£1,560** | **TV £135,500** |
| 80–81 | Gareloch | £750 | Sold to Alex Dennistoun |
| | Mussel Gatherers | £800 | Sold to Schwabe |
| | Lower sail | £210 | Sold to John Aitken (aka Lowering Sail) |
| | **1880–81 Sales** | **£1,760** | **TV £149,500** |
| 81–82 | The Island Harvest | £700 | |
| | The sand pit | £100 | |
| | Low tide at Port St Mary | £100 | |
| | Boats with nets & seagulls | £100 | |
| | Gravel shore at Port St Mary | £160 | |
| | **1881–82 Sales** | **£1,160** | **TV £97,500** |

| Year | Title (Hunter's own title or abbreviation) | £ | Note |
|---|---|---|---|
| 82–83 | A pebbled shore | £1,000 | Exhib RA 1883. The highest price painting Hunter ever sold. NIF |
| | Lobster fishers | £500 | Exhib RA 1883, possibly sold to S E Thompon, Belfast ? |
| | Iona shore | £130 | Water colour. Sold at the RI Exhibition 1883 to Mr Lewis Jarvis |
| | **1882–83 Sales** | **£1,530** | **TV £128,500** |
| 83–84 | The Herring Market at sea | £600 | Exhib RA 1884 |
| | The first arrivals | £200 | Sold to Agnews |
| | Summer twilight | £300 | Exhib RA 1884l Sold to Templeton; NIF |
| | Running water | £220 | Sold to Moore; NIF |
| | Unloading herring | £200 | Sold to Templeton; NIF |
| | **1883–84 sales** | **£1,520** | **TV £132,500** |
| 84–85 | Waiting for the Homeward Bound | £600 | Sold to the Adelaide Government, Australia |
| | Salmon Fishers | £500 | Sold to James Laing |
| | In search of sea drifts | £200 | |
| | The girl who baits the line | £250 | |
| | **1884–85 sales** | **£1,550** | **TV £90,873** |
| 85–86 | Summer fishing | £250 | Sold to Fairfax Rhodes |
| | Caller Haddies | £200 | Sold to Ian Reid |
| | When the boats come in | £350 | Sold to I? F Fletcher |
| | The Horseshoe Falls | £200 | |
| | **1885–86 sales** | **£1,000** | **TV £135,290** |
| 88–89 | The morning breeze | £500 | Exhib RA 1889 Sold to W J Wyllie |
| | The woman's bait | £700 | Exhib RA 1889 as Baiters S old to Watson |
| | Oscar Leslie Stephen[48] | £200 | Exhib RA 1889 |
| | ? | £50 | Sold to Tooth (Gallery) |
| | ? | £50 | Sold to J S Marten |
| | **1888–89 sales** | **£1,550** | **TV £139, 250** |
| 89–90 | Master Gordon Ness | £200 | Exhib RA 1890 (portrait) |
| | Sands of White Hills | £380 | Dundee Exhibition |
| | Etching for portfolio | £25 | |
| | Morven Hills | £525 | Exhib RA 1890 Sold to P Ness |
| | **1889–90 sales** | **£1,130** | **TV £101,500** |
| 90–91 | Loch Glendhu | £200 | Sold to Murray |
| | Iona shore | £200 | Possibly an etching sale |
| | Iona Crofters | £235 | Sold to McLean |
| | Rough sea | £200 | Sold to Shewlis ? Johnson |
| | Drying fish | £75 | Painting exhib RA 1888; This possibly etching sold to J Watson |
| | **1890–91 sales** | **£910** | **TV £80,800** |

---

48  Oscar Leslie Stephen 1819–1898

| Year | Title (Hunter's own title or abbreviation) | £ | Note |
|---|---|---|---|
| 91–92 | Scourie Bay | £250 | Exhib RA 1892; Sold to Stuart Hall |
| | The water carrier | £250 | Sold to Stuart Hall |
| | Sea Piece | £200 | Sold to John Keiller |
| | Oban | £250 | Sold to Knight |
| | **1891–92 sales** | **£950** | **TV £84,400** |
| 92–93 | Ireland | £630 | Exhib RA 1893 Sold to Wm A Donaldson |
| | Atlantic Islands | £150 | Sold to Dyce Brown |
| | Burial of the McDonalds | £487 | Exhib RA 1892 Sold to James Reid |
| | **1892–1893 sales** | **£1,287** | **TV £115,600** |
| 93–94 | Wintry weather | £250 | Exhib RA 1894 Sold to Sir Julian Goldsmid |
| | Gleanings of the herring harvest | £700 | Exhib RA 1894 Sold to Oyston |
| | ? | £125 | Sold to James Thompson |
| | **1893–94 sales** | **£1,075** | **TV £97,600** |
| 95–96 | Good night to Skye | £500 | Exhib RA 1895 Sold to Glasgow Corporation |
| | Fishers of the North Sea | £500 | Exhib RA 1888; possibly sold to F C Stop (Surrey) |
| | Irish Coast | £100 | Sold to Campbell |
| | ? [small picture] | £30 | Sold to Ness |
| | **1895–96 sales** | **£1,130** | **TV £105,000** |
| 96–97 | Kildonan | £210 | 40" × 28" Sold to H E M Davies |
| | The pool in the wood | £400 | Exhib RA 1897 Sold to Drew |
| | Waiting for the tide | £52 | Sold to Drew; probably an etching |
| | Helmsdale | £157 | 40" × 22" Exhib RA 1897 Sold to Adler |
| | A natural harbour | £150 | Exhib RA 1896 |
| | **1896–97 sales** | **£970** | **TV £88,000** |
| 98–99 | Helmsdale/Highland Waterfall? 36" × 21" | £200 | Aka Highland Waterfall? Sold to Miss Redcliffe |
| | Kyleakin, Skye 60 × 36 cm | £315 | Sold to Vivian |
| | Bringing home the bracken | £300 | Exhib RA 1898 |
| | London Bridge | £150 | |
| | Kinfauns Castle (Scotland) | £150 | |
| | **1898–99 sales** | **£1,115** | **TV £100,100** |
| 99–00 | Kildonan Castle | £300 | Exhib RA 1901 Sold to Donald Currie MP |
| | Loch Fyne | £231 | Sold to Henry Bell |
| | Beating to windward | £100 | Exhib RA 1896 Sold to McKinnon, Australia |
| | Kyles of Skye | £135 | Exhib RA 1899 Sold to Dumfries Council |
| | **1899–1900 sales** | **£866** | **TV £74,400** |

*Chapter 5*

# His London home, 14 Melbury Road, and family pictures

Colin Hunter was a member of a group of artists which became known as The Melbury Road Set and also as The Holland Park Circle. His home and studio, Lugar Lodge (often referred to also as Lugar House), was as magnificent as any other in the prestigious avenue of Melbury Road artists – all of which boasted wealth and success.

In 1896 more than twenty artists (including Royal Academicians) lived in Melbury Road and the adjacent Holland Park Road.

## The leading artists of the Holland Park Circle

All these artists lived in Melbury Road or Holland Park Road, and were Hunter's contemporaries, neighbours and friends

**Lord Frederic Leighton PRA**[49]
1830–96 (2 Holland Park Road) (now number 12)

**Valentine Prinsep RA**
1838–1904 (1 Holland Park Road)

**George Frederic Watts OM**
1817–1904 (6 Melbury Road)

**Sir Luke Fildes RA**
1841–1918 (11 Melbury Road) (now number 31)

**Marcus Stone RA**
1840-1921 (8 Melbury Road)

**Sir Hamo Thornycroft RA**
1850–1925 (2 & 4 Melbury Road)

**Colin Hunter ARA**
1841–1904 (14 Melbury Road)

**William Holman Hunt ARA OM**
1827–1910 (his last years at 16 Melbury Road)

**Sir James Jebusa Shannon RA**
1862–1923 (3 Holland Park Road)[50]

**William Burges**
1827–81 (9 Melbury Road) (now number 29)

---

49  PRA President of the Royal Academy; RA Royal Academician; ARA Associate Royal Academician; OM Order of Merit

50  Shannon's was the last of the studio houses to be built along Melbury Road and Holland Park Road.

## The Melbury Road Set

Those artists of the Holland Park Circle (above) who actually lived in Melbury Road were also known as The Melbury Road Set.

# The Melbury Road Set Important Aesthetic and Architectural Monuments

Most of the building plots in Melbury Road, built in the second half of the nineteenth century in Holland Park in west London, were bought by a group of artists who made this area the centre of a new aesthetic elite. They moved in fashionable society, and in keeping with their social and financial position – artists were never held in higher esteem than in the closing decades of the nineteenth century – they built themselves expensive and modish studio houses which stood out from the common run of suburban architecture around them. The fantastic interior of Leighton House, built by Lord Leighton, with its Arab Hall decorated with tiles he had brought back from his travels and cooled by an indoor pool, and Tower House, designed as a Gothic castle by the architect Wiliam Burges for himself, stand out as important aesthetic and architectural monuments of the period.

From The Roland Collection website (2005)

Holland Park and all the roads around it in Kensington, was always known as an affluent and fashionable area. When Melbury Road was created out of a corner of the Holland Estate, it was not surprising that it too attracted only the well to do. Even from the start, the homes that were built on the sold-off land were designed to be large and imposing – and expensive.

The Holland Estate was the forerunner of today's Holland Park. It had more than two hundred acres surrounding Holland House when it was bought in 1768 by Henry Fox, first Baron Holland. But before this the area had formed part of an even larger estate attached to Holland House, consisting of nearly five hundred acres and extended southwards, almost to Fulham Road.

In 1770 a survey of Holland Estate's 237 acres, showed very few buildings of any note. Apart from Holland House, there was a building called Little Holland House which stood in a small corner of the grounds, located approximately on the site now known as 14 Melbury Road. This was the dower house of Holland House. However, to avoid confusion, it is worth noting that there were two Little Holland Houses. The original was demolished in 1875 to make way for the newly created Melbury Road. George Frederic Watts built a new home and studio in Melbury Road (no. 6) and called it Little Holland House also because for a while he had lived in the original.

Holland House itself, in the shadow of which Hunter built his home and studio on the new Melbury Road, was a magnificent, lavish, Jacobean stately home. Under the 3rd Earl of Holland the house became a great centre of social, literary and political life with many famous visitors including Byron, Macaulay, Disraeli, Dickens and Sir Walter Scott.

The 4th Earl of Holland, Henry Edward Fox, died at the age of fifty-seven in 1859 without an heir (and hence the title became extinct). His widow who led an extravagant lifestyle was once referred to as "clever, eccentric and tiresome...[one] who had gathered round her at Holland House, an internationally famous circle of statesmen, wits and men of letters".[51]

The whole estate had been left to her by her husband but Lady Holland entertained lavishly and with little regard to whether she could afford to lead such an extravagant life style. She sold off great blocks of land on the western parts of her estate in her constant need for money to fund her social excesses including extraordinarily over-the-top garden parties. By 1873 Lady Holland was in desperate financial straits and the disastrous effects of living on capital rather than income were becoming increasingly apparent. She was on the verge of bankruptcy. Her financial adviser scolded her and wrote, "When you live at Holland House, you need not entertain all London."[52]

Lady Holland really needed to sell her late husband's family home to survive but it seems she could not bring herself to do that. Eventually, albeit undoubtedly very

reluctantly, she sought help from a distant cousin of her late husband's, Henry Edward Fox, the fifth Earl of Ilchester. After protracted negotiations he agreed to take the estate, subject as it was to a mortgage debt and a few small annuities, and in return he allowed Lady Holland to live in Holland House for the rest of her life. The formal conveyance took place in January 1874.

The Ilchesters took over the management of the estate (and its debts) and Lady Holland lived on in Holland House until she died in 1889.

Within a year of inheriting Holland Estate, the Ilchesters themselves had to raise money to pay off some of its considerable debt. The estate by then, or what was left of it after Lady Holland had already sold off many acres in the preceding decades, still stretched south from Holland House down to High Street Kensington and west to Addison Road. Another block of land had to be sold off. The Ilchesters cut a road through the south west corner and created a new estate – the Ilchester Estate – for development. Much to Lady Holland's dismay at the idea of having ever encroaching near neighbours, the land was divided into building plots and sold off under long leases with a new freeholder, the Earl of Ilchester. The Earl called the new road, Melbury Road, after one of his properties in Dorset. Two years later in 1876 Colin Hunter started building his new home at no. 14. Soon afterwards Hunter was able to look across Holland Estate towards Holland House where Lady Holland was almost imprisoned by her debt – although the high society garden parties in the grounds of Holland House continue unabated, now hosted by the new owner, the fifth Earl of Ilchester.

Despite all the sold-off tracts of land that had reduced the size of the Holland Estate in the 19th century so drastically, at the beginning of the 20th century Holland House still had the largest private grounds of any house in London, including Buckingham Palace. And even as Colin Hunter moved in to Melbury Road it was still possible to shoot woodcock in the grounds of Holland House – a practice that continued until 1905 – after Hunter's death.

Colin's son John walked to his junior school Linton House in Holland Park Avenue,[53] from 14 Melbury Road every day by crossing Holland House's parklike gardens via Holland

51 Sue Young Histories (.com)
52 British History Online, The Holland Estate

53 Linton House School is now a block of flats, still called Linton House.

Lane. This lane no longer exists today by name, but in fact it was the continuation of today's Ilchester Place leading up directly from 14 Melbury Road, through the Ilchester Place Gate and into Holland Park. As the lane approached Holland House it turned east and crossed in front of the house (as the park path does today) towards Holland Walk. Holland Lane used to lead directly from Holland House to the original Little Holland House before Melbury Road was created. In Hunter's day it was fenced off with iron railings through which, as late as the 1880s, John spotted not only woodcock in the grounds, but also pheasant. There were also strutting peacocks around the stately home which were easily spotted (and heard) along with the small Holland House clock in the turret that struck the hour on his way to school. Peacocks are still in the park to this day and frequently provide raucous accompaniment to the open-air opera performances held in in front of the ruins of Holland House every year.

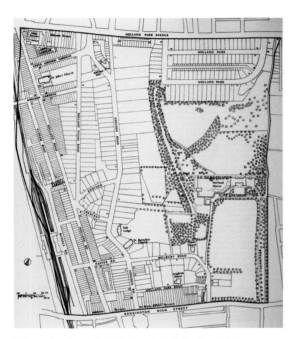

**The extent of the Holland Estate in 1768**

Image reproduced from British History Online british-history.ac.uk

The thick line denotes the extent of the estate in Kensington purchased by Lord Holland in 1768. Based on the Ordnance Survey of 1894–6.

It was then 237 acres, including one nine-acre field on the Hammersmith side of the parish boundary. Apart from Holland House itself, there was Little Holland House approximately on the site of the present No. 14 Melbury Road.

Holland Park in 1768 then extended from today's Holland Park Avenue south to Kensington High Street, east to present day Holland Park Walk and west to the present day railway line (Olympia). There was no Abbotsbury Road, Addison Road, Warwick Gardens, Holland Road, Melbury Road, Holland Park Road – and several more. All were originally part of the huge Holland Estate/ Park. And well before 1768 the estate was even larger – extending south to Fulham Road.

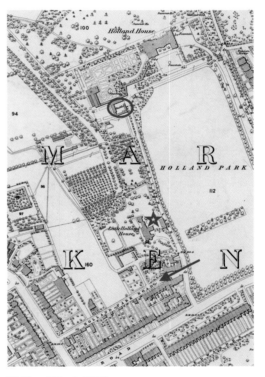

**Holland Park 1869**

Reproduced by permission of the National Library of Scotland

This old map shows Holland Park six years before Melbury Road was created. Today's 14 Melbury Road is located approximately where the original Little Holland House stood (marked with a blue star).

Holland Lane runs north passing the stables (blue oval) of Holland House. This was the route that a few years later, John Young-Hunter would take to walk to his school. Holland Lane no longer exists but the southern part of the lane became the southern part of Melbury Road.

By 1872 Lady Holland had already started selling off parts of the Holland Estate as her financial situation worsened. Note that Holland Park Road (blue arrow above) (where Leighton built his studio) was there first. Melbury Road followed, no doubt when even more capital needed to be released for the Holland Estate.

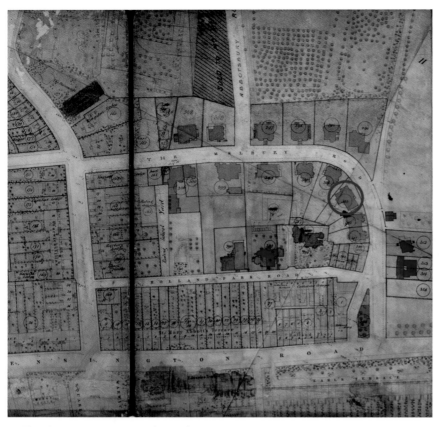

**Holland Estate late 1870s (detail)**

Image: London Metropolitan Archives, © Ilchester Estates

Map shows:

**Plot 305, circled in blue, 14 Melbury Road – home and studio of Colin Hunter**

*also:*

Plot 298, 8 Melbury Road home and studio of Marcus Stone
Plot 299, 6 Melbury Road, New Little Holland House, home and garden studio of G F Watts
Plot 294, 11 (today 31) Melbury Road home of Luke Fildes
Plot 295, Tower House 9 (today 29) Melbury Road, home of William Burges
Plot 290, Holland Park Road, home and studio of Frederick Leighton

After Lady Holland's death the Ilchesters lived in Holland House until the second world war. Holland House enjoyed its last hours of glory in 1939 when King George VI and Queen Elizabeth (the current queen's mother) dined there followed by a grand ball attended by the cream of society. In 1940, in the London Blitz, Holland House was bombed and largely destroyed by fire. In the same assault of enemy action on London just two days later in another bombing raid over Kensington, 14 Melbury Road was also hit and the late Colin Hunter's home was obliterated. Several years after the end of the war the Earl of Ilchester sold the Holland House ruins and its grounds to the London County Council in 1952 for £250,000. They were preserved as Holland Park for the enjoyment of the public. Two years later, the plot at 14 Melbury Road, now cleared of the bombed ruins of Colin Hunter's original home, was sold to developers. In 1955 they built the block of flats there today. The wife of the developer still lives there.

Little Holland House which stood near or on the site of the future 14 Melbury Road was demolished in 1875 to make way for the Earl of Ilchester's planned subdivisions. George Frederic Watts RA (1817–1904) had lived in Little Holland House and the first house to be built on the new Melbury Road was for Watts who named his new home Little Holland House for nostalgic reasons (sometimes referred to as the new Little Holland House). Later, when numbers were assigned, this became no. 6. One of Watts' most famous sculptures that can still be seen today, is the tremendous bronze statue of man on horseback called Physical Energy in Kensington Gardens. He started the sculpture at 6 Melbury Road.

Other artists' houses in Melbury Road which were begun in 1875 or 1876 were for (Sir) Hamo Thornycroft, Marcus Stone, William Burges and (Sir) Luke Fildes. The last artist to take a plot in Melbury Road during the initial phase of house building there was Colin Hunter. He engaged the architect J J Stevenson to provide the designs and tenders for building were received in August 1876. The lowest, for £4,965, was accepted and work began at once.

Hunter lived there under the terms of the Ilchester Estate lease until he died. Today, the area is still known as Ilchester Estate but because of a change in recent English law, the freehold had to be offered to resident tenants if they wished to buy it. No. 14, now a block of flats, was sold to shared freeholders as recently as 2012.

*"Everything in Colin Hunter's house is exquisite ..."*

## Round the Studios

*From our London correspondent.*

… Artists, as a class, are exceptionally open-handed. If they make money easily, they are, with few exceptions, ready to disburse it with at least an equal ease.

Perhaps this is one of the reasons why the studios are as attractive as they are to the visitor with artistic taste. There is no limit to the lovely things which Sir Frederick Leighton, Alma Tadema, Edwin Long and a host of others have brought together within their homes. How many thousands of pounds Sir Frederick has spent on tiles and tapestries from Rhodes and Cyprus perhaps he himself hardly ventures to calculate.

… Close to Sir Frederick Leighton's stand a group of houses occupied by artists. The adjoining house is occupied by Val Prinsep. Val Prinsep is one of the biggest and burliest of his craft.

… A turn in the road, after leaving Val Prinsep's, brings you to the splendid red brick abodes of Marcus Stone, Luke Fildes and Colin Hunter, and to the less ambitious habitation of Mr Watts RA. The three first named painters are all associates of the Academy, Colin Hunter being elected to that coveted honour only a few weeks ago. A plain-looking, plain-spoken Scotchman, with a simple, pleasant Scotch wife, Colin Hunter is one of the most popular because one of the least ostentatious, of painters. Yet if any man had a right to glory in his house it is he. Everything in it is exquisite. The capitals of Europe have been laid under tribute to fill it with rare and beautiful things. Colin Hunter paints sea pieces vigorously and freshly, but he would not place himself in the front rank. Fortune, nevertheless, in its most tangible shape, has smiled upon him.

*The Age*, Melbourne, 17 May 1884.

Colin Hunter named his new home and artist's studio at 14 Melbury Road Lugar House or Lugar Lodge. It is unclear which name Hunter originally intended because references to both "house" and "lodge" are numerous. The reason for the choice of "Lugar" has never been firmly established. It was a huge house and very grand – his son believed it was the most beautiful house in the road out of many beautiful houses – although one might have to forgive the bias in his opinion. It had many rooms, an enormous artist's studio of course, but also a nursery (which later became John's studio), a billiard room, his mother's boudoir, many bedrooms for family and for servants. When the house was put up for sale after Hunter's death the brochure described it as an "exceedingly choice residence, containing ten bed and dressing rooms, two bath rooms, a noble studio and

suite of entertaining rooms". John Young-Hunter recalled that he was born into a household with "the colourful and fragrant atmosphere of paint and turpentine" and a house in which he was surrounded by "his father's friends, the Royal Academicians of Britain". Colin was particularly good friends of Luke Fildes, Marcus Stone and Val Prinsep and John recalls that they were frequently entertained in Lugar House.

The gracious Mrs Colin Hunter entertained her husband's Royal Academician friends lavishly and frequently at 14 Melbury Road. Her dinner parties were said to be flawless, from the food to the flowers.

Linley Sambourne (1844–1910), the famous English cartoonist and illustrator who lived in Stafford Terrace just across Holland Park from Melbury Road, was also a good friend of Hunter's. In his personal diary entry of Wednesday March 28th 1883, Sambourne wrote "... After, to Colin Hunter's ..." and on the next day "... after, went with Colin Hunter to dine at Walter Lethbridge's.[54] 15.[55] *Met no one worth mentioning.*"[56]

Sambourne's house was decorated in the fashionable 'aesthetic' style of the day and familiar to Linley via the houses of successful artist friends such as Luke Fildes and Colin Hunter.[57] The décor of Colin Hunter's house was widely admired and a talking-point for many locals.

Not only was Colin Hunter a thoroughbred Scot, he was also the head, the firm patriarch, of a typical Victorian and well-to-do family. In the household were his glamorous and highly sociable wife and esteemed hostess, four children, servants, and circles of friends most of whom were successful artists and celebrities. It was a grand house at 14 Melbury Road and it was run as such. Colin of course was a successful artist himself and moved in distinguished circles.

---

54  Probably Walter Lethbridge 1845–1907, wine merchant
55  Is this the number of guests?
56  Italics: written in red ink
57  www.historicengland.org.uk

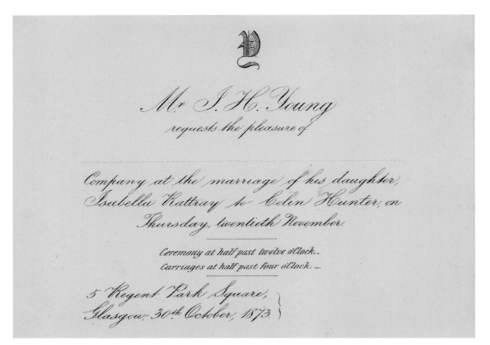

The invitation to Colin Hunter & Isabella Young's wedding

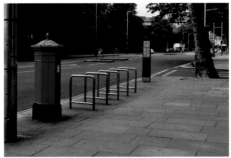

The Victorian pillar box on the corner of Melbury Road and High Street Kensington, to which young John Hunter was regularly despatched by his father from Lugar House to post the family letters. It is still there today and in use.

Photo 2018: Julio Carlos Alves Da Silva

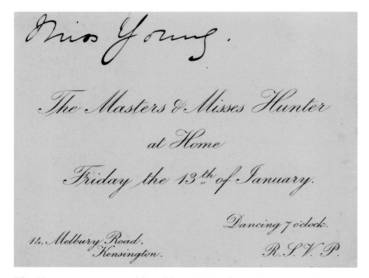

The Hunters entertained lavishly at 14 Melbury Road. Isabella was a supreme hostess, but here it appears that even the children were highly sociable and holding their own "dancing at 7 o'clock".

At the bottom of Melbury Road at the intersection with High Street Kensington, stands a red Victorian pillar box. It has stood there since Colin Hunter's day and is still in use, despite its frustratingly small slot which was fine for the tiny envelopes of Queen Victoria's era but not for the larger envelope sizes today. Young John tells how he was regularly sent down to that box to post the daily letters.

Because he was somewhat obsessive he used to circle the box two or three times to make sure he had not dropped any letters before he wandered back up Melbury Road to his home.[58] The author never looks at or uses that same pillar box today without thinking of the Hunter family at number 14.

It is not quite known why Melbury Road and Holland Park Road off it became an enclave of distinguished artists, architects, sculptors, writers (and, today, film directors and pop stars) but it did. Perhaps it was because Lady Holland loved the arts so much (and artists perhaps). All of them were well-to-do and the homes and studios they built there one after the other in the 1870s and 1880s were very grand. But with Leighton, the most esteemed of all late Victorian artists and President of the Royal Academy also building

58 *Reviewing the Years*, John Young-Hunter

there the whole area was assured to become a mecca for aspiring artists.

The importance of this small corner of the Holland estate as a centre for the artist 'establishment' is indicated by the fact that in 1896, when Leighton died, six Royal Academicians were living in Holland Park Road and Melbury Road (Leighton, Prinsep, Thornycroft, Watts, Stone and Fildes) as well as one associate member (Hunter). J J Shannon was also to become an associate in the following year and a full Academician later. Of other artists who were not member of the Royal Academy, the most famous was probably Phil May, the cartoonist and illustrator. In that year over twenty residents of these two streets were identified as artists.

The artists who lived in the homes and studios of Holland Park Road and Melbury Road became known as 'the Holland Park Circle'. Most of the artists opened their studios on Sunday afternoons (Watts opened his studio also on Wednesday afternoons). The open studios attracted many visitors and many families including mothers or nannies with perambulators who filled the pavements of Melbury Road. It was a smart and stylish social event to meet in Melbury Road and visit the studios of successful artists, nearly all of whom were Royal Academicians. No doubt it was also an important event for the artists themselves who hoped to sell some of their works to the wealthy promenaders.

The activities in the homes of the artists and their neighbours were also highly sociable events as well as numerous. Artists and celebrities of all kinds eagerly joined the social circles of the august residents of Holland House, Holland Park Road and Melbury Road when they could. Many were Americans. Apart from the Sketch Club (see page 30) in the 1880s a circle of friends formed a small and exclusive society called The Kinsmen and frequently met together in Colin Hunter's house. Amongst this clique were Frank Millet, Alfred Parsons, Edwin Abbey, William Black, George Boughton, Lawrence Barrett, Linley Samborne, W S Gilbert (the dramatist of Gilbert & Sullivan fame), Luke Fildes, Alma-Tadema, and John Singer Sargent – all of whom would have been considered close friends of Hunter's.

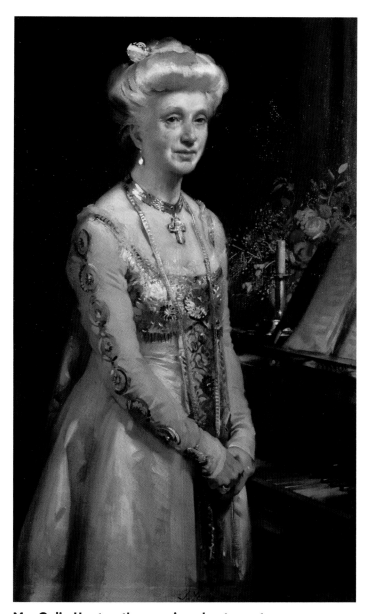

**Mrs Colin Hunter, the gracious hostess at 14 Melbury Road**

Portrait by her son John Young-Hunter
Family by descent, great great grandson Scott Kuster
Image courtesy Marcia Rider

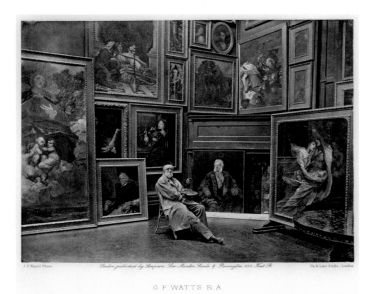

G F WATTS R.A.

**G F Watts in his studio at the new Little Holland House, 6 Melbury Road**

© National Portrait Gallery, London

This is a wonderful photograph of an artist's studio in Melbury Road, typical of those found in neighbouring homes. Although this photograph is archived as Watts' "studio" it may have been his art gallery – separate from his painting studio.

Thomas Thornycroft (1815–85), sculptor, lived at 2 Melbury Road, with his wife and three children, all of whom were artists. And, of course, three servants. He was most noted for his sculptor Boadicea in her chariot, at Westminster Bridge.

At 8 Melbury Road lived Marcus Stone, artist, with his wife and again, three servants, to run the huge home in keeping with his neighbours.

The 1881 census shows Colin Hunter lived at 14 Melbury Road with his wife and three children and the household had four servants.

Sir Luke Fildes ARA (in 1881 but later RA) (1843–1927) lived opposite Colin Hunter at 11 (today, 31) Melbury Road. In 1881 he was living with his wife and baby son Frederick, and in the house also was another artist, his brother-in-law Henry Woods, also ARA. Accompanied by four servants.

At 9 Melbury Road (today 29) in the extraordinary Tower House was William Burges (1827–81), one of the greatest Victorian English architects. He was single but he, too, lived with servants. He was also ARA.

## A summary of all Hunter's neighbours

The following table is based on the 1881 census. Interesting to note is the dairy farm and dairy farmer just on the corner of the plush Melbury Road and Holland Park Road homes and studios.

| 1 Melbury Road | Coach house with rooms over. Coachman and his wife and 3 grooms |
|---|---|
| 2 Melbury Road | Thos Thorneycroft, sculptor Living with wife and children all of whom were artists. And 3 servants. Thomas 64yo; Daughter Mary, 35yo single, painter & artists Son William, single 31yo sculptor ARA Daughter Teresa, 16yo single, artist |
| 3 Melbury Road | Being built |
| 4 Melbury Road | Elizabeth Bagshot, widow |
| 6 Melbury Road | Geo F Watts, artist painter |
| 8 Melbury Road | Marcus Stone, 40 yo artist painter ARA Living with wife and 3 servants |
| 9 Melbury Road (now 29) | Tower House William Burges, 54yo, single, architect Living with married couple servants, housekeeper (Belgian) and butler |
| 11 Melbury Road (now 31) | Luke Fildes, 36yo artist painter ARA. Born Liverpool Married living with wife Fanny Son Frederick 1yo Brother-in-law Henry Woods ARA 31yo, artist painter 4 servants: cook, house maid, parlour maid, nurse |
| 10 & 12 Melbury Road | Lady's School (with staff and boarder scholars) |
| 14 Melbury Road | Colin Hunter, not at home at time of census Isabella, wife, 28yo, born Scotland In residence with 3 children, John Y, Allan and Colina, all born Scotland; 4 servants |

| | |
|---|---|
| 16 Melbury Road | John Henry Sylvester, surgeon 1891 census<br>(Hunter painted his portrait)<br>William Holman Hunt after 1901 until his death 1910 |
| 18 Melbury Road | Charles Stuart & Jane M Stuart<br>Married couple, both artist painters.<br>Both 42yo<br>Living with son E E Gordon 10yo student at School of Art<br>Son William Arthur<br>3 servants |
| 1 Holland Park Road | Valentine C Prinsep, 43yo, single, painter ARA<br>Living with 3 servants and one servant couple's children 3yo, 1yo 0yo<br>One servant was nurse maid, no doubt for other servant's young children |
| 2 Holland Park Road | Leighton House<br>Frederick Leighton, 50yo single, President of the RA, born Scarborough<br>Living alone |
| "The Farm" Holland Park Road | Edwin Teddall, dairy farmer |
| Rowsley House<br>20 Holland Park Road | James A Goldingham, artist |

## The London artists' quarter

Beyond the Melbury Road hub, more artists of one discipline or another lived close to it.

The wider circle of artists who lived or met in or around Holland Park in Victorian times constituted such a cluster it deserved the recognition as "the London artists' quarter".

All these people were contemporaries of Colin Hunter's and lived in his neighbourhood of Kensington and Holland Park.

| | |
|---|---|
| Abbey, Edwin | Artist; American muralist, illustrator & painter |
| Alexander, Wm Cleverley | Artist; local philanthropist, artist and patron of the arts |
| Archer, James | Artist |
| Barrie, JM | Novelist and playwright |

| | |
|---|---|
| Boughton, George | Artist, exhibited annually at the RA from 1863 |
| Burges, William | Artist, architect, designer of furniture & jewellery |
| Cole, George | Artist |
| Corbet, Matthew | Artist |
| Davis, Sir Edmund | His home, Lansdowne House, built as an artists' colony |
| Dickens, Charles | Regularly met at Holland House as member of literary group |
| Dicksee, Sir Frank | Artist |
| Dillon, Frank | Artist |
| Fildes, Sir Luke | Artist |
| Frith, Wm | Artist, admitted to RA at age of 21 |
| Galsworthy, John | The future Nobel Laureate |
| Gilbert WS | Wrote 33 plays |
| Hardy, Thomas | Novelist |
| Hassall, John | Children's book illustrator; poster artist |
| Hunt, William Holman | Artist; founder member of pre-Raphaelite movement |
| Hunter, Colin | Artist |
| Laszlo, Philip | Artist; portraitist |
| Leighton, Frederick, Lord | Artist; President of the Royal Academy |
| May, Phil | Artist; cartoonist |
| Sambourne, E Linley | Cartoonist; illustrator of *Punch* |
| Turner, JMW | Artist; regularly painted in Campden Hill Square |
| Watts, George F | Artist & sculptor; house guest of Lord Holland's |

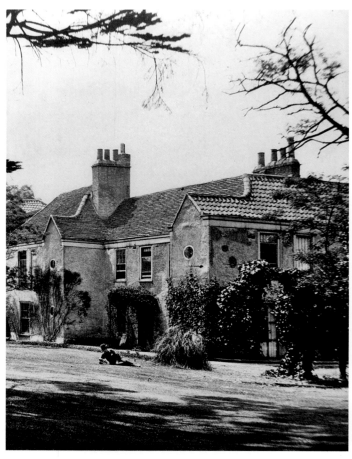

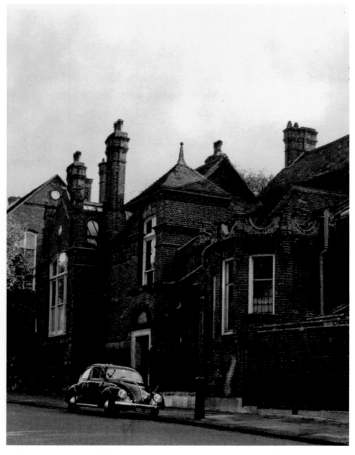

**The original Little Holland House, the dower house of Holland House**

Photo courtesy of The Royal Borough of Kensington & Chelsea Libraries

This house stood in the south west corner of the Holland Estate and was surrounded by open fields and farmland. Not far away further to the south west, Lady Holland had already sold off some of the estate in the 1860s which saw the creation of Holland Park Road. Here Leighton and Prinsep's son had bought plots.

But more of the land was to be sold off, and this time the new Melbury Road was created in 1875 cutting right through the grounds of Little Holland House and near to the house itself. Little Holland House which stood approximately where 14 Melbury Road is sited today was demolished. George Frederick Watts who lived here for several years with the Prinsep family had to find a new home. He built on the new Melbury Road, no. 6, and in a sentimental gesture to his lost former home, named it (the new) Little Holland House.

**The new Little Holland House, 6 Melbury Road (early 1960s)**

Courtesy of The Royal Borough of Kensington & Chelsea Libraries

Despite all-out efforts to preserve 6 Melbury Road in recognition of the fact that it was the acclaimed artist's home, Watts' Little Holland House was demolished *c*.1966 and replaced with a block of flats which is today called **Kingfisher House** (below).

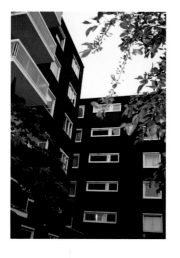

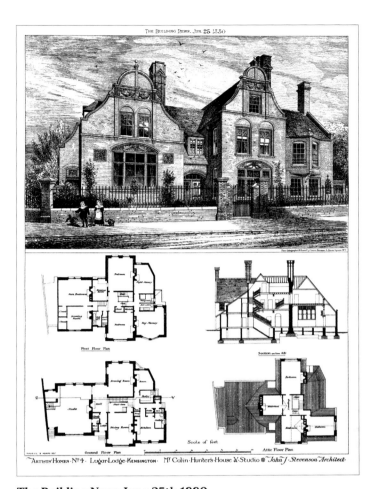

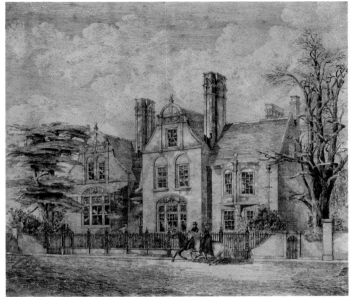

Image above courtesy Marcia Rider.
Artist's impression of 14 Melbury Road. Pen and ink on paper.
Artist unknown.

## The Building News June 25th 1880

Courtesy Royal Borough of Kensington & Chelsea Libraries.

When Colin Hunter moved into his new home and artist studio at 14 Melbury Road in 1876, he named it Lugar Lodge. But it was also known as Lugar House. Where the name Lugar came from is unknown.

Hunter's home and studio was designed by architect John J Stevenson (1831–1908). It is likely that Stevenson was a friend of Hunter's as he was a fellow Glaswegian who also moved to London around the same time as Hunter did (1870). Stevenson died at 4 Porchester Gardens in Bayswater, London.

The two windows upstairs on the right were the windows of the nursery. The children could look out at an angle both ways up and down the street.[59] The Hunters had four children and the Fildes family opposite had six. While their artist fathers were busy at their easels, the children of Luke Fildes and Colin Hunter would wave to one another from their nursery windows on either side of Melbury Road.[60]

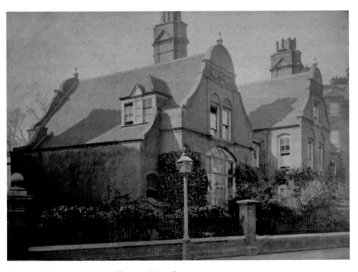

**Lugar House, 14 Melbury Road**

Photo, courtesy Marcia Rider

---

59  Marcia Rider's mother, Gabrielle, Colin Hunter's granddaughter, recalled this personal memory.

60  *Kensington Past*, Barbara Denny & Carolyn Starren, 1998

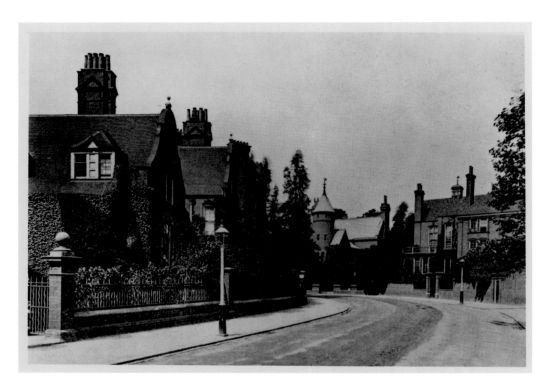

**Melbury Road *c.*1900**, showing Lugar House, no. 14, on left (Colin Hunter), Tower House around corner on other side of the road (William Burges's home until his death) and no. 11 (today no. 31) (Luke Fildes's home) opposite.

Photo courtesy of The Royal Borough of Kensington & Chelsea Libraries

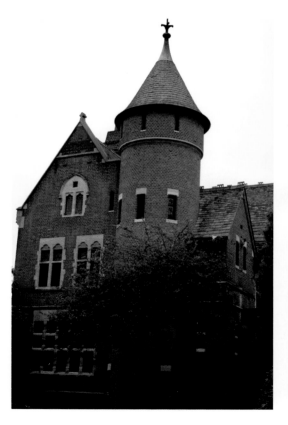

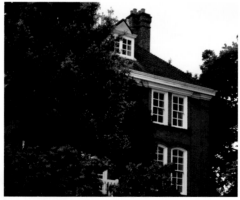

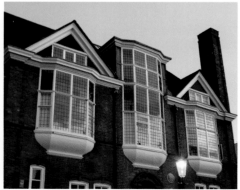

**Three of Colin Hunter's neighbours**

William Burges in the Tower House no. 29, today no. 9 (left)
Luke Fildes in no. 31, today no. 11 (top right)
Marcus Stone in no. 8 (bottom right)

Melbury Road today continues to attract celebrities:
Jimmy Page, the English guitarist and rock band Led Zeppelin star
Robbie Williams, English singer, songwriter originally from pop group Take That
Until 2013 Michael Winner, English film director and producer lived in no. 31
Don Black, English lyricist for many famous musicals, movie themes and hit songs

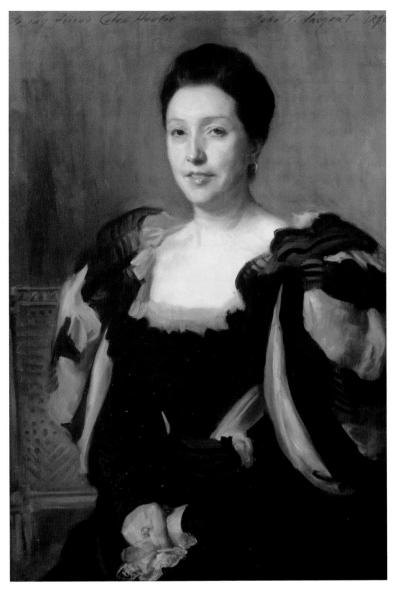

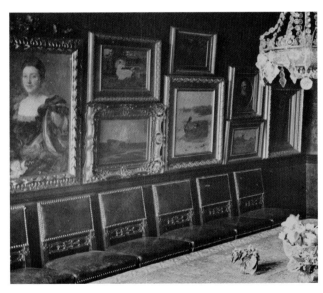

**Portrait of Mrs Colin Hunter, Isabella Rattray Hunter (née Young)**

1896, oil on canvas, 94 × 62.2 cm, 37" × 24.5"
John Singer Sargent
Courtesy The Utah Museum of Fine Arts, Salt Lake City
Exhibited Royal Academy 1896

The photo on the right shows the same portrait hanging in the Hunters' dining room 14 Melbury Road

Isabella was a gifted socialite who staged medieval and renaissance costume parties at 14 Melbury Road. This portrait shows her in one such costume.[61]

61  The Art of John and Mary Young-Hunter, Pyms Gallery, 2000

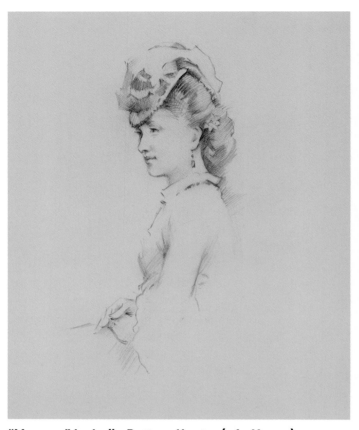

## "Mamma" Isabella Rattray Hunter (née Young)

Pencil sketch by John Young-Hunter of his mother or by Colin Hunter of his wife,[62] 26 × 21 cm, 10.25" × 8.25"

Published in *Reviewing the Years* John Young-Hunter

**Provenance**
Estate of the artist
Family by descent

**Isabella Hunter**
Photo courtesy Marcia Rider.

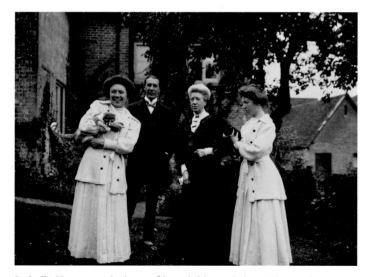

Isabella Hunter with three of her children, Colina, Alan and Agnes outside 14 Melbury Road (between 1904 and 1913 – after Colin's death and before Alan's; John would have been in the USA)

Photos courtesy of Marcia Rider.

---

62 Despite the claim to the contrary in *Reviewing the Years*, a descendant of the artist believes this drawing is by Colin of his wife, not by her son.

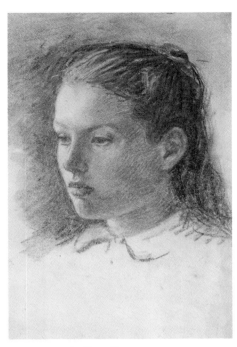

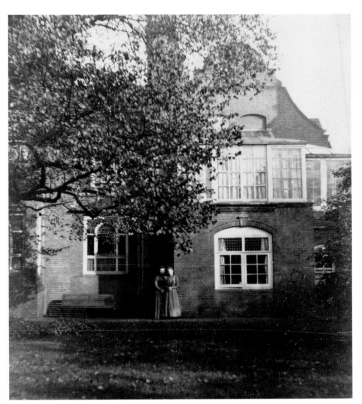

## Agnes or Colina Hunter

(One of Colin Hunter's daughters), Colin Hunter
Pencil sketch, 24 × 18 cm, 9.5" × 7"

**Provenance**
Estate of the artist
Family by descent

There is some doubt as to which daughter it is, although family descendants say they would opt for it being Agnes if a decision had to be made.

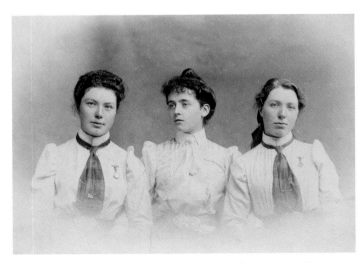

Colina Hunter (left), unknown cousin (centre) and Agnes Hunter (right), Colin Hunter's two daughters

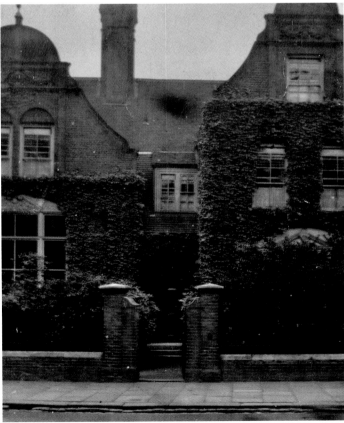

A rare view of 14 Melbury Road taken in the back garden (top) and the front door (bottom)

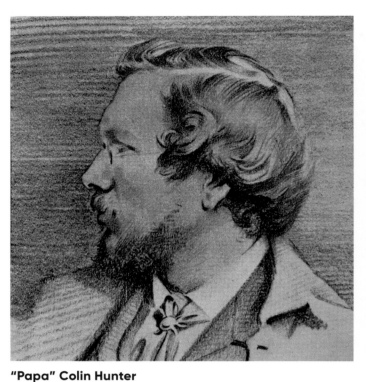

**"Papa" Colin Hunter**

Pencil sketch by John Young-Hunter of the artist's father

Published in *Reviewing the Years*, John Young-Hunter

Provenance: Estate of the artist, family by descent

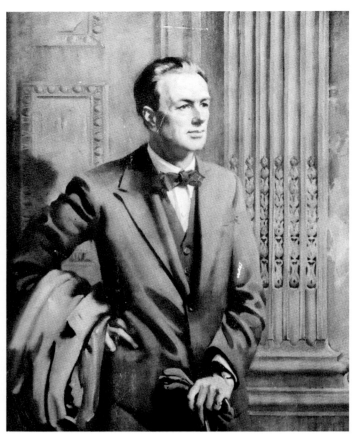

**John Young-Hunter self portrait**

Colin Hunter's eldest child

Estate of the artist, family by descent

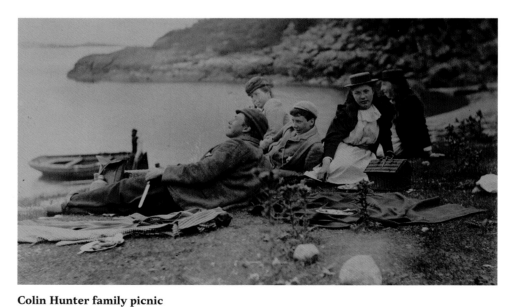

**Colin Hunter family picnic**

Left to right: Colin Hunter, Isabella, Alan, Colina, Agnes
A rare photo of the family together. Probably taken by son John.
Courtesy Marcia Rider

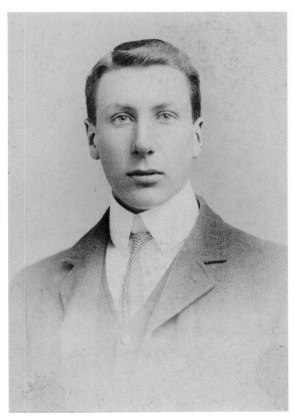

**Alan Hunter (1878–1913)**

Colin Hunter's second child and second son
Photo courtesy Marcia Rider

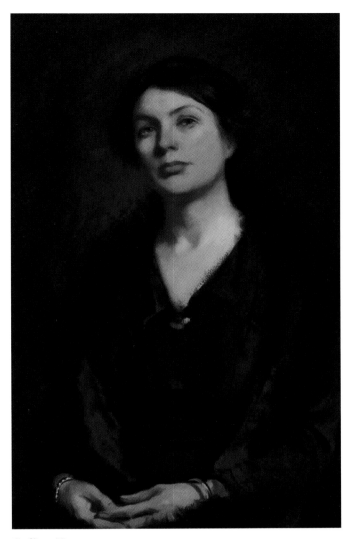

## Colina Hunter

1915, oil on canvas, 91.4 × 66 cm, 36" × 26"
John Young-Hunter

Exhibition label on stretcher: 'Miss Colina Hunter' and is inscribed 'John Young Hunter 28 Addison Road'. The artist used this address from 1915–20 and exhibited a portrait of his sister at the Royal Academy in 1915.

John painted this on one of his return visits to Britain. Colina and John were particularly close. Colina lost her fiancé in the Great War and she never married.

**Provenance**
Estate of the artist
Family by descent

**Published**
Pyms catalogue p.89, 2000

Painted in the style of a John Singer Sargent, one of John Young-Hunter's teachers at the Royal Academy Schools. Singer Sargent was also a friend of the Hunter family (hence, his portrait of John's mother, see page 57).

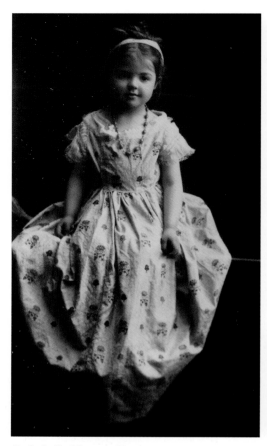

**Gabrielle Young-Hunter,
Colin Hunter's granddaughter**

All photos on this and next two pages courtesy
Marcia Rider

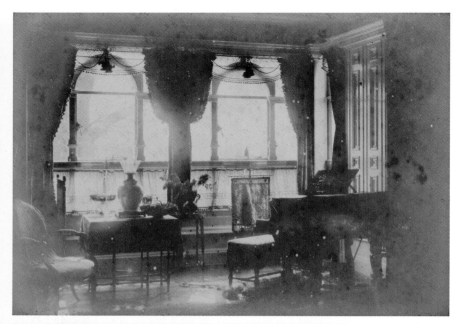

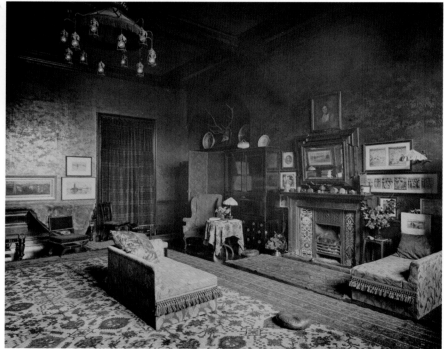

**The interiors of Lugar House, 14 Melbury Road.**

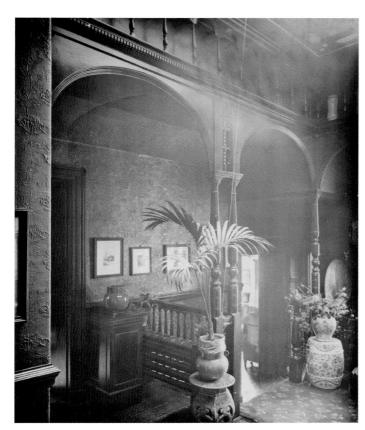

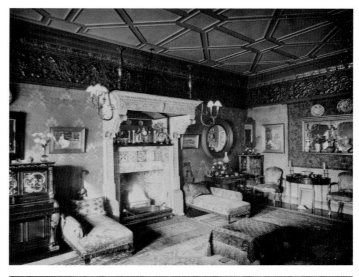

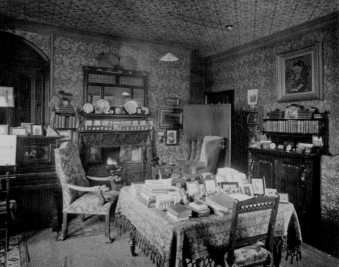

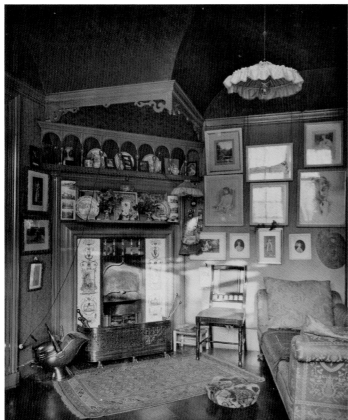

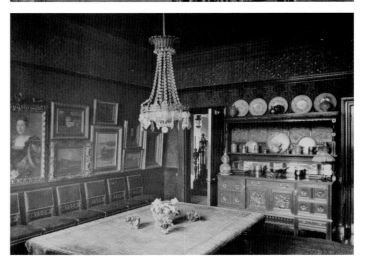

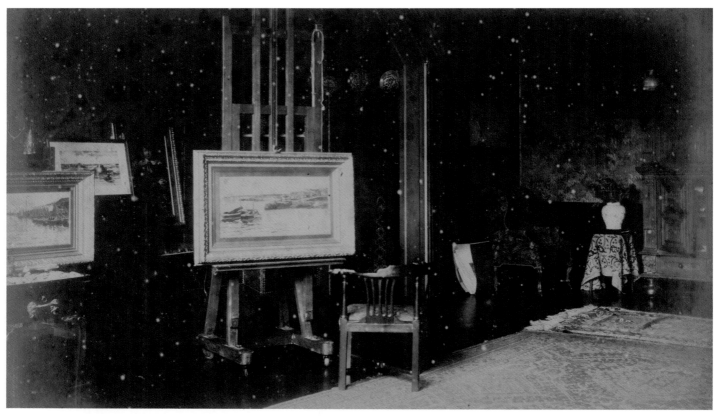

**Colin Hunter's studio, 14 Melbury Road.**

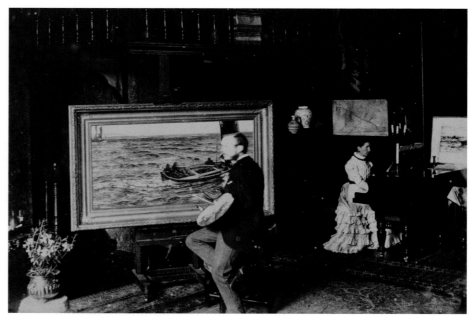

**Colin Hunter at easel and wife Isabella at piano, 14 Melbury Road.**

(This could be a staged photograph because it is not believed this was Colin's studio despite the easel and palette.)

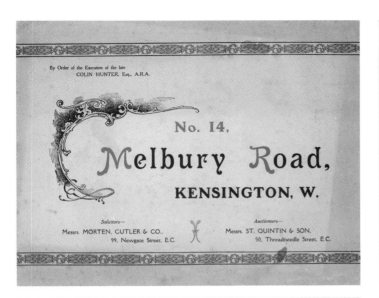

By Order of the Executors of the late
COLIN HUNTER, Esq., A.R.A.

## No. 14,
# Melbury Road,
### KENSINGTON, W.

Solicitors—
Messrs. MORTEN, CUTLER & CO.,
99, Newgate Street. E.C.

Auctioneers—
Messrs. ST. QUINTIN & SON.
50, Threadneedle Street. E.C.

PARTICULARS.

THE

# Highly-Attractive Residence

KNOWN AS

## No. 14, MELBURY ROAD,
### KENSINGTON,

in an exceptionally favourite position overlooking the Grounds of Holland House, close to numerous Railway Stations, and combining quietude and comparative seclusion with close proximity to the centres of fashion.

### ❖ THE HOUSE ❖

was erected and artistically completed by Mr. COLIN HUNTER, for his own occupation; it is of handsome elevation in red brick, partly creeper-clad, is well screened from the road, and contains the following accommodation:

3

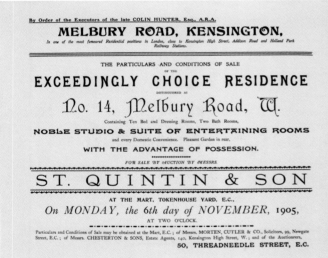

By Order of the Executors of the late COLIN HUNTER, Esq., A.R.A.

## MELBURY ROAD, KENSINGTON,

In one of the most favoured Residential positions in London, close to Kensington High Street, Addison Road and Holland Park Railway Stations.

THE PARTICULARS AND CONDITIONS OF SALE

OF THE

# EXCEEDINGLY CHOICE RESIDENCE

DISTINGUISHED AS

## No. 14, Melbury Road, W.

Containing Ten Bed and Dressing Rooms, Two Bath Rooms,

### NOBLE STUDIO & SUITE OF ENTERTAINING ROOMS

and every Domestic Convenience. Pleasant Garden in rear.

### WITH THE ADVANTAGE OF POSSESSION.

FOR SALE BY AUCTION BY MESSRS.

# ST. QUINTIN & SON

AT THE MART, TOKENHOUSE YARD, E.C.,

## On MONDAY, the 6th day of NOVEMBER, 1905,

AT TWO O'CLOCK.

Particulars and Conditions of Sale may be obtained at the Mart, E.C.; of Messrs. MORTEN, CUTLER & CO., Solicitors, 99, Newgate Street, E.C.; of Messrs. CHESTERTON & SONS, Estate Agents, 140, Kensington High Street, W.; and of the Auctioneers,

### 50, THREADNEEDLE STREET, E.C.

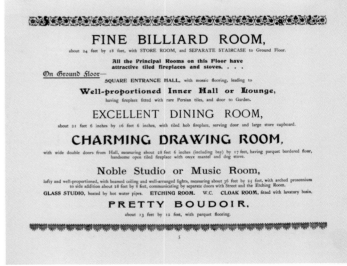

## FINE BILLIARD ROOM,

about 24 feet by 18 feet, with STORE ROOM, and SEPARATE STAIRCASE to Ground Floor.

**All the Principal Rooms on this Floor have attractive tiled fireplaces and stoves. . . .**

On Ground Floor—

SQUARE ENTRANCE HALL, with mosaic flooring, leading to

### Well-proportioned Inner Hall or Lounge,

having fireplace fitted with rare Persian tiles, and door to Garden.

## EXCELLENT DINING ROOM,

about 21 feet 6 inches by 16 feet 6 inches, with tiled hob fireplace, serving door and large store cupboard.

## CHARMING DRAWING ROOM,

with wide double doors from Hall, measuring about 28 feet 6 inches (including bay) by 17 feet, having parquet bordered floor, handsome open tiled fireplace with onyx mantel and dog stove.

### Noble Studio or Music Room,

lofty and well-proportioned, with beamed ceiling and well-arranged lights, measuring about 36 feet by 25 feet, with arched proscenium to side addition about 28 feet by 8 feet, communicating by separate doors with Street and the Etching Room.

GLASS STUDIO, heated by hot water pipes. ETCHING ROOM. W.C. CLOAK ROOM, fitted with lavatory basin.

## PRETTY BOUDOIR.

about 13 feet by 12 feet, with parquet flooring.

5

The fascinating sales particulars of 14 Melbury Road when it was put up for sale after Colin Hunter's death in 1904.

*Chapter 6*

# His art

## Hunter's studio sale after his death

After Hunter died in 1904 he still had some fine art works in his studio, including some that had been exhibited in the Royal Academy, that had not yet been sold.

The executors of his estate (his son, John Young-Hunter and daughter Colina) put them up for sale at Christie's Auctioneers (then called Messrs Christie, Manson & Woods), at 8 King Street, St James's Square, London, on 8th April 1905.

The old catalogue of that sale has not been easily reproduced but extracts are shown below. We are grateful to Christie's for looking deep into their archives to find it.

The catalogue revealed some surprises, such as **Voices of the Sea** having been exhibited in St Louis in 1904, which the author had not discovered before.

Disappointingly, not all works were identifiable by the names given and there were no images of the lots. It is quite possible that some of the works in the catalogue are in fact reproduced in this book but under a different name. An attempt has been made to find matches with the scene suggested by the catalogue title, the date and the dimensions – but without much joy. If any reader does recognise any of the unidentified works in the catalogue the author would be grateful to learn of it via contact with the publisher.

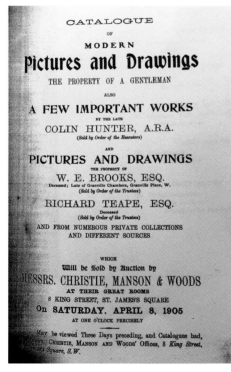
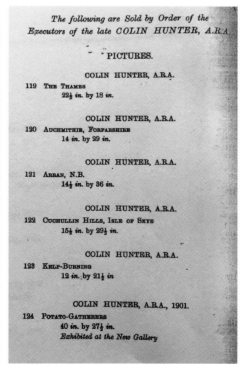
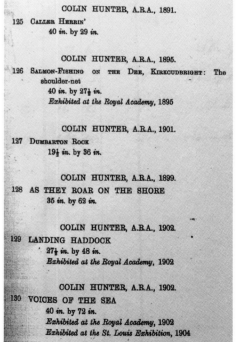

Catalogue images by courtesy of Christie's Fine Art Auctioneers.
Note: In Lot 121 above, "N.B." stands for North Britain.

## Hunter's copper plates

As well as being a painter, Hunter was a highly skilled engraver and etcher. An art critic in *The Art Journal* April 1885 praised his etching **Lowering Sail** saying that this etching "showed to the full Hunter's facility in composition, and his power of giving motion to ships, clouds, waves and other moving things".

Copper was the preferred plate to use with etchings and engravings (although steel and wood plates were also used). The main difference between etching and engraving is that etching requires drawing the picture in wax and then using acid while engraving uses a tool to cut straight into the plate.

Hunter's descendants inherited some of the original copper plates which have been in storage for more than one hundred years. Some are one hundred and thirty years old. The poor quality of some of the copper plate images published in this book may simply be due to age.

Engravings were usually inspired by Hunter's original oil on canvas works. However once prints were made from the plates and gifted or sold widely (some plates may have produced 500 impressions), owners frequently gave the prints their own titles quite unaware of the name and likeness associated with the original art work. Even etchings held in museum and art gallery collections have occasionally been given titles that do not suggest any link with the original art work.

All copper plate images are © Colin Hunter family estate.

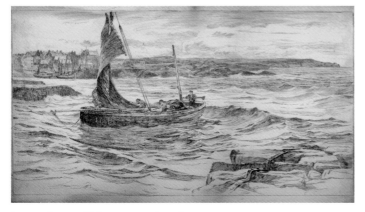

**Lowering sail (copper plate)**

Original copper plate, 33 × 58.4 cm, 13" × 23"

© Colin Hunter family estate

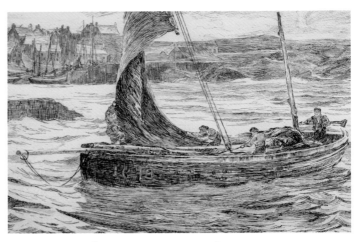

**Lowering sail (copper plate detail)**

This close-up of the copper plate for **Lowering sail** shows clearly the artist's skill with the etcher's needle.

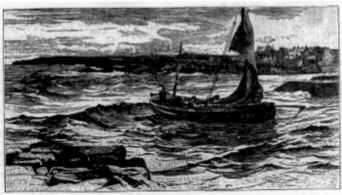

*Lowering Sail. Engraved by R. Paterson, from an Etching by Colin Hunter, A.R.A.*

**Lowering sail**

*c.*1884 (engraving)

Engraving by R Paterson, from an etching by Colin Hunter

It appears that R Paterson made an engraving from one of Hunter's etchings. Perhaps he did not have access to the original painting which had been sold.

According to Hunter's accounts the original painting (not found) which inspired this engraving was painted in 1881 and sold to John Aitken for £210 (today's value £24,150). But the engraving and etchings must have been *c.*1884, because the caption above quotes Hunter as ARA. The image of this etching was published in *The Art Journal* April 1885 and in *The Windsor Magazine* 1912 No. 214.

One of the original etchings on paper from this engraving is held in the Aberdeen Art Gallery & Museums Collection but with the title **Fishing port**.

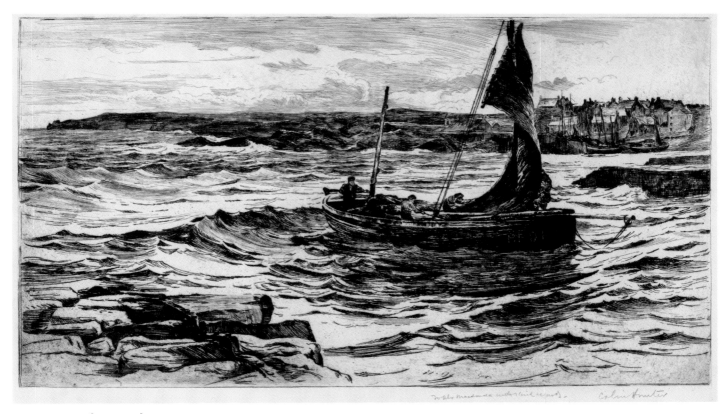

### Fishing port (etching)

(originally, **Lowering sail**)

Etching on paper

Aberdeen Art Gallery & Museums Collections

Bequeathed by Alexander Macdonald, 1901

Inscription on mount: "To Alex Macdonald with kind regards Colin Hunter"

This is the second etching bequeathed by Alexander Macdonald to Aberdeen. See **Loch scene** (**In the gloaming**) on page 73. Once again it appears that either Macdonald or Aberdeen changed the etching's title from Hunter's original.

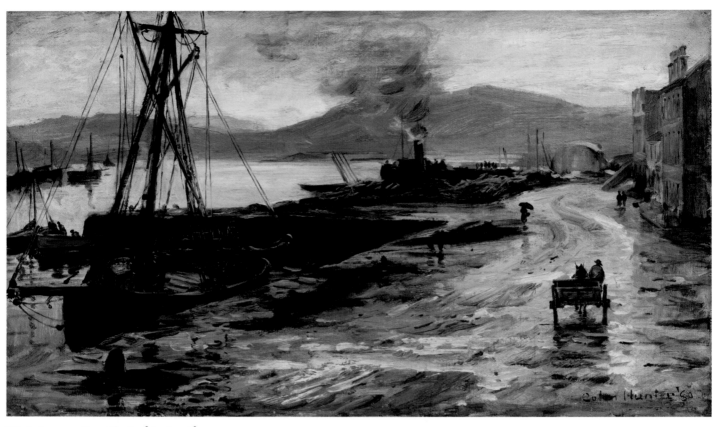

## Wet day on the Clyde (Tarbert)

1880, oil on canvas, 30.8 × 50.8 cm, 12.1" × 20"

© CSG CIC Glasgow Museums Collection

**Provenance**
Gift to Glasgow from Mrs Maitland Ramsay, 1953

Note the similarities and differences between the original oil on canvas and the engraving.

Why was the painting called **Wet day on the Clyde** and the engraving of it **Tarbert**?

They are in fact the same location – the Argyll coast line on the Clyde. From a little east of Helensburgh (Hunter's childhood home town) to Campbeltown on the south of the Mull of Kintyre is all part of the Clyde estuary. The area also includes the sea lochs and their associated towns and villages such as Gare Loch, Loch Goil, Loch Fyne – and Tarbert.

However, it is interesting to note that Hunter himself originally called his engraving **Tarbert wet day** (see Appendix 2, page 286) – which provides a close match to the title of **Wet day on the Clyde**. The "wet day" seems to have been subsequently dropped from the title of his etchings.

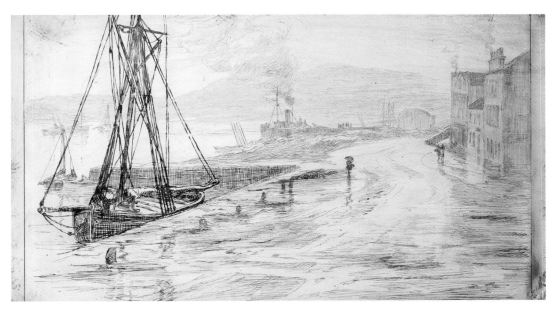

**Tarbert, Loch Fyne (copper plate)**

Original copper plate, 12.7 × 22.9 cm, 5" × 9"

© Colin Hunter family estate

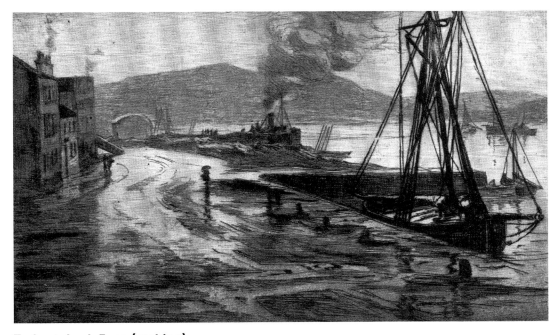

**Tarbert, Loch Fyne (etching)**

Etching derived from the original painting **Wet day on the Clyde** shown opposite.

Image from *The Windsor Magazine* 1912 no. 214

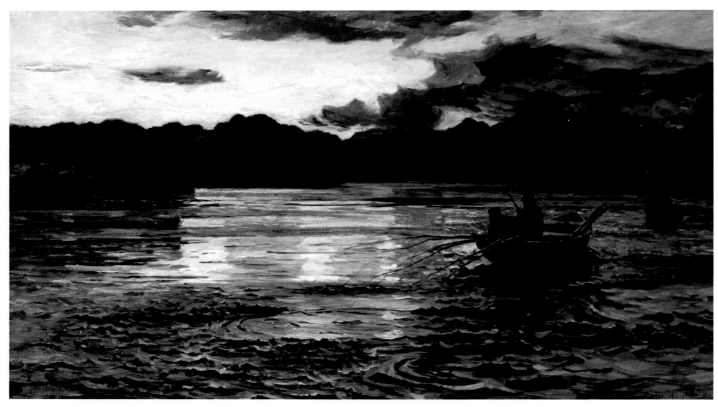

## Summer fishing

(mistakenly named **Summer fishing Skye**)
Also known as **In the gloaming**, **Loch scene**, **The Gare Loch**
1881, oil on canvas, 47 × 90 cm, 18.5" × 35.4"

© The Burton Art Gallery and Museum, Bideford, Devon

At some point this painting was mistakenly entitled **Summer fishing Skye**. But you will see the identical scene named as **The Gare Loch** by Hunter himself and the Gare Loch is not in or near Skye. Moreover, Hunter himself never added Skye to the title. In his personal accounts of 1885 in his own handwriting, he called it simply **Summer fishing**.

Sold by Hunter for £250 (today's value £22,400) to Fairfax Rhodes, 1885
Bequeathed to Burton Art Gallery from the Hubert Coop Collection, 1951

Hunter made an engraving of this scene and called it **The Gare Loch** (or **Gareloch**). According to his own accounts 1880–81 he sold it for £750 to Alex Dennistoun of Golfhill, Glasgow.

Hunter submitted an original etching of **The Gare Loch** as his diploma work to the RE (Royal Society of Painter-Etchers and Engravers, today the Royal Society of Painter-Printmakers) on his election in 1881. The RE subsequently loaned it to the Ashmolean in Oxford. See right.

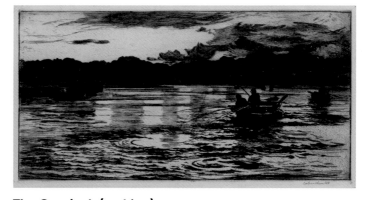

## The Gareloch (etching)

Also known as **Loch Scene**, **In the gloaming**, **Summer fishing**
Etching, 30.2 × 57.6 cm, 11.9" × 22.7" (excluding mount)

By permission of the Ashmolean Oxford

Loaned to the Ashmolean (accession no. LI300.18) by the RE.

Note the identical scene to **Summer fishing**.

See copper plate engravings opposite.

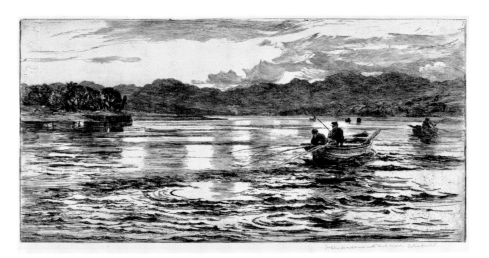

### Loch scene (etching)

(as named by Aberdeen Art Gallery)

Also known as **In the gloaming**, **The Gare Loch** (or **Gareloch**), **Summer fishing**

Undated but probably *c.*1881, etching on paper, 30 × 57 cm, 12" × 22.5"

Aberdeen Art Gallery & Museums Collections

The etchings produced from the original copper plate above **In the gloaming**, were frequently given other titles. On the mount of the Aberdeen etching (above) Colin Hunter wrote "To Alex Macdonald with kind regards Colin Hunter".

It was bequeathed to Aberdeen by Alexander Macdonald in 1901. It is surprising that he or Aberdeen gave it the name **Loch Scene** when Hunter's title must have still been around: in 1912 it was published as **In the gloaming** in *The Windsor Magazine* 1912 No. 214

Another etching of this scene sold by Peter Wilson Auctioneers, Nantwich, 2015.

Personally sold or gifted etchings by Colin Hunter were often signed on the mount. Another etching of this scene is signed: "To James Richmond with the etcher's kind regards and best wishes".

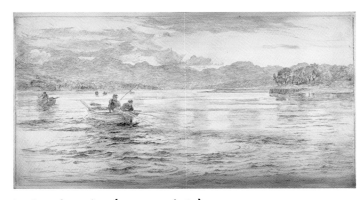

### In the gloaming (copper plate)

Original copper plate, 33 × 61 cm, 13" × 24"

© Colin Hunter family estate

The engraving **In the gloaming** was inspired by the painting **Summer fishing**.

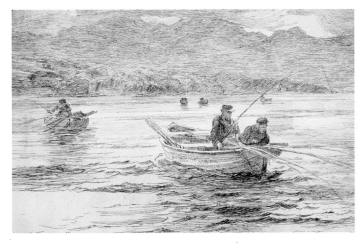

**In the gloaming (copper plate detail)**

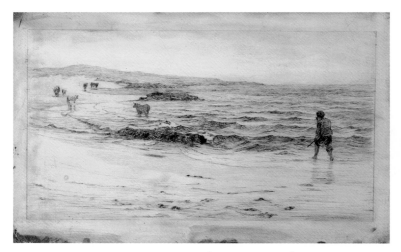

**Highland cattle in the shallows (copper plate)**

Original copper plate, 17.8 × 27.9 cm, 7" × 11"

© Colin Hunter family estate

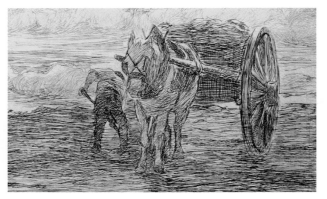

**Harvesting seaweed with horse and cart (copper plate detail)**

Original copper plate engraving, 33 × 24.1 cm, 13" × 9.5"

© Colin Hunter family estate

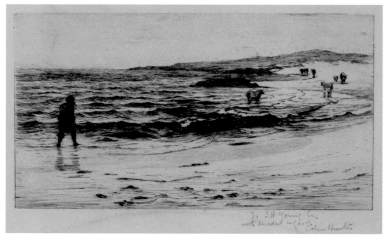

**Highland cattle in the shallows (etching)**

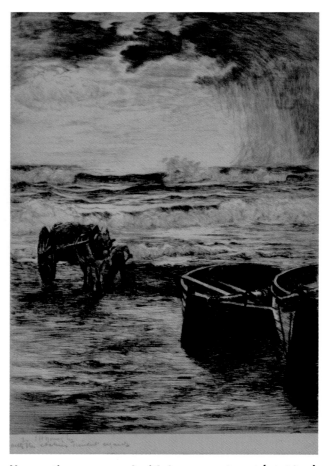

**Harvesting seaweed with horse and cart (etching)**

Handwritten caption on print reads *To J H Young with the etcher's kindest regards.* J H Young was Colin Hunter's father-in-law.

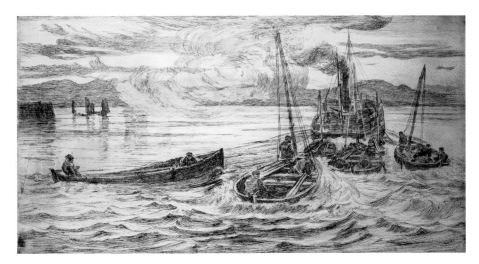

**Day's work done (copper plate)**

Original copper plate engraving, 19.1 × 34.3 cm, 7.5" × 13.5"

© Colin Hunter family estate

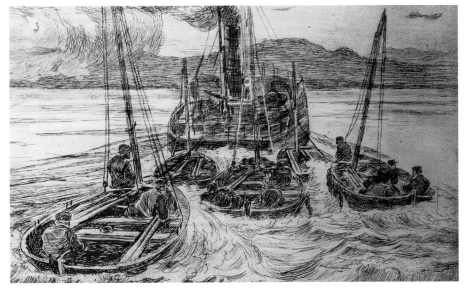

**Day's work done (copper plate detail)**

The etcher's needle work is "very fine" (as on a handwritten note by Gabrielle Kuster, Hunter's granddaughter, on the paper wrapped around this copper plate).

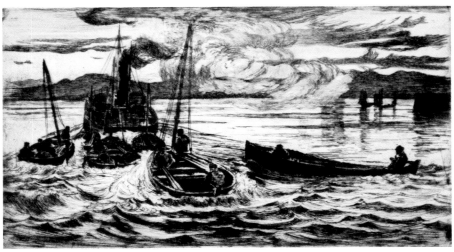

**Day's work done (etching)**

Signed on mount by Colin Huter

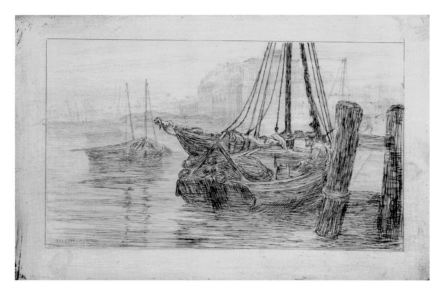

**In harbour (copper plate)**

Original copper plate engraving, 10.2 × 15.2 cm, 4" × 6"

© Colin Hunter family estate

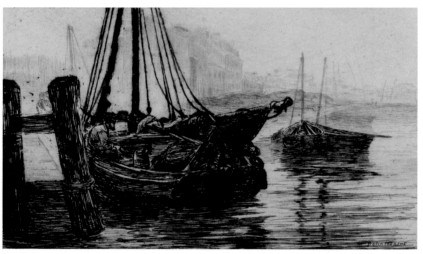

**In harbour (etching)**

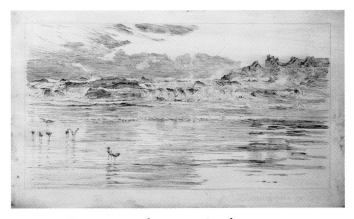

**Seven gulls on beach (copper plate)**

Original copper plate engraving, 15.2 × 24.1 cm, 6" × 9.5"

© Colin Hunter family estate

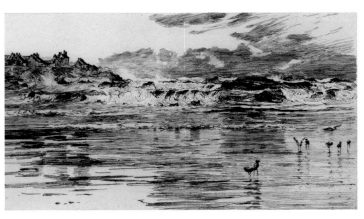

**Seven gulls on beach (etching)**

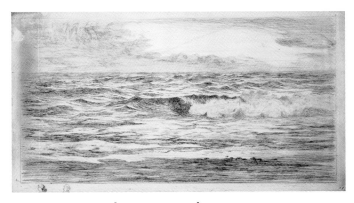

**The restless sea (copper plate)**

Original copper plate engraving, 21.6 × 38.1 cm, 8.5" × 15"

© Colin Hunter family estate

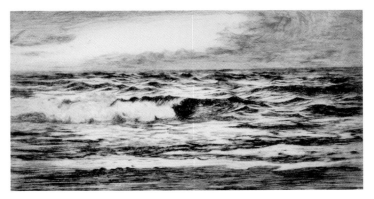

**The restless sea (etching)**

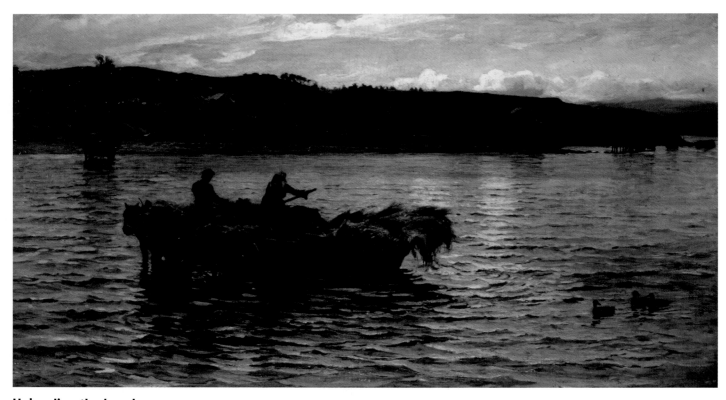

## Unloading the bracken

Also known as **Carting seaweed on a Scottish loch**

1881 (date indistinct), oil on canvas, 86 × 152 cm, 33.9" × 59.8"

Signed and dated LR

Image courtesy Sotheby's

Sold, Sotheby's, Gleneagles Hotel, 02 Sep 1998 Lot 1332

This painting has also been recorded elsewhere with the date of 1861. It is believed that 1881 is the correct date but after cleaning or damage the date has been misread as 1861.

It is believed that this painting was incorrectly titled **Carting seaweed**. If you compare the painting **Bringing home the bracken** – as named by Hunter himself – (see page 223) the similarity is striking. There is a wispiness of the bracken cargo. Compare this with the cargo of seaweed in **Their only harvest** (see page 124). The way the seaweed has been painted there is very different to the painting of the bracken.

The oil on canvas painting inspired the copper plate engraving and etching opposite.

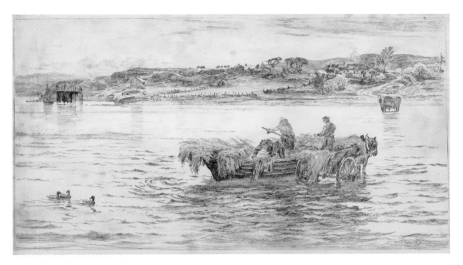

**Unloading the bracken (copper plate)**

*c.*1881, original copper plate engraving,
33 × 58.4 cm, 13" × 23"

© Colin Hunter family estate

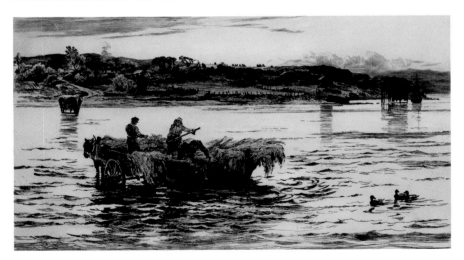

**Unloading the bracken (copper plate detail)**

The detail shows clearly the skill of the etcher's needle

**Unloading the bracken (etching)**

*c.*1881

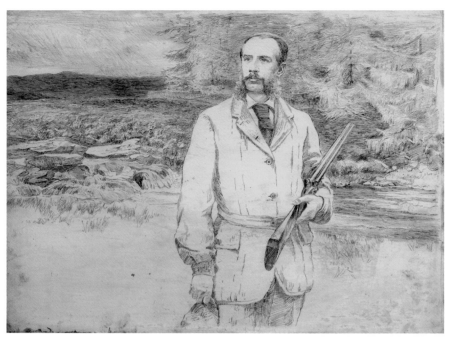

**Good shot (copper plate)**

Original copper plate, 44.5 × 58.4 cm, 17.5" × 23"

© Colin Hunter family estate

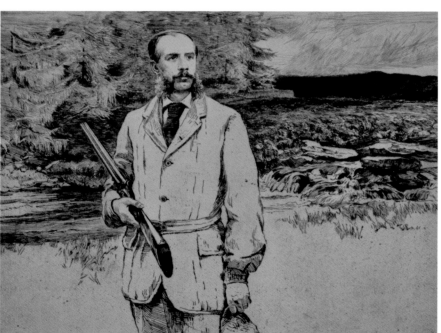

**Good shot (etching)**

Colin Hunter was known to be an ardent yachtsman, fisherman, golfer and shot.[63]

For this reason it was queried whether or not this man with a gun was Colin Hunter himself. But family descendants were not convinced although a family likeness could not be dismissed. Colin Hunter's father (1804–78) or his Uncle Colin (1810–92) may have been good shots too? If either of them shared this sport with Colin, perhaps he took the opportunity to draw this scene.

63  Review, *New York Times*, Sunday 24th July 1898

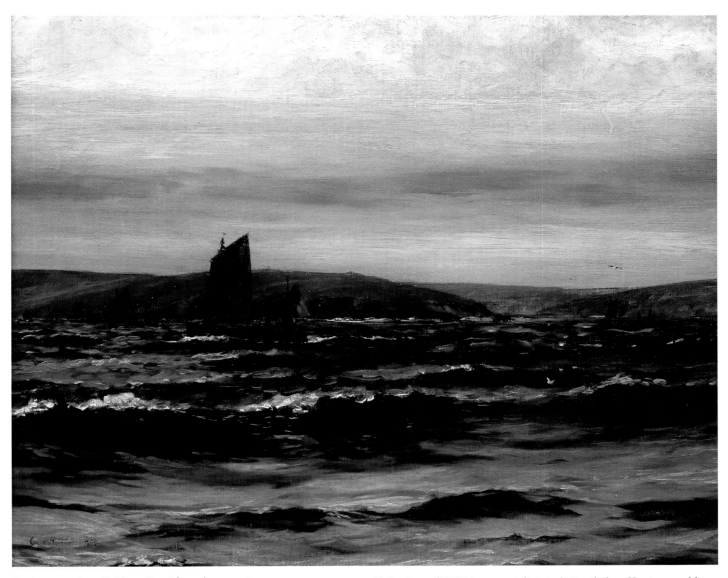

## Early morning fishing fleet leaving port

1860(?), oil on canvas, laid on board, 45 × 56 cm, 17.5" × 22"

Signed Colin Hunter, indistinctly dated 1860 LL

Image courtesy Bonhams International Auctioneers & Valuers

Sold, Bonhams, Chester, 2013

**Provenance**

2013 Painting came from estate of a dealer in Yorkshire who left his chattels to the benefit of York Museums. They retained quite a number of pieces and sold the remainder. The dealer had been active really through the 1970s and 1980s and not done much buying or selling since. (Courtesy, Bonhams)

If the date of 1860 is correct (it is indistinct) then Hunter would have been nineteen years old when he painted this and it would be one of his earliest known works. He was probably living at Princes Street, Helensburgh at this time.

# The Gare Loch (or Gareloch)   A sea loch that opens into the Firth of Clyde near Helensburgh

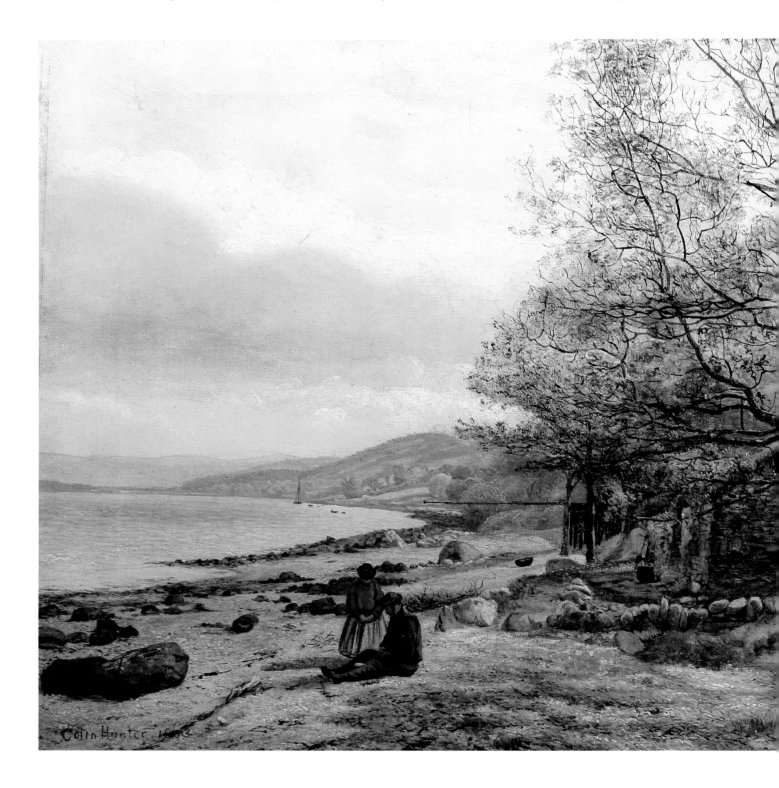

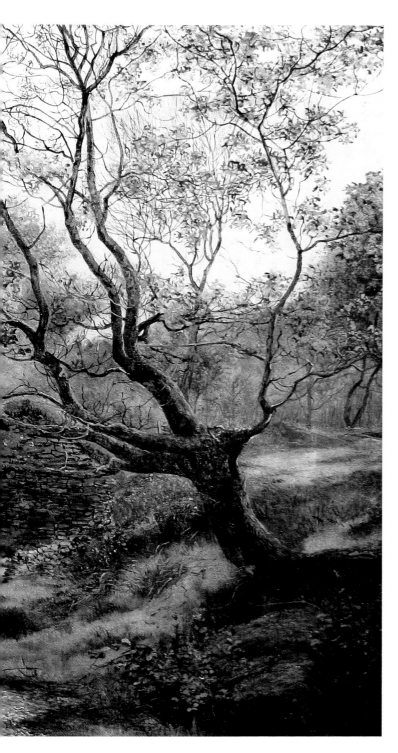

## On the Gare Loch near Shandon Ferry by Rhu, Dumbartonshire, nr Helensburgh

(Has also been sold as **Figures on a shore**)
1863, oil on canvas, 40 × 60 cm, 16" × 24"

Signed, dated and titled verso

Image courtesy Bonhams International Auctioneers & Valuers

Private collection

One of Hunter's earliest dated works. He would have been 21 or 22 years old.

See similar work and location **Row (now 'Rhu'), Gare Loch** in following images.

Sold, Bonhams, London (entitled **Figures on a shore**), 2008

Not sold, McTear's, Glasgow, 2014

Sold, Wright Marshall, Knutsford, 2017

It is not surprising that Hunter frequently painted the Gare Loch early in his career as his home town of Helensburgh was at its mouth.

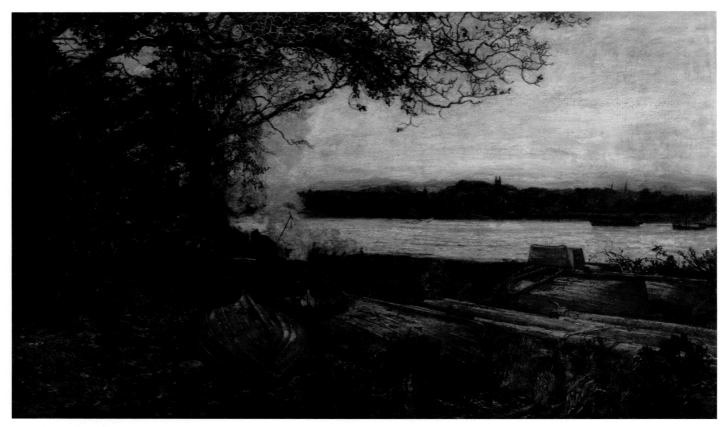

## Row (now 'Rhu'), Gare Loch

Undated but possibly 1860s, oil on canvas, 107 × 185 cm,
42.1" × 72.8"[64]

By permission of East Ayrshire Council/East Ayrshire Leisure

**Acquisition**
Gifted 1924 by Sir Alexander Walker, grandson of the famous
Johnnie Walker (whisky). He was a major donor of art works and
other items to the East Ayrshire collections.

'Row' became 'Rhu' in the 1920s.

The painting's viewpoint seems to be over the water from Rhu, on
the Rosneath side of the loch and this is apparently also known as
the Rhu Narrows. The current Rhu and Shandon Parish Church
which appears in the painting was built around 1851.[65] (See similar
work **On the Gare Loch near Shandon Ferry** 1863 on page 82)

---

64  Dimensions vary according to some records, but these dimensions
    have been confirmed by East Ayrshire Leisure
65  Acknowledgement: Jason Sutcliffe, East Ayrshire Leisure, Kilmarnock

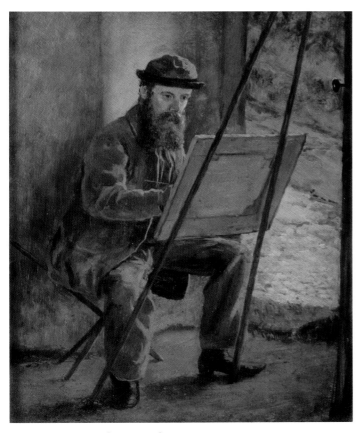

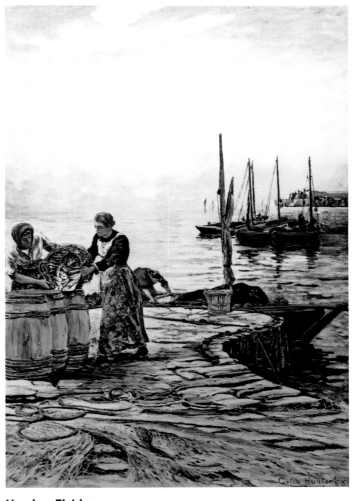

## J Milne Donald (1819–66), Sketching

Undated but possibly c.1861, oil on millboard, 25.4 × 20.3 cm, 10" × 8"

© CSG CIC Glasgow Museums Collection

### Provenance

Gift from G. Telfer Bear (1874–1973), artist, 1940

When Hunter was still a young man, John Milne Donald was his Scottish artist friend albeit a rather ungracious mentor. It is likely that Hunter painted this portrait before he left Helensburgh to live in Edinburgh (c.1863). Hunter was about 25 years old when Milne died in 1866 and by then Hunter had been living in both Edinburgh and Glasgow.

Apparently, Milne Donald did not share much with Hunter when it came to offering training to the budding artist. Milne Donald was an old landscape painter who printed off his landscapes and sold them for a few pounds. He was a Highlander and full of the true Celtic jealousy. He guided Hunter but little, even though he allowed Hunter to accompany him on his sketching rambles.[66]

## Herring Fishing

Also known as **Women sorting fish**

1865, hand coloured antique print, 100.3 × 69.8 cm, 39.5" × 27.5"

Private Collection

Sold, 30 October 2013 as an oil on canvas and dated 1885[67]

If 1865 is the correct date, this was painted when Hunter was 24 years old. He was probably living in Edinburgh.

---

66  *The Art Journal*, April 1885

---

67  The hand coloured print is dated 1865, the oil on canvas as 1885. One of the dates must be incorrect.

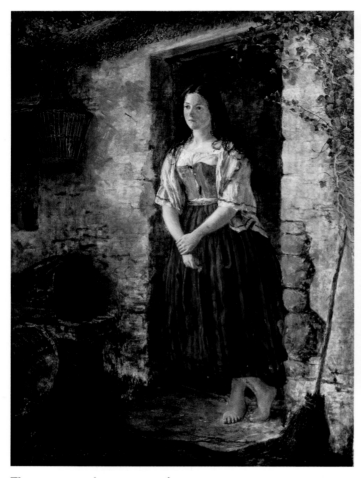

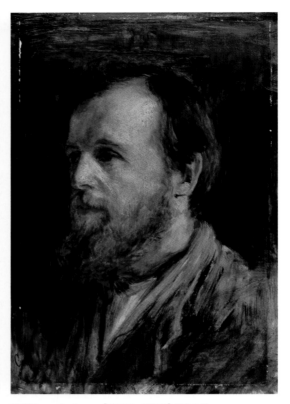

## The cottage door, a reverie

1869, oil on canvas, 67 × 49 cm, 26.5" × 19"

Signed Colin Hunter LL

The date appears to read 1869 although somewhat indistinct[68]

Private collection

Sold, Bonhams, Edinburgh, 2011

At this time, Hunter was probably living at 12 St Andrew's Square, Edinburgh

## William Leiper (1839–1916) RSA[69]

1869, oil on canvas, 31.5 × 21.6 cm, 12.4" × 8.5"

Aberdeen Art Gallery & Museums Collections

**Provenance**
Bequeathed to Aberdeen by James Dunn, 1928

An early work and one of the few portraits Hunter painted. He would have been 28 years old and at this time was probably living in Edinburgh where he had a studio at 12 St Andrew's Square or travelling frequently between there and Helensburgh.

It is unlikely that this painting was a formal commission as Hunter was not known as a portraitist. Probably Hunter painted Leiper as a friend because he knew him as both a local artist and architect. Leiper was well known for his domestic architecture in and around Hunter's hometown of Helensburgh. In addition to his architecture Leiper shared Hunter's love of art. Leiper went on to become an accomplished watercolourist in the late 1870s when he took a break from architecture to pursue painting.

Also see **Black's Tower**, page 35

---

68  Bonhams condition report 2011

69  Royal Scottish Academy of Art & Architecture

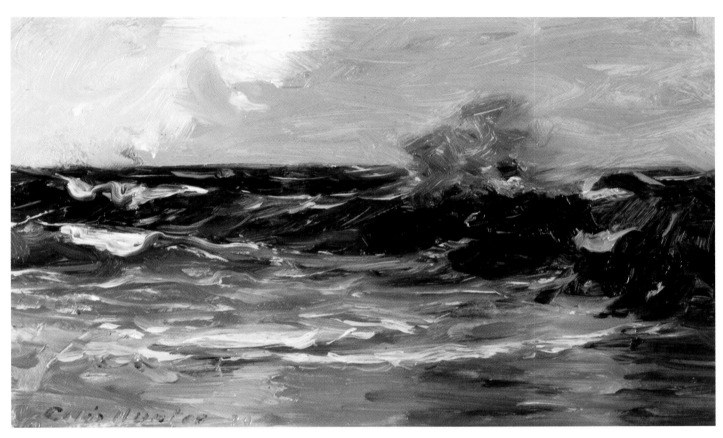

**Breakers**

1870, oil on board, 12 × 19.5 cm, 4.8" × 7.6"

© Dundee City Council (Dundee's Art Galleries and Museums)

**Provenance**
Purchased from James Guthrie Orchar's niece, Miss A M Douglas, 1924
Gifted to Dundee Art Galleries and Museums, 1987

In 1870 Hunter was probably living at 54 George Square, Glasgow

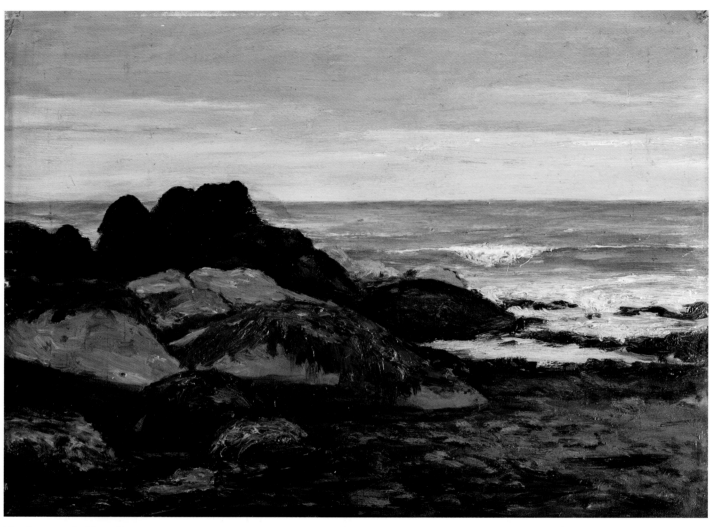

**Rocky coastal landscape**

1870, oil on board, 20.3 × 30.5 cm, 8" × 12"

Signed Colin Hunter verso

Private collection

Sold by Lawrences Auctioneers, Bletchingley, Surrey, 2012

At this time, Hunter was probably living at 54 George Square, Glasgow

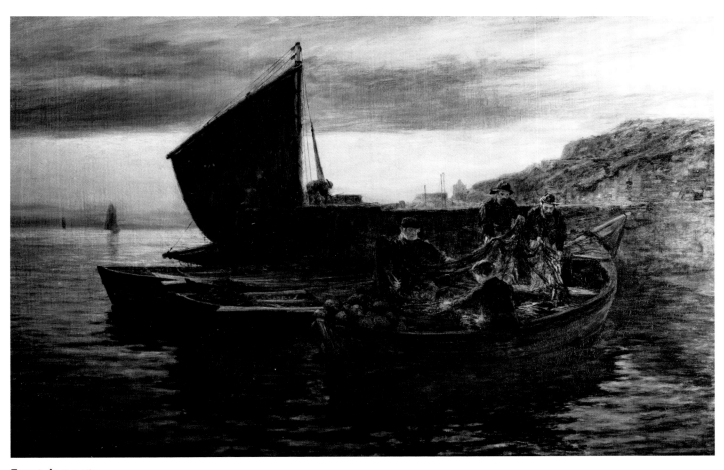

## Emptying nets

Also known as **Fisherman drawing in nets in coastal waters**

1871, oil on canvas, 75 × 121cm, 29.5" × 47.5"

Signed and dated 'Colin Hunter 1871' LL

Private collection

Sold, Bonhams, Edinburgh, 2010

Restored by Simon Gillespie Studio, London, 2010

At this time, Hunter had a studio in London and was probably living at 2 Langham Place, Chiswick.

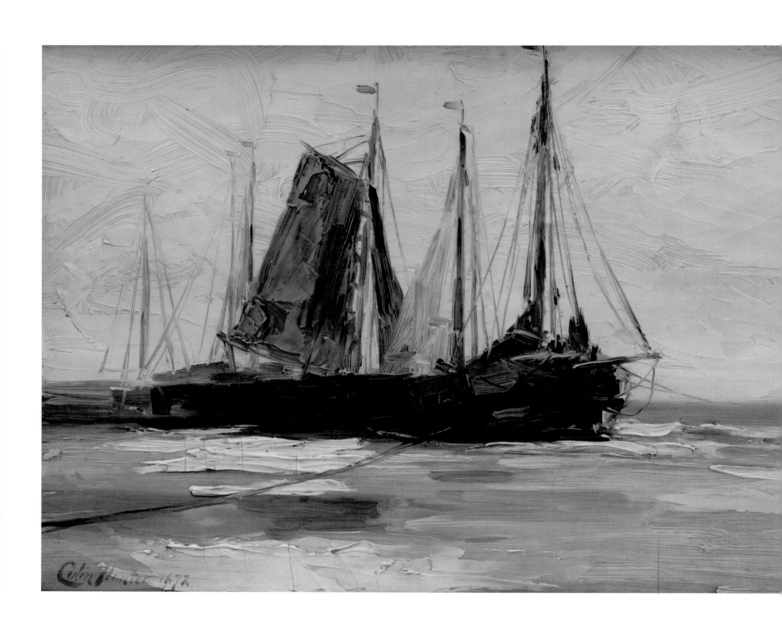

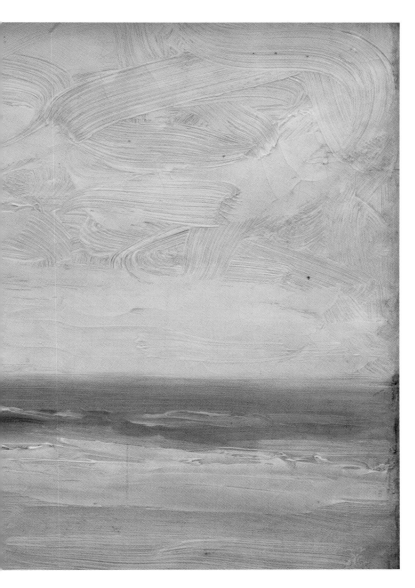

**Waiting for the tide**

1872, oil on canvas, 28 × 55 cm, 11" × 21.7"

Art Gallery of New South Wales, Sydney

**Provenance**
Purchased from Ernest Thurlow, 1940

**Bibliography**
Renee Free, *Art Gallery of New South Wales catalogue of British paintings*, Sydney, 1987

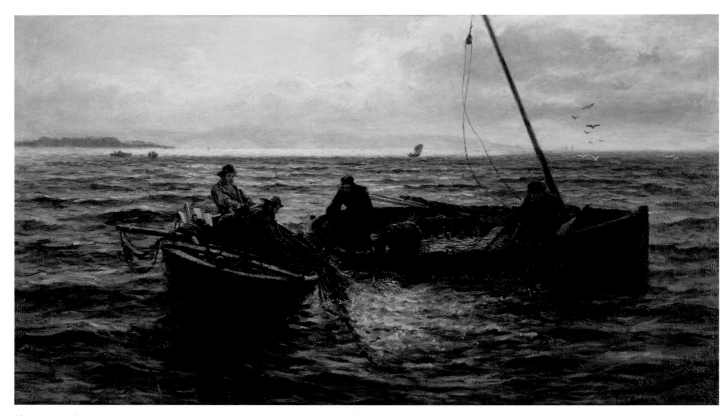

## Harvest of the sea

1872, oil on canvas, 71.1 × 121.9 cm, 28" × 48"

Image courtesy of and © Waddington's Auctioneers and Appraisers, Toronto, Canada

Sold, Waddington's, Toronto, 2012

Note the etching made of this painting but called **Herring fishing** (see right).

'... the sea pictures of Colin Hunter ... who uses the palette-knife to load the lights of the waves till the impasto actually defines the line of the water as if with a solid crest. This tells with tremendous effect while the light falls from above, but with a low or side light falsifies instead of intensifying the truth. But it cannot be denied that this method gives irresistible force to such a picture as Colin Hunter's **Harvest of the Sea** (1872) and to his other pictures **The Leeshore** and **The Village of Aroch** (1878), when seen at the distance and under the light for which they are calculated.'

*The Times*, 26th May 1879

Location is not known, but it is not in Scotland:

'Mr Hunter does not forget his Scottish origin, and with a single exception, **The Harvest of the Sea**, has always gathered his subjects, as in this instance, from the shores of his fatherland.'

*The Art Journal*, London, July 1881

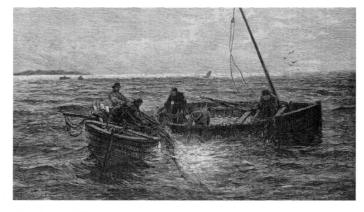

## Herring fishing

Also known as **Herring trawlers**
c.1872, engraving by R Paterson after picture by Colin Hunter, engraved surface, 29.2 × 50.2 cm, 11.5" × 19.8"

Image reproduced from unidentified magazine

Courtesy Marcia Rider

See the painting above, **Harvest of the sea**, from which this etching was made.

At this time, Hunter had a studio in London and was probably living at 2 Langham Place, Chiswick.

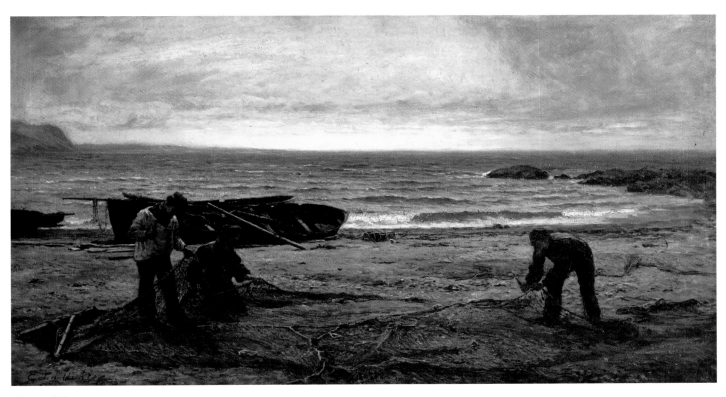

**Three fishers**

1873, oil on canvas, 66.4 × 123 cm, 26.1" × 48.4"

New Walk Museum & Art Gallery, Leicester/Bridgeman Images

Exhibited RA 1873

**Provenance**
Purchased at Christie's, 1891

1873 is the year Hunter married Isabella Young in Glasgow. At the time of his marriage he gave his address as Parklee, Helensburgh.

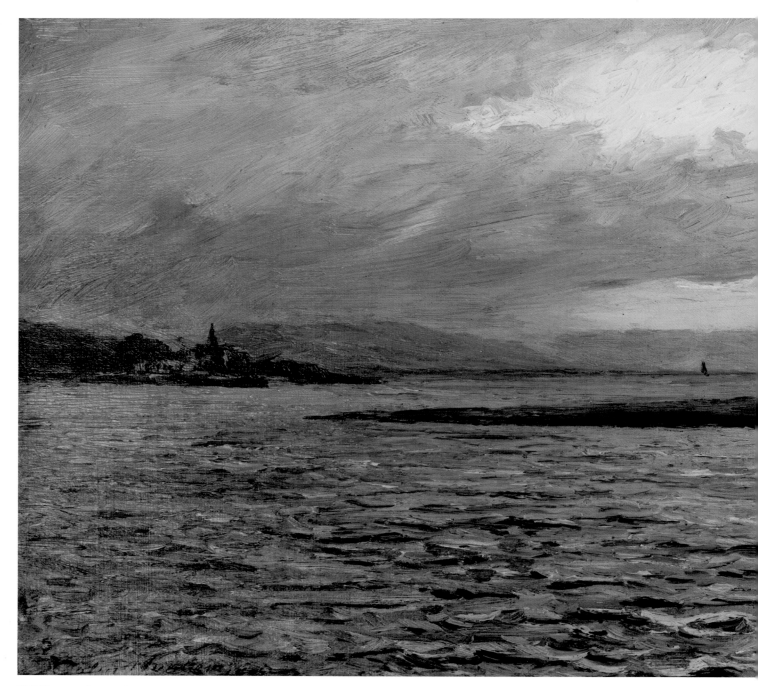

**Off the west coast**

1873, oil on canvas, 38 × 75cm, 15" × 30"
Signed and dated

Private collection

Sold, Lyon & Turnbull, Edinburgh, 2009

This is the year Hunter married Isabella Young in Glasgow. At the
time of his marriage he gave his address as Parklee, Helensburgh.

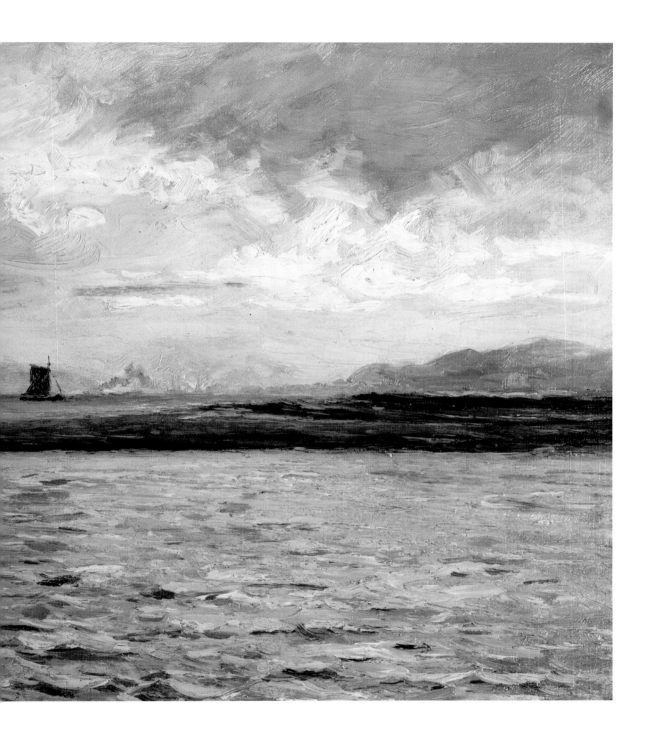

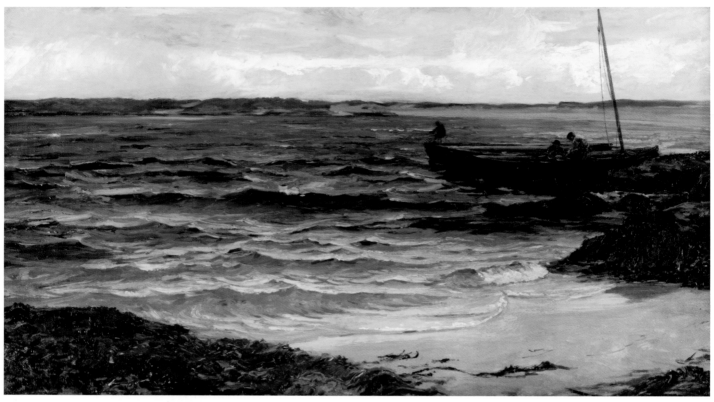

**On the west coast of Scotland**

1879, oil on canvas, 49.5 × 88.9cm, 19.5" × 35"

© Dundee City Council (Dundee's Art Galleries and Museums)

**Provenance**
Collected by James Guthrie Orchard; presented to Dundee Art
Galleries and Museums 1987

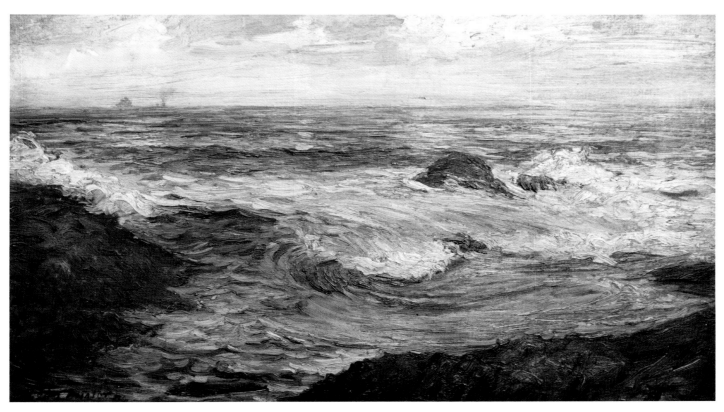

**Stormy seas**

1874, oil on board, 34.3 × 58.4 cm, 13.5" × 23"

Signed and dated, Colin Hunter 74

Private collection

Sold, Bonhams, Edinburgh, 2011

At this time, Colin and Isabella were probably living at 61 Carlton Hill, St John's Wood, London.

# COMING ASHORE.

### COLIN HUNTER.

THE following little poems by Barry Cornwall form a fitting accompaniment to "Coming Ashore." This picture was exhibited at the Royal Academy in 1874.

"How silent are the winds! No billow roars:
But all is tranquil as Elysian shores!
The silver margin which aye runneth round
The moon-enchanted sea, hath here no sound:
Even Echo speaks not on these radiant moors!

"What! is the Giant of the ocean dead,
Whose strength was all unmatch'd beneath the sun?
No; he reposes! Now his toils are done,
More quiet than the babbling brooks is he.
So mightiest powers by deepest calms are fed,
And sleep, how oft, in things that gentlest be!"

"A perilous life, and sad as life may be,
Hath the lone fisher on the lonely sea,
O'er the wild waters labouring, far from home,
For some bleak pittance e'er compelled to roam:
Few hearts to cheer him through his dangerous life,
And none to aid him in the stormy strife:
Companion of the sea and silent air,
The lonely fisher thus must ever fare;
Without the comfort, hope,—with scarce a friend,
He looks through life, and only sees—its end!"

Mr. Colin Hunter has acquired a well-earned reputation as a painter of coast scenes, and has been a regular contributor to the Royal Academy for many years. Amongst his most successful works may be mentioned "Trawlers waiting for Darkness," 1873; "With Wind and Tide," 1874; "Kelp Burning," 1876; "Store for the Cabin" and "Ebbing Tide," 1878. To this year's Exhibition he sent "Their only Harvest," which has been purchased by the Royal Academy under the terms of the Chantrey bequest.

## Coming Ashore

1874

Coming Ashore was exhibited in the Royal Academy in 1874 but no image of it has been found. This is the only reference to it, a poem that "forms a fitting accompaniment to it".

This piece was probably published in 1879 because the last sentence refers to the year Colin Hunter sent **Their Only Harvest** to the RA for exhibition – 1879.

Note the references to **Trawlers waiting for darkness, With wind and tide, Kelp burning, Store for the cabin** and **Ebbing Tide**.

Courtesy Kate Rider

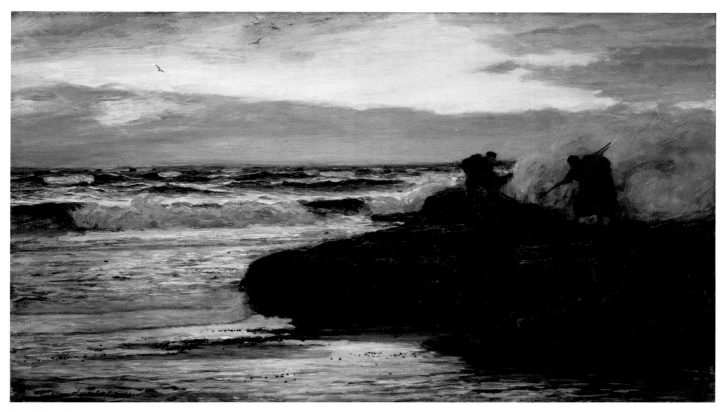

## Seaside fire

Possibly **Kelp burning**

1876, oil on canvas, 54.6 × 95.3 cm, 21.5" × 37.5"

Signed and dated LL

Private collection

**Provenance**

Sold in Texas 2018 and exported to England

This may be a painting called Kelp burning which Hunter exhibited in the Royal Academy in 1876. Unfortunately, no image or dimensions were available from the RA archives to confirm this.

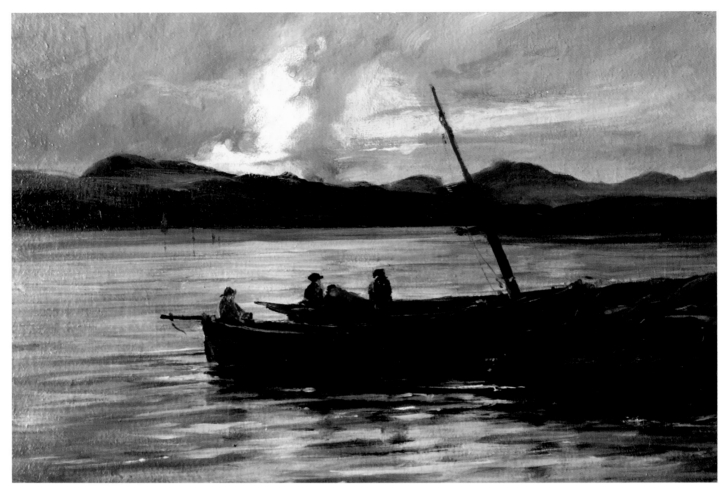

**Fishing boats at dusk**

Undated but likely *c.*1873, oil on canvas, 23.5 × 33 cm, 9.3" × 13"

Probably a copy of, or second version of **Trawlers waiting for darkness** (see opposite)

Signed

Private collection

Sold, Swan & Turne, 2015

Note similarity to **Trawlers waiting for darkness** (see page 103). Because of the similarity with **Trawlers waiting for darkness** which was dated 1873, it is a good guess that this picture was painted at the same time and in the same location.

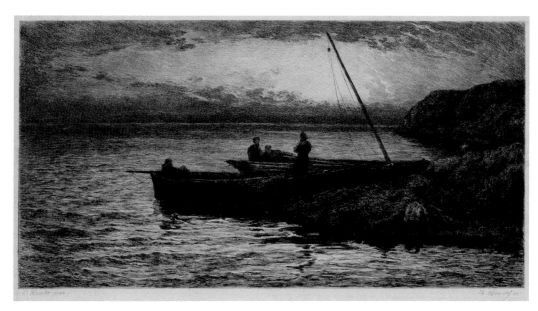

## Trawlers waiting for darkness

1873, etching/engraving, 19 × 34.5 cm, 7.5" × 13.5"

C. Hunter pinx. Th. Chauvel sc.

Courtesy Marcia Rider.

Theophile Chauvel (1831–1909) engraved this from Colin's original oil that was exhibited in the Royal Academy 1873 and the Royal Scottish Academy 1874.

See similar scene opposite, **Fishing boats at dusk**.

The original **Trawlers Waiting for darkness** in oil 1873, is recognised as Hunter's first major success and brought him significant public recognition.

Another **Trawlers waiting for darkness** was exhibited in 1870 in the Royal Scottish Academy – but no image of that painting has been found to establish if it is the same picture as this one. It was priced at £80 which suggests a large, probably oil painting but there is no record of whether it was oil or watercolour. Dimensions are not recorded either which would help identify whether it was the same painting as was exhibited in 1874. There is no record of the 1870 painting having been sold.[70]

The original painting has not been found. Neither Academy has an image of it. Considering it was hailed as one of Hunter's best paintings (see below) it is particularly disappointing that it has not been traced.

Hunter frequently painted around Tarbert and Loch Fyne.

'Tarbert, coyly hiding itself in a winding, lake-like inlet [of Loch Fyne], fretted by rocky promontory and isle, is a fishing village, crouched at the feet of a ruined keep which Robert Bruce inhabited.

Quarter of a century ago it was the St Ives of the Scottish painter; today the taste for yellow wrack and fishing skiffs is somewhat in abeyance, but the same spirit, pensive mystery, and expectation haunt the place as Colin Hunter found in his **Trawlers waiting for darkness**. It is only a narrow neck of land that keeps Loch Fyne from the appealing arms of the Atlantic.'

*Journeys in Scotland: The Clyde River and Firth*,
Neil Munro (1863–1930)

'It is in pictures such as **Trawlers waiting for darkness** (1873) ... where the sentiment of dying light is associated with some incident of sea-toil with its perils and uncertainties, that this pathetic quality is most marked ...'

*Scottish Painting, Past and Present*, 1620-1908,
James Lewis Caw. 1908

"**Trawlers waiting for darkness** is in all ways one of Hunter's best works. Both the act and the sentiment of waiting, of patient expectation, are thoroughly well suited to treatment in paint. There is nothing to make us rebel against the immobility of the material, and when the subject allows us to see not only the men who wait but the event for which they wait, the perfection of a theme is reached. Mr Hunter has used his opportunity in the happiest way. As we look at this picture we enter into the feelings of the silent fishermen in the foreground; we watch the light upon the cloud edges, and we almost expect to see it die away and the brawny arms and chests set to work to start the boats down to the darkened water.'

*The Art Journal*, April 1885

---

70  Agnes Wood, RSA Collections Volunteer

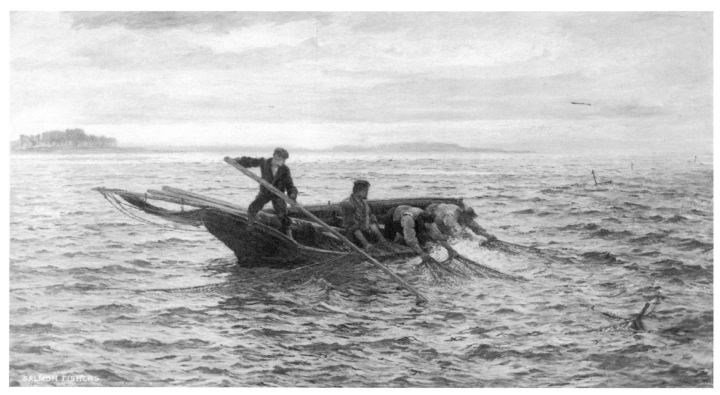

**The salmon fishers, Loch Fyne or The salmon fishers**

Originally **Salmon stake nets**

1874, oil on canvas, 114 × 203 cm, 45" × 80"

Image courtesy National Art Gallery of New South Wales, Sydney, State Library NSW.

In the image produced in the Art Gallery of New South Wales *Illustrated Collection Catalogue* 1899, the label under the painting reads "The salmon fishers" and then, indistinctly, "Colin Hunter, purchased 1881".

Exhibited Royal Academy 1874

Exhibited Melbourne International Exhibition 1880 (opened 1st October)

Purchased by Sydney Art Gallery 1881 for £900. A reference is made to the purchase in the New Zealand newspaper the *Bruce Herald*, 25 March 1881, page 3, in an article on The Melbourne Exhibition:

"The Sydneyites are also negotiating for the purchase of the Colin Hunter, entitled **Salmon Fishers, Loch Fyne** ... So far, Victoria has not made a single acquisition to help enrich her collection of works of art."

It therefore appears Sydney bought the painting after it appeared in the Melbourne Exhibition.

Sold by National Art Gallery of NSW 18th February 1959 through the auctioneer firm James R Lawson for £474.4.0.[71]

Included in the *Illustrated Catalogue* of the National Art Gallery of NSW in 1917.

The Sydney Art Gallery has a record of a telegram sent from London recorded in the Trustees Minutes March 1881. It reads: "Telegram from (Sir H. Sandford) to Mr Montefiore states the picture Salmon Fishers was secured for £900."
Unfortunately, the original telegram has not been found and the name of the sender in the minutes is difficult to decipher. However, the gallery believes it may be Sir Herbert Sanford, who was involved in organising various exhibitions in Australia and who had been acting Assistant Director at the South Kensington Museum.[72]

'In Colin Hunter's **Salmon Fishers, Loch Fyne**, we have a representative of the realistic art of the present Scottish school; and certainly there is in the whole Exhibition no finer specimen of vigorous brushwork, nor any more masterly interpretation of nature.'

> From an article on the Melbourne International Exhibition 1880 in The Pamphlet Collection of Sir Robert Stout, Vol 41, published Victoria University of Wellington Library, Wellington, New Zealand

---

71  Art Gallery of NSW Trustee Minutes

72  Acknowledgement: Kay Truelove, Librarian, Art Gallery of New South Wales

There is an unresolved puzzle about this painting and that named **Salmon stake nets**. The Royal Academy exhibited a painting entitled **Salmon stake nets** in 1874. However, no image of a painting with this name has been traced. Then in the 1959 catalogue of paintings for sale by the National Art Gallery of New South Wales, Colin Hunter's **Salmon fishers, Loch Fyne** was found and the listing clearly stated that it was exhibited in the Royal Academy in 1874. Until, and unless, another painting comes to light proving that **Salmon stake nets** and **Salmon fishers, Loch Fyne** are two different paintings, it can only be assumed that, at some unknown point, the painting adopted a new name.

Furthermore, in The Art Journal, April 1885, it is stated, "In 1874 Mr Hunter's chief picture was **Salmon stake nets**, now in the Sydney Museum".

This leads to the conclusion that sometime after 1874 the picture was re-named.

The picture is included in the NSW Government Printer series – Art Gallery. Unfortunately and confusingly in the State Library catalogue it is called **The Salmon Fishers** (without Loch Fyne) and the date of the work 1896 is presumed to be a mistake.

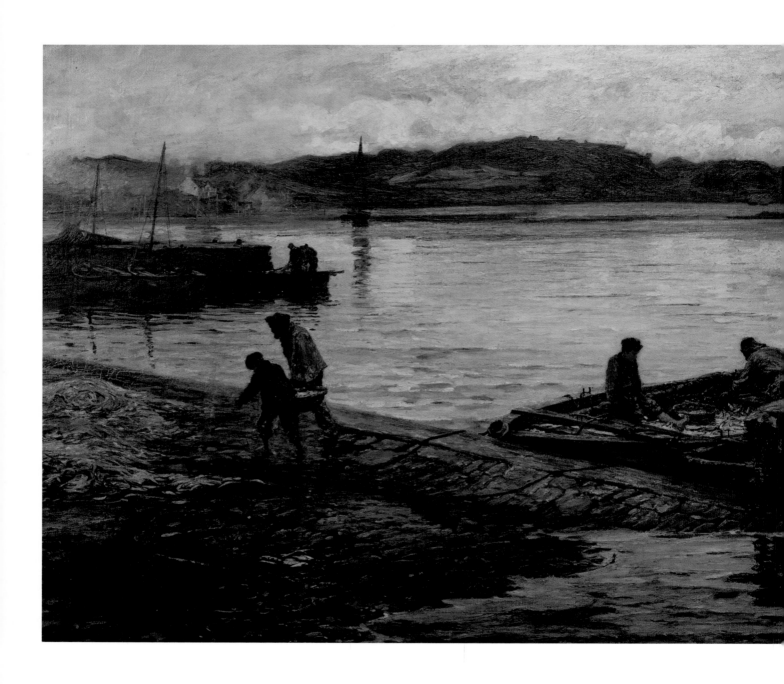

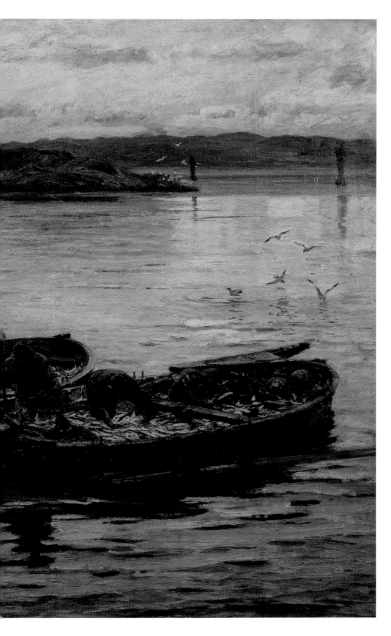

## Silver of the Sea

Also known as **The Silvery Sea**
Subtitle: **Herring fishing in Loch Fyne**
1880, oil on canvas, 86 × 158 cm, 33.9" × 62.2"

© Iziko Museums of South Africa Art Collections. Photography by Carina Beyer.

**Provenance**
Exhibited Royal Academy, 1880
Sold by Hunter to Donald Currie MP for £750 (today's value £63,000), 1880
Exhibited Royal Scottish Academy. Lent by Donald Currie MP, 1881
Presented to Iziko Museums of South Africa by Sir Donald Currie, 1899
Exhibited "British Pictures" arranged by the South Africa Fine Arts Association at the Drill Hall, Darling Street, Cape Town (no. 127), 1899

Plaque on frame reads: "Presented to The Cape Colony by Sir Donald Currie GCMG"

Sir Donald Currie GCMG 1825–1909, a Scottish steam ship owner (Union Castle Line), politician and philanthropist.

'Colin Hunter, one of the most Scottish of our sea painters, never tempts a fall by seeking southern sea subjects. He sticks to the West Highland seas and sea lochs, and so vividly brings them before us in either their grim grayness or milder steel colour that we accept the roughness of his impasto, and the summariness of his execution both of sea and boats, fish and figures, because we have received a keen, picturesque impression of the subject.

His **Silver of the Sea** is a smooth estuary with herring boats anchored in the middle distance and a foreground group of them with their crews, unloading their gleaming freight of "fush".'

*The Times*, 18th May 1880

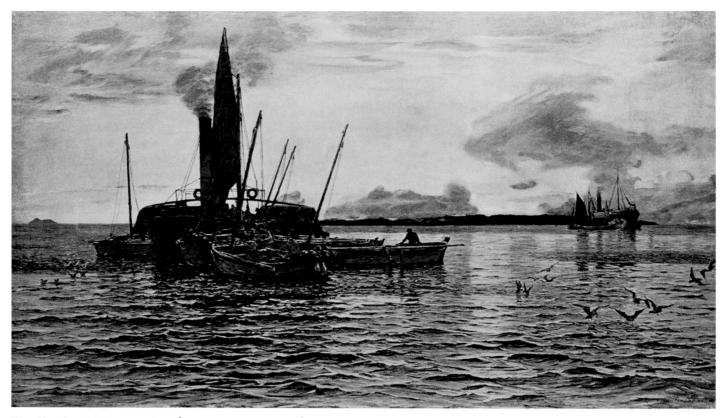

## The Herring Market at Sea (on Loch Fyne Argyll)

1884, oil on canvas, 108.3 × 183.5 cm, 42.6" × 72.2"

Image credit: SOTK2011 / Alamy Stock Photo

Royal Academy Autumn Exhibition 1884

Manchester Art Gallery

Another painting, called **Fishing at Sunset** also painted in 1884, but smaller at 56 × 102 cm, 22" × 40.2", was offered for sale at Sotheby's on 13 December 1989. Apart from being smaller, this painting was almost identical to the one above but there was no figure in the small boat in the centre of the picture. Regrettably Sotheby's no longer have an image of this painting in their archives.

The fishing on the west coast of Scotland, is primarily for herring and mackerel. They are caught by nets not by baited line. Most Scots are familiar with Loch Fyne herring which are smaller and sweeter than average herring. They were plentiful in Hunter's day on this beautiful loch. The fishing fleet was often concentrated at Tarbert. Picturesque small boats with tanned sails and slanting masts filled the harbour as they set forth for a night's fishing.

Owing to the congested area of the harbour, the market of the night's catch often took place in the open sea outside the harbour. Hunter painted this picture of a trading vessel from Glasgow surrounded by fishing craft. The picture is of early morning with reflections of the boats and the sky on the rippling surface of a calm sea.[73]

'By **The herring market at sea**, Hunter thoroughly justified his election to the Royal Academy in the early months of the same year. Like all the rest of his works it was a strong, honest study from reality. For weeks he went out to the fishing grounds of the mouth of the Clyde to paint and study the scene as he has presented it to us. The time is not long after dawn, in summer, and for day after day the painter was before his canvas and at work by four in the morning. This love for art and thoroughness in its pursuit will always lead to great results ...'

*The Art Journal*, April 1885

'**The Herring Market at sea** was painted on Loch Fyne, where steamers follow the boats to their fishing ground in order to take the fish whilst quite fresh to Glasgow and Greenock markets. To paint this scene, Colin Hunter chartered an old tug, past active service, and used to go out as early as 4am to paint the scene of the sale of the fish, which begins at dawn. **Waiting for the homeward bound** was painted under similar conditions off Ailsa Craig, where tugs lie-to in readiness to tow incoming ships up the Clyde.'

*The Windsor Magazine*, 1912

---

73 *Reviewing the Years*, John Young-Hunter

**Gossip**

'From the *Whitehall Review*

The air is still thick with art gossip. Mr Colin Hunter has been entertaining the friends who lately entertained him, and still has found time to finish two magnificent pictures for the Academy. The most important is called **The Herring Market at Sea** and shows us a small fishing steamer surrounded by a cluster of boats, from which the night's catch is being transferred. The sea is nearly calm; the rosy light of early morning suffuses the scene; and over all there is a glamour, a velvety transparency (if such a term may be used) which few other artists could achieve. The other picture [not identified] is one of waves breaking on the beach in a rock-bound bay and is full of colour and motion.'

*The Morning News*, Belfast, 15 April 1884

A copy of **The herring market at sea** was painted and signed by J R Bilenacker (?) which was sold as "After Colin Hunter" in May 2018 by Golding Young & Mawer Auctioneers, Bourne, Lincolnshire.

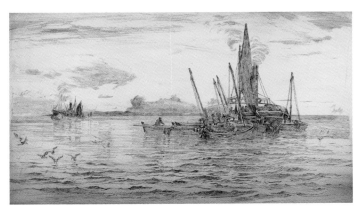

**The herring market at sea (copper plate)**

The original copper plate, 34.9 × 59.7 cm, 13.8" × 23.5"

© Colin Hunter family estate

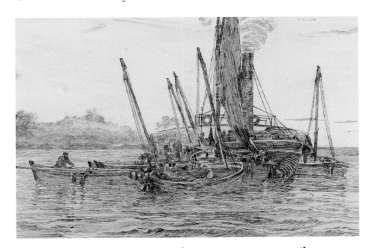

**The herring market at sea (copper plate detail)**

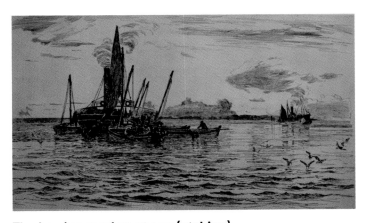

**The herring market at sea (etching)**

1884, etching, 33.5 × 57.5 cm, 13.2" × 22.6"

Image Kate Rider

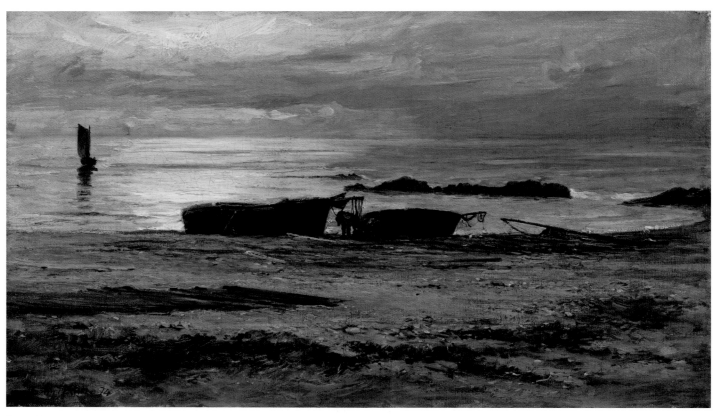

**Beach scene**

1874, oil on canvas, 35.7 × 61.2 cm, 14.1" × 24.1"

© CSG CIC Glasgow Museums Collection

Gifted to Glasgow Museums by Miss Birkmyre, 1956

In 1874 Colin and Isabella were probably living at 61 Carlton Hill,
St John's Wood, London.

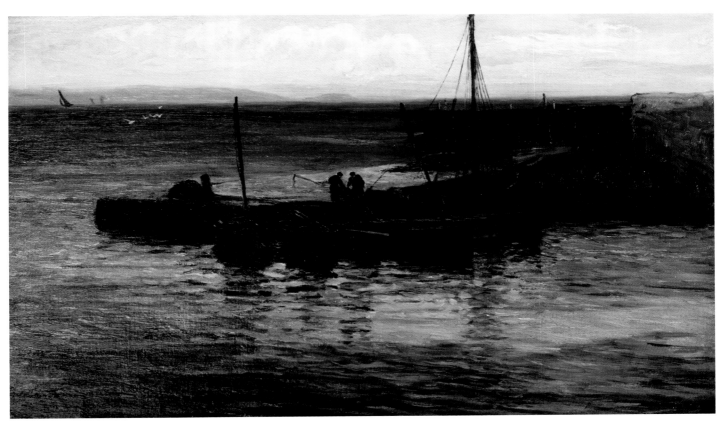

### Carradale Harbour

Also known as entitled on frame **Carradale Pier**
1874, oil on panel, 48 × 75 cm, 18.5" × 30"

Signed and dated Colin Hunter 74

Private collection

Sold by Bonhams Edinburgh, 2008

Restored by Simon Gillespie Studio, London, 2009

At this time, Colin and Isabella were probably living at 61 Carlton Hill, St John's Wood, London.

Carradale on Scotland's west coast is situated on the east coast of Kintyre overlooking the Isle of Arran. Thirteen miles north of Campbeltown, Carradale is a small fishing village with some of the most tranquil and peaceful areas in Scotland such as by Dunvalanree at Port Righ.

Carradale pier is actually a harbour wall these days. In years gone by it was a pier. The dark hills of the Isle of Arran can be seen beyond the small harbour where its fishing fleet gathers.

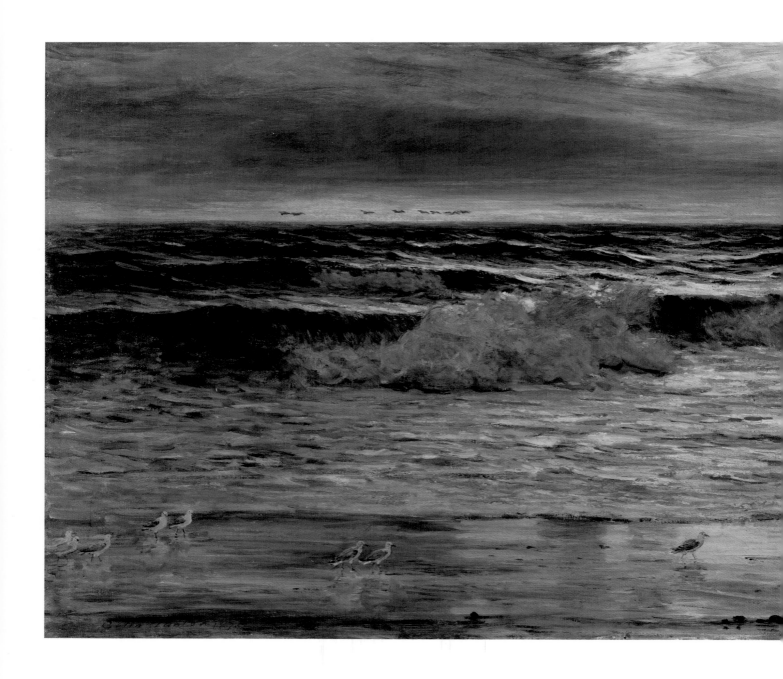

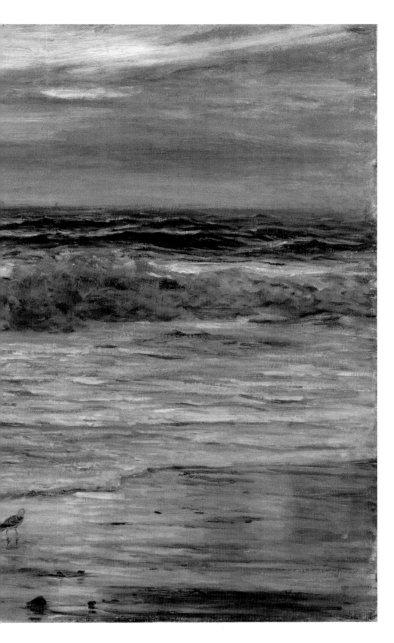

## Sea Piece, Dawn

1875, oil on canvas, 64.8 × 120.7 cm, 25.5" × 47.5"

© CSG CIC Glasgow Museums Collection

**Provenance**
Bequeathed by Adam Teacher, 1898

Another painting, called **Sea Piece**, was exhibited and sold in the Fine Art Exhibition in the Victoria Art Galleries[74] in Dundee in 1892. The Dundee Courier on 27 February 1892, described it as "the masterly and charming Sea Piece (no. 173) by Colin Hunter ARA, was sold to Mr Keiller". However, an image of this painting has not been found, and only the title gives any link to the one above.

---

74  Renamed The McManus in 1984

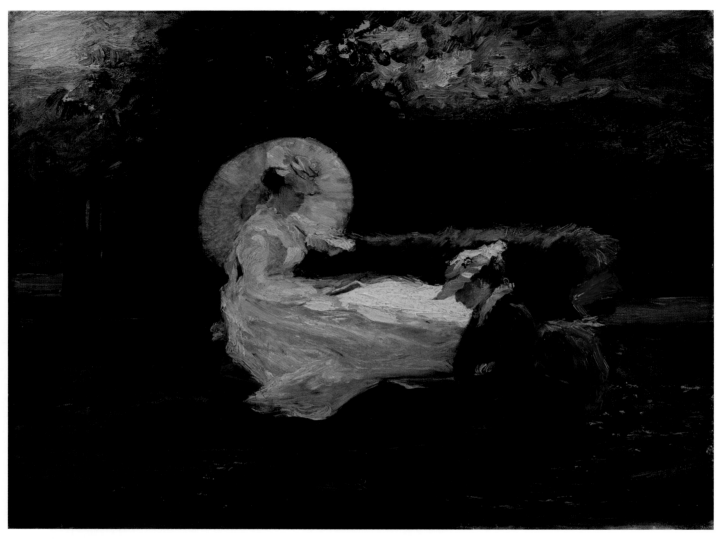

## Ladies in the Garden

1875, oil on canvas, 33 × 43 cm, 13" × 16.9"

Courtesy Marcia Rider

**Provenance**
Family inheritance

Below, the same painting hanging in the Hunters' dining room,
14 Melbury Road

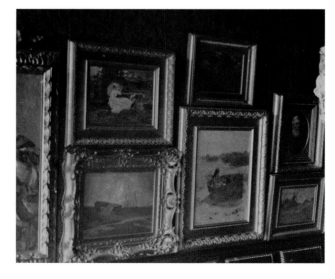

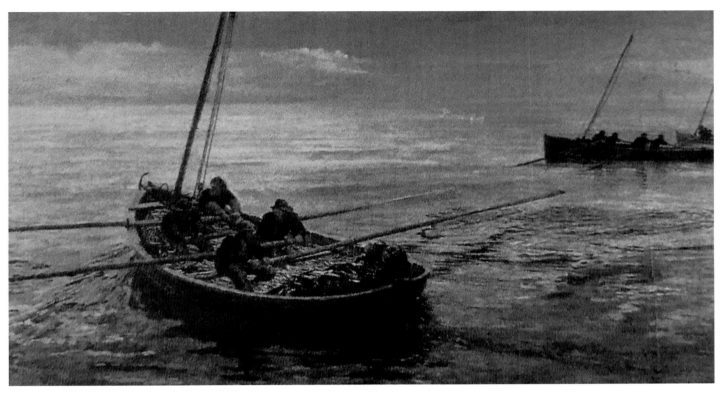

## Give Way

1879 (1875), oil on canvas, 90 × 157 cm, 35.5" × 62"

Signed and dated

Image courtesy Bonhams, reproduced from Phillips 2001 catalogue.

Sold, Phillips (now Bonhams), Edinburgh, 2001

According to Hunter's 1875 accounts **Give Way** was sold (together with **Hours of Rest**) to E.F. White for £800. This contradicts the date given to this painting of 1879 – unless it is a second painting of the same name. Alternatively, it may be that at some point the date on the painting became indistinct and was mis-read as 1879.

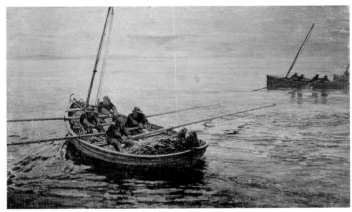

This black and white photo of **Give Way** shows a little clearer detail of the fishermen in the boat.

Image courtesy Kate Rider

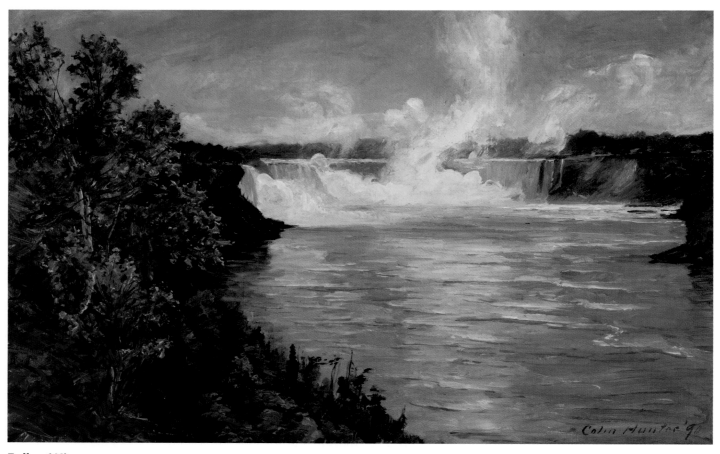

## Falls of Niagara

1890, oil on canvas, 44.5 × 69.9 cm, 17.5" × 27.5"

Signed Colin Hunter 90

© CSG CIC Glasgow Museums Collection

View of the Horse Shoe Falls, with spray rising in clouds in front of the falling water; trees to left. (As described by Scottish Art Galleries *1935 Catalogue of Pictures*)

**Provenance**
1898 Bequeathed to Glasgow by Adam Teacher.
There appear to be several paintings or etchings relating to the Niagara Falls.

1. **The rapids of Niagara above the Falls**, 1884 (Exhibited Royal Academy 1885) (aka **The Horse Shoe Falls**)

2. **Falls of Niagara**, 1890, 44.5 × 69.9 cm (Glasgow Museums) (above)

3. **Niagara Rapids**, 1901, oil on canvas, 147.3 × 330.2 cm (Glasgow Museums)

4. **Niagara Rapids**, etching, 40 × 89 cm (from the original)

It is believed (but not certain) that Hunter visited Niagara Falls only once (1884), but he returned to painting the subject years after his first visit.

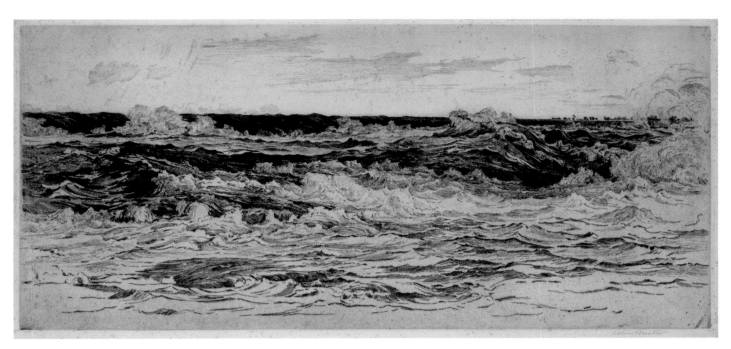

**Niagara rapids**

Etching, 40 × 89 cm, 15.7" × 35"

Signed on mount Colin Hunter.

Image courtesy family by descent

'From the original in the Glasgow Art Gallery.'

*The Windsor Magazine*, 1912

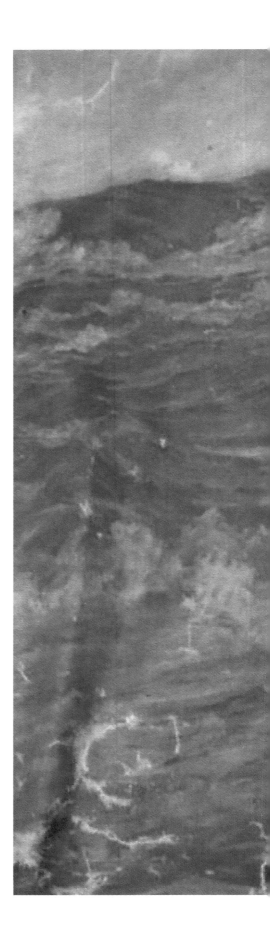

?

## The rapids of Niagara above the Falls

Also known as **The Horse Shoe Falls**
1884. No image found

Exhibited Royal Academy 1885

Sold by Hunter for £200 (today's value £18,000), 1885

Disappointingly no image of this work has been found, but there are several references to this original "Niagara":

Hunter's first works of Niagara were painted from a tiny rock in the middle of the foaming current.[75]

'One of the sensational pictures of the year in London will be Mr Colin Hunter's **The rapids of Niagara above the Falls**. Last autumn Mr Hunter went out to Niagara and annexed, pro tem., a small islet – a mere table of rock – which stands out in the rushing water above the fall and is separated by a yard or two from Goat Island. There he set up his easel almost on a level with the water and painted the waves as they tumble against the sky and take all kinds of fantastic shapes before falling into the gulf below. The St James's Gazette says, "The picture is very large, some twelve feet wide and five high. It is practically all sky and water; for a distant hint as the opposite bank and the dark trees upon it is no more than a hint ..."'
*The Boston Evening Transcript*, 6 Apr 1885

'... we look forward to the completion of the ambitious work Mr Hunter has now in hand. This is **the rapids above Niagara**. Last autumn [1884] Mr Hunter went to Niagara and had the luck to find a small spot of unoccupied land, hardly bigger than a good-sized table, out in the furious water above the fall. This he managed to have connected with an outlying spur of Goat Island by a temporary and rather crazy bridge, and after a fortnight of hard work he completed the study he is now enlarging. Besides this he brought home several very exquisite studies of the fall itself; these were made from various points on the Canadian shore.'
*The Art Journal*, April 1885

'... But of the third election [to the Royal Academy as an Associate] what shall we say, when we know that the artist chosen is Edward Burne-Jones.[76] This is Saul amongst the prophets with a vengeance. Fancy the "Annunciation" hung above Colin Hunter's "The rapids of Niagara above the Falls" ...'
*The Spectator*, 13 Jun 1885 p.16

---

75  Obituary, *The Press*, Christchurch, New Zealand, 1st October 1904
76  Sir Edward Burne-Jones ARA (1833–1898) British artist and designer.

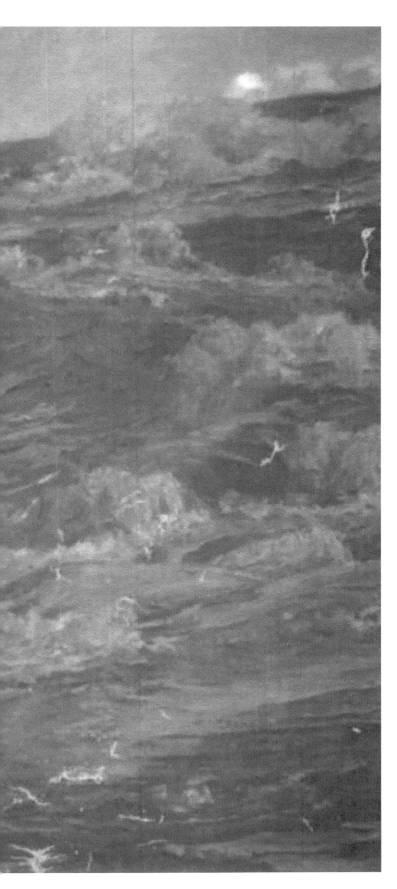

## Niagara Rapids (detail)

1901, oil on canvas, 330.2 × 147.3 cm, 10' 9" × 4' 9"

Signed Colin Hunter 1901

This is an enormous canvas. It is rolled up in storage in the Glasgow Museums collection. It is so large that it needs more than one person to unroll it safely.

Courtesy Glasgow Museums Resource Centre (GMRC)

**Provenance**
Gift from Sir Donald Currie "in a ruinous state" 1901

The Rapids where the river suddenly narrows and is thrown into violent commotion before being precipitated over the Falls. (As described by Scottish Art Galleries *1935 Catalogue of Pictures*)

Two other Niagara paintings exist, one exhibited in the Royal Academy 1885, **The rapids of Niagara above the Falls**, and another **Falls of Niagara** 1890 (see page 116). This one (left) was a reminiscence of Hunter's visit to America in 1884.

Despite the 1885 exhibited Niagara (no image found) and this 1901 one left, both were described as "huge canvases". There must remain doubt over whether this detail above is in fact part of the original "huge canvas" of 1885.

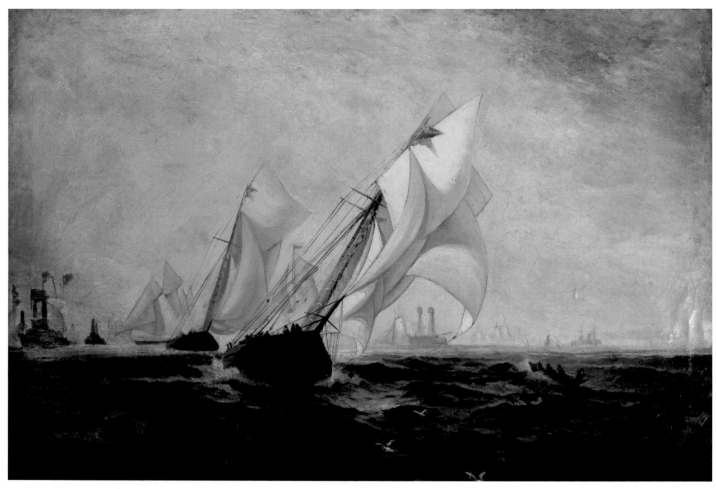

## America's Cup The Third Challenge

Also known as **Twin vessels at full sail and Sea storm**
1876, oil on canvas, 71 × 99 cm, 28" × 39"

Signed Colin Hunter/RA undated

New York Yacht Club's schooner "Madeleine" leading the Royal
Canadian Yacht Club's "Countess of Dufferin"

Private collection

1. Sold as **Twin vessels at full sail** by Brunk Auctions Asheville
   NC, USA 2011 (from private collection).

2. Sold as **Sea storm** by Leslie Hindman Chicago, 2013.

3. Sold as **America's Cup The Third Challenge** by Bonhams,
   London 2013 (from a UK private collection; vendor bought it in
   Chicago; it had been in America "a long time").

'In 1851 an American syndicate brought over to England a radical
schooner yacht with the aim to challenge the yachting supremacy
of the English. Finding little competition, they took part in a race
around the Isle of Wight for a 100 guinea silver ewer, donated
by the Marquis of Anglesey, which they won decisively. Finding
no further challengers, they returned to America and in 1857 the
syndicate donated the trophy to the New York Yacht Club as a
perpetual challenge trophy to be called the America's Cup.

No challenges were made until 1870 when James Ashbury
unsuccessfully challenged with the schooner yacht *Cambria* followed
by a further unsuccessful attempt in 1871. It was not until 1876 that
a further challenge on behalf of the Royal Canadian Yacht Club,
was mounted in the 221 ton schooner *Countess of Dufferin*. The
Americans responded with the smaller schooner *Madeleine* which
defeated the challenger 2-0. The course of the races was set in New
York harbour and featured the Sandy Hook light ship, which can be
seen in the right of the picture.

Attracting huge popular interest, the races were attended by
fleets of spectator vessels which can be seen at the margins of the
course.

The New York Yacht Club retained the trophy despite numerous
challenges until it was finally wrested from them by the Australian
challenger *Australia II* in 1983. Since then Swiss, Australian, New
Zealand and American syndicates have held the Cup, which is still
being competed for today.'

Bonhams catalogue, The Marine Sale, 2 Oct 2013

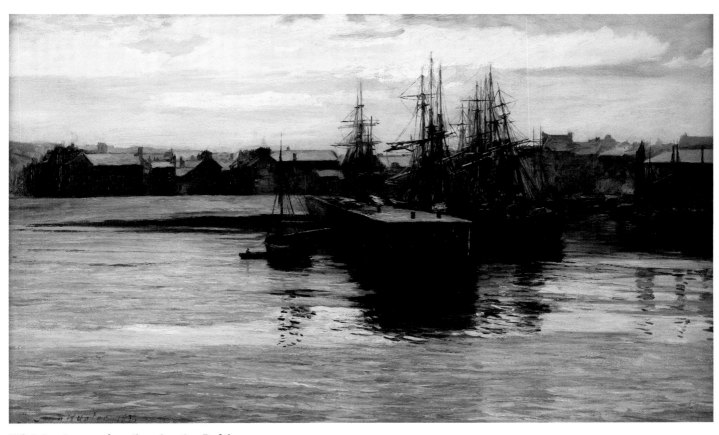

## Wick harbour – loading for the Baltic

Previously entitled **A busy harbour (possibly Wicklow)**
1876, oil on canvas, 45.7 × 77.5 cm, 18" × 30.5"

Signed and dated

**Provenance**
Sold by Bonhams, Edinburgh to Fine Art Society, 2008
Sold by Fine Art Society to private buyer in London, 2014

Bonhams sold this painting as **A busy harbour (possibly Wicklow)**. Subsequently the Fine Art Society (Edinburgh) renamed it **Wick harbour – loading for the Baltic**.

It is not known why the Fine Art Society renamed it or what evidence they relied on for the new title. However, whatever the reason, it is quite significant as Wick is in northeast Scotland and Wicklow is in Ireland.[77]

---

77  Acknowledgement: Jamie Mackinnon, Fine Art Society, Edinburgh

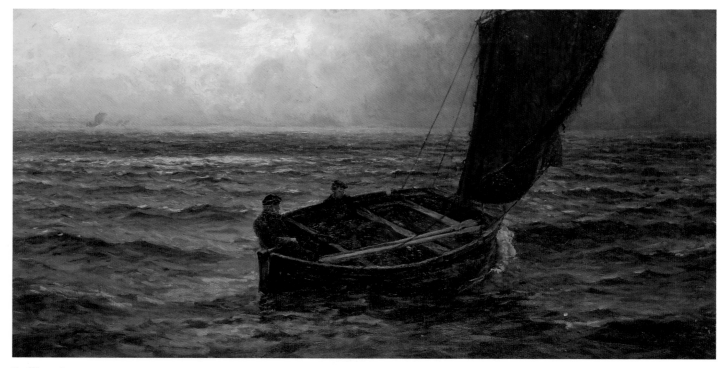

## Sailing free

Probably 1872, oil on canvas, 52 × 97.5 cm, 20.5" × 38.3"

Signed, original frame inscribed with title and artists' name

Also inscribed on the artist's original label verso and numbered "2" together with his address

Figures in a fishing boat, remainder of fleet in distance

Image courtesy of Harry Middleton, for Tennants Auctioneers, Leyburn, North Yorkshire

Possibly exhibited at the Royal Academy 1872

### Provenance
Thomas Agnew & Sons, Old Bond Street Galleries, Piccadilly, London
Exchange Street, Manchester
Dale Street, Liverpool

Sold, Tennants Auctioneers, Lot 1127, March 2007

Hunter exhibited a painting called **Sailing free** at the Royal Academy. However, the additional note verso on this painting, with number "2" may suggest he did a second painting of this name, or a second version of it. Therefore, it cannot be certain this is the actual painting exhibited. However, because Hunter sold several of his RA exhibited paintings to Thomas Agnew, it is a strong possibility that this is indeed the RA work.

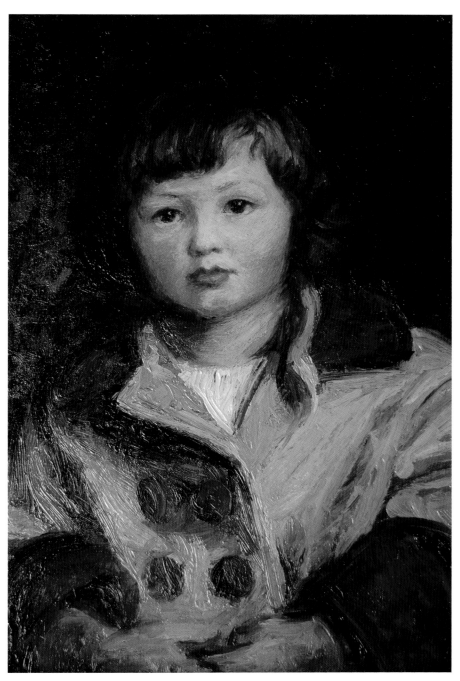

**John Young Hunter (later Young-Hunter), portrait of the artist's son**

c.1877, oil on panel, 59 × 46 cm, 23.2" × 18.1"

Unsigned

**Provenance**
Estate of the artist
Family by descent

Courtesy Kate Rider

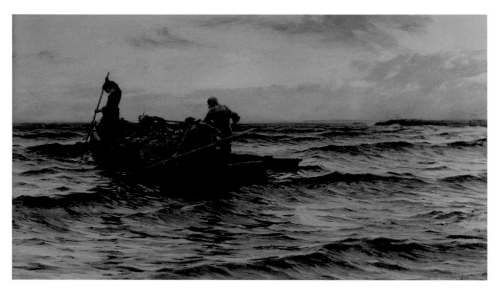

## Their only harvest (1)

1879, oil on canvas, 105 × 182 cm, 41.3" × 71.5"

© Tate London 2018. (colour image not available – painting requires restoration and new photography)

Exhibited at the Royal Academy, 1879

Purchased in 1879 from the Chantrey Fund[78] by the Council of the Royal Academy

Painted in Connemara on the west coast of Ireland, County Galway.

Similar to **Hauling in the nets at sunset**. See page 126

The scene shows the boat loaded with seaweed which, after being dried on the beach and converted into kelp, is sold for fuel at about two pounds a ton.

'Prominent in the strong school of Scotch landscape, and peculiar as being a painter of sea, rather than of moor and mountain, like the great number of his contemporary compatriots, Mr Colin Hunter produces every year work which is truer, fresh and more vivid than what he has done before. **Their only harvest** unites uncommon beauties of colour, composition and light; its group of figures is in rare harmony of line and form with the shapes of sky and ocean; the waves have a vitality of movement, and in their colours reflect at different angles the different passages of the sky in a manner which shows intimate and faithful study from nature. The seaweed in the boat is rich with its tawny brown tones. These few words are needful in order to remind the reader of the complete beauties of a picture which, beside being fine in colour, has yet other qualities, which make of it so good an engraving. The nature is grave and strong in sentiment, while the humanity contributes an element of masculine pathos, without overstraining effort at emotionalism. The health of the sea-breezes is keen in the whole work.'

*The Royal Academy catalogue*, 1879

'A picture in the Tate Gallery, bought by the Royal Academy on the terms of Chantrey's bequest, is a representative example of my father's best work. It was painted on the west coast off Connemara in Ireland, and its title, **Their Only Harvest**, is both explanatory and poetic. A crop of sea-weed may not seem to be indicative of affluent circumstances, but "kelp" which it becomes after being burned, is a very satisfactory fertiliser and the crofters made a living thereby.'

John Young-Hunter writing on his father's work, from *"Reviewing the Years"*

Hunter's 1878–79 accounts (written in his own hand) show he sold **Their Only Harvest** to the Royal Academy for £735. That is £61,000 today's value.

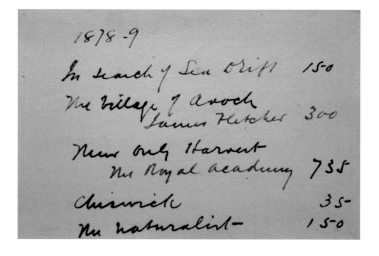

---

78  The sculptor Sir Francis Chantrey (1781–1841) bequeathed a fortune and asked that the income on the money be used to buy paintings and sculpture made in Britain. The fund is administered by the RA and the first work was bought for the collection in 1877 following the death of Lady Chantrey.

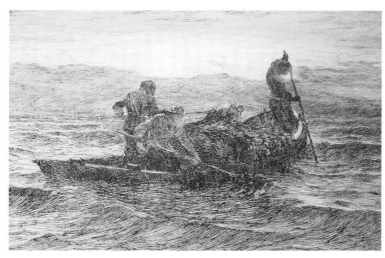

**Their only harvest (copper plate detail)**

Original copper plate, 21.6 × 38.1 cm, 8.5" × 15"

© Colin Hunter family estate

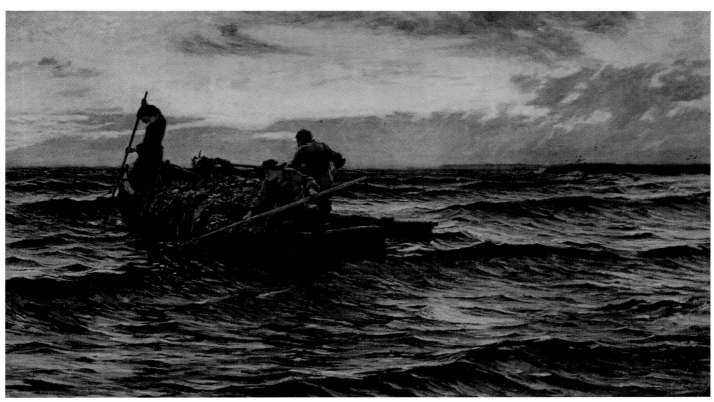

**Their only harvest (2)**

1879,[79] oil on panel, 51 × 71 cm, 20" × 28"

Photo courtesy Marcia Rider

Kirkcaldy Museums & Art Gallery, Fife Council
Purchased 1939

A second painting called **Their only harvest** and in the same year. This painting is almost identical to the one in Tate Britain, but it is much smaller.

'Kelp gathering and manufacture died out very rapidly from about 1830 although it did not cease entirely ... there are numerous paintings of various stages of kelp manufacture, all of which are dated a few decades after the industry is acknowledged to have virtually ceased. Colin Hunter, for example, depicted the active gathering of seaweed in **Their Only Harvest** in 1879.

... The heightened emotional appeal indicated by the title ... may be evocative of the tough conditions and hard work, offering little economic return in a dying industry ...'

*Painting Labour in Scotland and Europe,*
*1850–1900,* John Morrison

---

79  As dated in *Painting Labour in Scotland,* John Morrison, page 119, although the painting itself is undated.

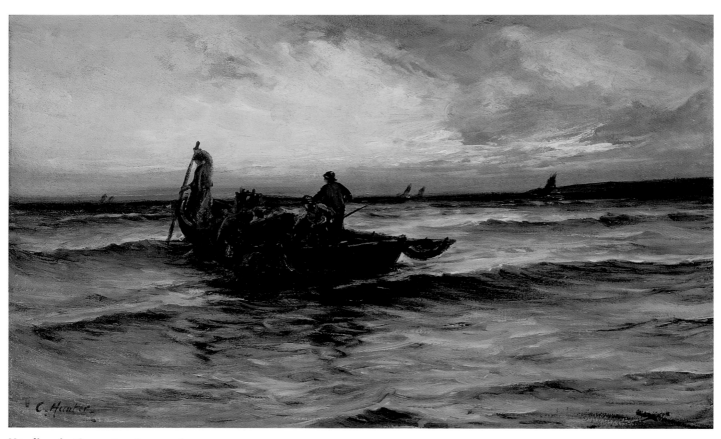

**Hauling in the nets at sunset**

Also known as **Gathering Kelp**

Undated, oil on board, 36.8 × 58.4 cm, 14.5" × 23"

Signed C Hunter LL

Photo © Christie's Images/Bridgeman Images

Sold in original frame under glass at Lawrence's Crewkerne, 21st January 2011

Sold at Christie's, South Kensington, London, 24th November 2011

This is yet another painting very similar to **Their Only Harvest** 1879 (see pages 124 & 125). It is much smaller again and the horizon view has changed. A particular difference is the addition of a sailing boat on the horizon.

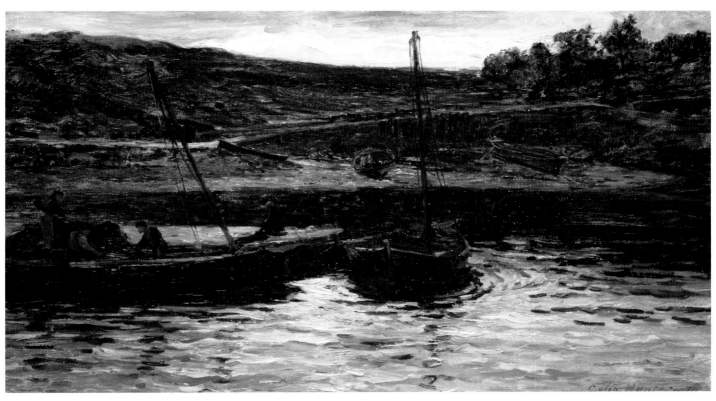

### Fishermen

1874, oil on canvas, 35 × 61 cm, 14" × 24"

Signed and dated LR

Private collection

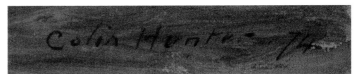

**Provenance**
Bought from private collection, Belgium, exported to England for a private collection, 2018.
Sold by Simon Itsvan (deceased), antique dealer in Charleroi, Belgium, to a private collector, *c.*2008.
Before 2008, Simon Itsvan had an antique dealer business in London where it is likely he bought or held this painting.

A painting with the title of **Fishermen** has not been traced in Colin Hunter's own records, nor in any exhibition or gallery. Of course, once again, the painting may have been renamed over the years as it changed hands. Other paintings which were also painted in 1874 and for which no image has been found to identify them clearly include **Coming Ashore** and **English port**. Such "unattached" paintings always pose the question, "Could it be this one?"

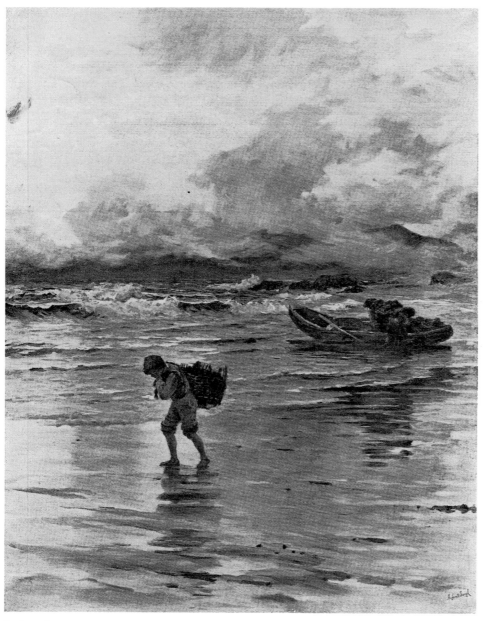

## Ireland

1893, oil on canvas, 160 × 124.5 cm, 63" × 49"

Reproduced from *Royal Academy Pictures 1893*.

Exhibited Royal Academy 1893

Sold to Wm. A. Donaldson for £650, 1893. Today's value £58,400.

'... here, as in the larger picture in the seventh room, **Ireland**, Mr Hunter has, not for the first time, proved himself to be the most dexterous of those who paint "the melancholy ocean" and its barren shores.'

*The Times*, May 6, 1893

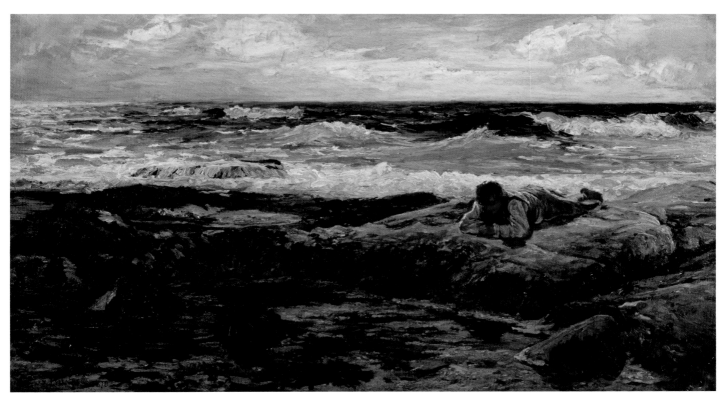

### The Naturalist

1878, oil on canvas, 50.8 × 91.4 cm, 20" × 36"

Courtesy of Perth Museum & Art, Perth & Kinross Council

**Provenance**
Gift to the council from Colin Hunter's daughter, Colina I. Hunter, 1950

Hunter's 1878–79 accounts (written in his own hand) show he sold **The Naturalist** for £150. Today's value £12,500.

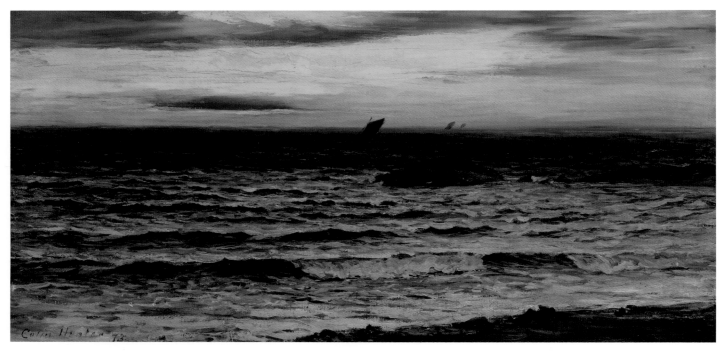

**With wind and tide**

1874, oil on canvas, 38 × 76 cm, 15" × 29.9"

Image courtesy John Moran Auctioneers, Los Angeles, California, USA

Sold, Moran Auctions, Los Angeles, 2009

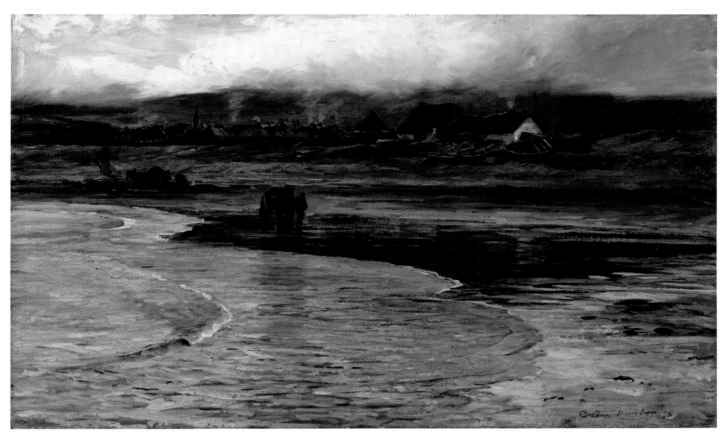

### Ebbing tide

1877, oil on canvas, 54.6 × 90.2 cm, 21.5" × 17.5"

Signed Colin Hunter 78 (if correct it may have been signed the year after he finished painting it – see below)

© CSG CIC Glasgow Museums Collection

Exhibited at Royal Academy 1878

**Provenance**
Bequeathed by Adam Teacher, 1898

Painted in 1877 while staying in Connemara.[80]

'Highland crofter village on the West Coast, tide receding from the shore, on which are several kelp-gatherers, with horses and carts.'
Scottish Art Galleries, 1935 Catalogue of Pictures.

If the Art Journal reference is correct that it was painted in 1877 in Connemara (Ireland), this is a complete contradiction of the Scottish Art Galleries catalogue entry saying it was painted on the west coast of Scotland with the highland crofter village in the scene.

---

80 *The Art Journal*, April 1885

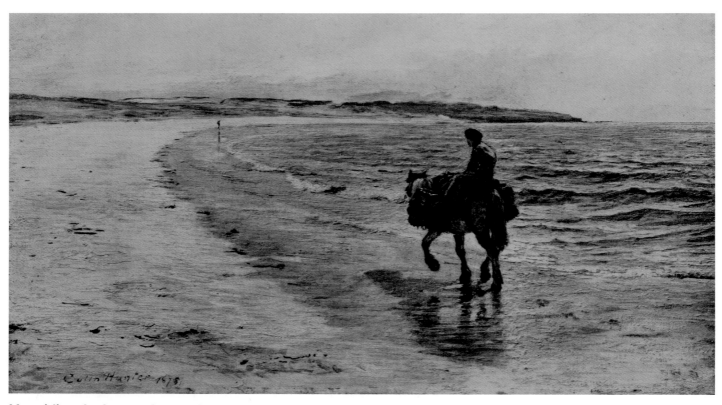

**Man riding donkey on the seashore**

1878, oil on canvas

Signed and dated

Hunter's title and dimensions not known

Image courtesy family by descent

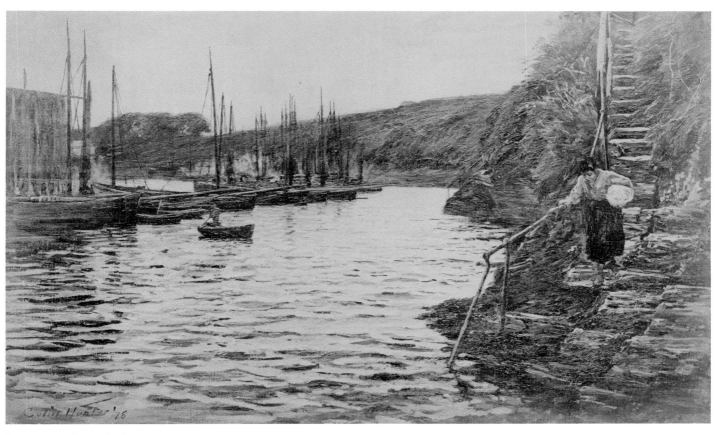

**Long way down to the quay**

1878, oil on canvas

Signed and dated

Hunter's title and dimensions not known

Black & white photo of oil painting

Image courtesy family by descent

Location possibly western shores of Argyll or the highlands.[81]

81  Acknowledgement: Iain McIntyre, local historian Argyll and Bute,
    Scotland. Thanks too to Dr James Paterson, Argyll and Bute Council.

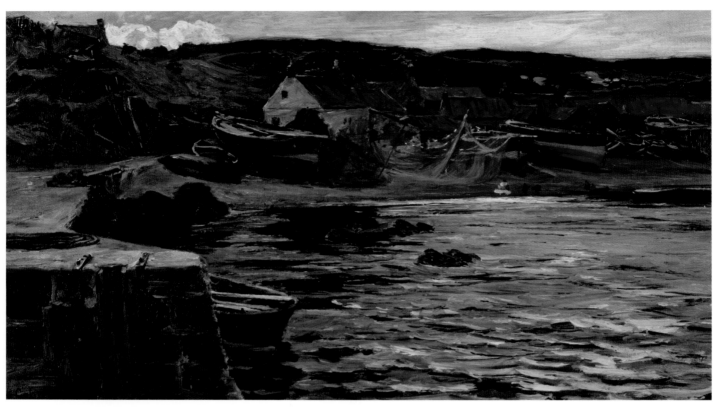

**Boats at rest, Coldingham**

1879, oil on canvas, 40.6 × 71.1 cm, 16" × 28"

Courtesy of Perth Museum & Art, Perth & Kinross Council

**Provenance**
Gift to the council from Colin Hunter's daughter, Colina I Hunter, 1950

Is this the same location as the following four paintings?

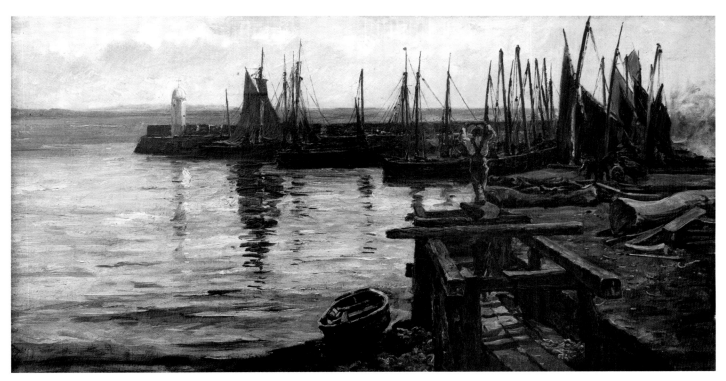

**Harbour scene, possibly Coldingham?**

1887, oil on canvas, 40 × 76 cm, 16" × 30"

Signed and dated Colin Hunter 1887

Private collection

Sold, Clarke Auction Gallery, Larchmont New York, 2016

**Provenance**
2016 From a Carmel New York home to an English home.

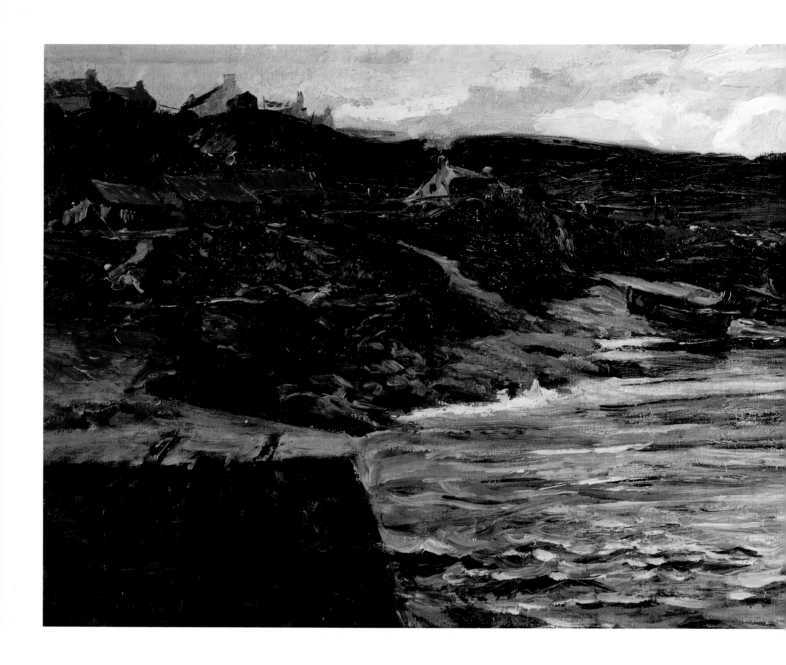

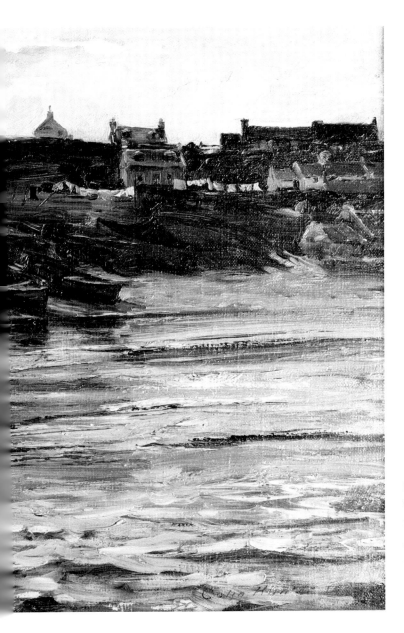

## Fishing boats moored on the shore, probably Coldingham

1885 or 1889, oil on canvas, 41 × 77 cm, 16" × 30"

Signed indistinctly dated LR (but probably 1885)

Private collection

Sold, Christie's London, 2007

Is this also Coldingham? See image on page 134.

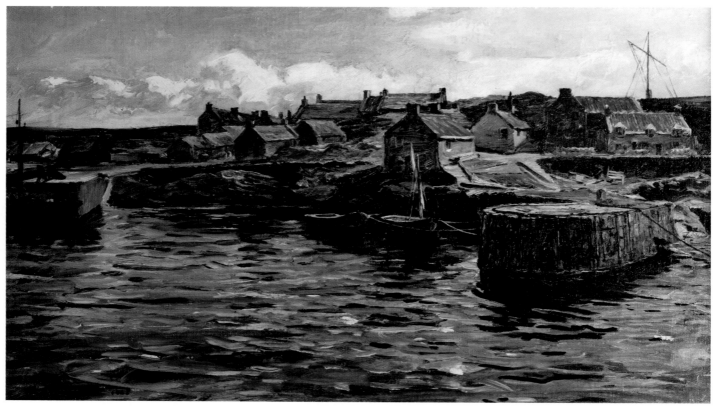

**A fishing harbour, possibly Coldingham**

Also known as **Fishing boats in harbour**
1865 or 1885, oil on canvas, 36 × 61 cm, 14" × 24"

Signed and dated 'Colin Hunter 1885' (1865?) LL

See previous two paintings. Could this arguably also be Coldingham from another viewpoint? (Has Hunter moved from one side of the harbour to the other?) What is possibly the Coldingham Priory can be detected on the skyline in all three paintings attributed here to Coldingham.

Private collection

Sold, Bonhams, Edinburgh from a deceased estate on west coast of Scotland, 2004

Date is indistinct and could be 1865. However, the painting was cleaned prior to the auction, and in cleaning the 1885 could have been damaged so it may now appear 1865. Bonhams believe that 'stylishly' it is 1885.[82]

If the date was taken to be 1885, this is the same period as the previous two images that may be Coldingham: 1879, 1885 or 1889. However, if it is to be 1865 then it would be harder to be sure of the location.

---

82  Acknowledgement: Chris Brickley, Bonhams, Edinburgh

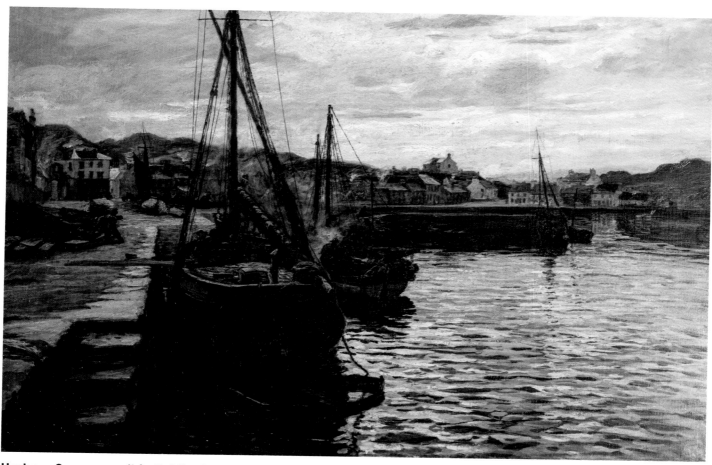

**Harbour Scene, possibly Coldingham**

Also known as **Scottish harbour**

Undated, possibly late 1880s, oil on canvas, 66 × 100 cm, 26" × 40"

Signed Colin ... , lower centre

Private collection

Sold, Sotheby's, London from a private collection, 2010

**Provenance**

In 2010 auction sale, vendor purchased it from the deceased estate of Ian Scott, known as Oskotsky, who was a cartoonist and agent who represented Gerald Scarfe.

Arguably this is another painting of Coldingham. Although there is no firm evidence, the similarities in other Coldingham paintings are striking.

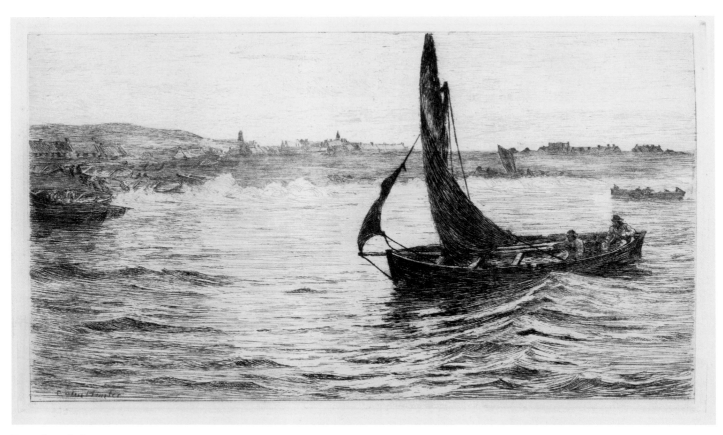

**Running Ashore**

1880, etching, 26.6 × 37.6 cm, 10" × 14.8"

Fine Arts Museums of San Francisco

Plate 33 in the book, *The Etcher* (London: Sampson Low ... , 1880)
vol 2 (bound in same volume as vol 1, 1879)

There are some similarities in this etching with **Lowering sail** and
**Fishing port**. See pages 68 & 69

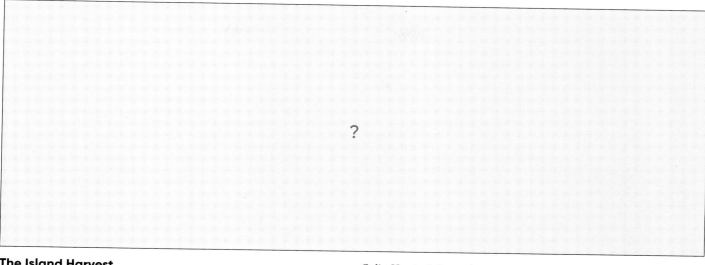

?

## The Island Harvest

1881. No image found

Exhibited at Fine Art Society Rooms 1881

| Among the better known of his pictures are: | | |
|---|---|---|
| Trawlers waiting for darkness | exhibited in R.A. | 1875 |
| Salmon fishers | " " | 1874 |
| Give way | " " | 1875 |
| Digging bait | " " | 1876 |
| Store for the Cabin | " " | 1877 |
| Their only Harvest   the property of the Trustees of the Chantrey Bequest Fund  " | | 1878 |
| Silver of the Sea | " " | 1879 |
| Mussel Gatherers<br>    & In the Gloaming | " " | 1880 |
| The Island Harvest | exhibited in Fine Art Society Rooms | 1881 |
| Waiting for the homeward bound | exhibited in R.A. | 1882 |
| A pebbled shore | " " | 1883 |

Extract of Hunter letter dated 4th February 1884

Original letter held at the Victoria & Albert Museum

Colin Hunter's letter (extract transcribed, left) was written on 4th February 1884 from 14 Melbury Road. Unfortunately, it is unclear who Hunter is writing to as the original handwritten letter in the Victoria and Albert Museum, begins simply "Dear Sir".

But it is plain that Hunter is providing the recipient with suggested copy for a profile of some kind on his works, because he puts himself in third person (*Among the better known of his pictures are ...*).

In the list of his "better known pictures" that follows is **The Island Harvest** and he clearly says it was exhibited at The Fine Art Society Rooms in 1881. Situated in the heart of Mayfair, The Fine Art Society has operated as an art dealer since 1876 and from 1881 three floors of galleries ("the rooms") have been permanently open to the public for exhibitions.

Despite Hunter's letter saying **The Island Harvest** was exhibited there, his name cannot be found in The Fine Art Society records. This is probably because Hunter sold the painting in 1881 to an unknown purchaser who may have subsequently loaned it to the Society for a seasonal show – perhaps under his or her own name. If so, this would explain why Hunter's name does not appear in the Society's stock books for that year.[83]

It is disappointing that no image of this "better known picture" has been found although two others in Hunter's own list, also have not been found – **Store for the Cabin** and **A pebbled shore**.

Hunter sold **The Island Harvest** in 1881 for £700. Today's value £59,500.

83  Acknowledgement: Patrick Duffy, The Fine Art Society

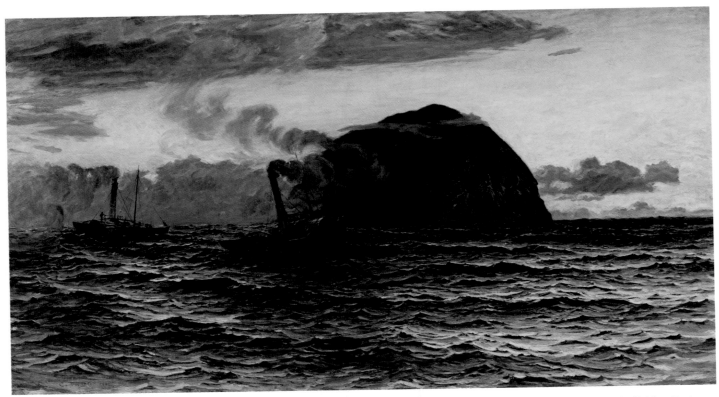

### Waiting for the homeward bound, off Ailsa Craig, Firth of Clyde

1882, oil on canvas, 100.3 × 181.1 cm, 39.5" × 71.3"

South Australian Government Grant 1885

Courtesy Art Gallery of South Australia, Adelaide

Exhibited Royal Academy 1882

Sold by Hunter to the Adelaide Government in 1884 for £600 (today's value £52,000).

Ailsa Craig is a volcanic island in the Firth of Clyde ten miles off the Ayrshire coast. The island is home to Europe's biggest gannet colony and an increasingly significant number of puffins.

'**Waiting for the homeward bound** refers to the two Glasgow tugs, which have gone out to the open water about Ailsa Craig to intercept incoming ships and tow them home. To paint this picture Mr Hunter had to charter a small steamer for a month. Every morning he went out to a point a mile or two from the rock and carried on his work as well as the swaying of his platform would let him. His early life had made him a good sailor under ordinary conditions, but he found that to stand still for hours a day on a lifting deck with a canvas to be covered before him, was more than trying, and the picture was carried on in the intervals of *ce terrible mal de mer*.'

*The Art Journal*, April 1885

'**Waiting for the homeward bound** was painted off Ailsa Craig, where tugs lie-to in readiness to tow incoming ships up the Clyde.'

*The Windsor Magazine*, 1912

'I heard him {Colin Hunter] smilingly relate one incident. The picture he was painting was a large one, eight feet by four feet, and the subject he called **Waiting for the homeward-bound**. He had hired two tugboats to manoeuvre near the rock called Ailsa Craig in the Firth of Clyde, he himself standing on the deck of a third boat, all of them rocking on a turbulent sea. Now my father was a good sailor, usually impervious to sea sickness; but on this occasion the rocking of the boat, in fact, the unsteadiness of everything, including himself and his picture, contributed to the necessity of his visiting the gunwale at frequent intervals.

The picture, now in the National Gallery of South Australia, Adelaide, Australia (and for which he received a particularly large gold medal), turned out to be one of his best, a very fine picture too.'

John Young-Hunter talking of his father Colin in '*Reviewing the Years*'.

'The new painting hung on Thursday morning in the National Gallery and bearing the title of **Waiting for the homeward bound** by Colin Hunter ARA, is a companion picture to **The salmon fishers Loch Fyne** which was purchased for the Sydney Gallery for £900. Although heavily handicapped by being hung where there is not sufficient room for it to be seen to advantage, this latest addition to our somewhat mixed collection of works of art cannot fail to impress the careful critic favourably after due study. It is not the fault of the gentlemen under whose directions this painting was placed that it is so disadvantageously situated, because they have no choice in the matter, and have really done the best they could under the circumstances. It is one of those class of paintings that must be hung almost on a level with, or rather below, the eye, and being broadly and boldly executed, as well as large, it needs to be viewed at some distance by the spectator.

It is a sea piece, and at first sight it does not impress one favourably, because the artist belongs to the school favouring the broad and what may be termed harsh treatment of such subjects rather than the delicate handling of each detail with minuteness of finish.

Here we have Ailsa headland standing bluffly out against a grey sky, which, low down on the horizon, is gilded by the sun's rays, softened by a foggy medium. Lightened up by those beams is a wide stretch of uneasy ocean, the irregular ridges of the waves catching the golden light in fanciful fashion, the brighter bits being in strong contrast to the shadowy hollows. The headland casting the huge shadow forward darkens the water in its way, and here the artist has shown remarkable skill in the treatment of a most difficult piece of painting. With so high and dark a bluff occupying the best part of the picture, he has had to carry out the design with some nicety so as to avoid heaviness and want of transparency where the water lies.

Looking at the production for the first time it does strike one that there is this fault to find with it, but viewed at the proper distance and examined as a whole, the foresea is crisp and full of motion – in fact, one almost seems to see the sunlight dancing on that restless stretch of sea. Where the light comes past the point and meets the shadow of the headland the contrast is fine.

There are two steam tugs tossing under the lee of Ailsa, rather roughly painted, but in unison with the surrounds and in accordance with the style. There is a nice artistic touch where the smoke streaming from the funnel of one of them is caught by the eddy of wind round the point and is turned back upon itself till it lifts and mingles with the cloud above. By-the-way, that cloud is perhaps the worst piece in the picture. It is natural, no doubt, but being stiff in outline and coarse- looking it tends to spoil some of the general effect.

The picture was painted in 1883 [sic] and the artist paid £250 for the use of steam boats as studies. The price given for this acquisition to our Gallery was six hundred guineas, and it is better worth the money than some of our art possessions for which prices in proportion were paid.'

*South Australian Register*, 6 March 1885

'The chief work in the Adelaide section is **Waiting for the Homeward Bound, off Ailsa Craig, Firth of Clyde**, by Colin Hunter ARA. Remarkable is the firm and luminous treatment of the water, as also the way in which the gloom of approaching night is suggested by the blackness of the headland, and the darkly outline pilot boats, whilst yet the sky holds fast the saffron hints of the dying day.'

Written under the National Art Gallery column,
*Sydney Morning Herald*, 24th April 1896

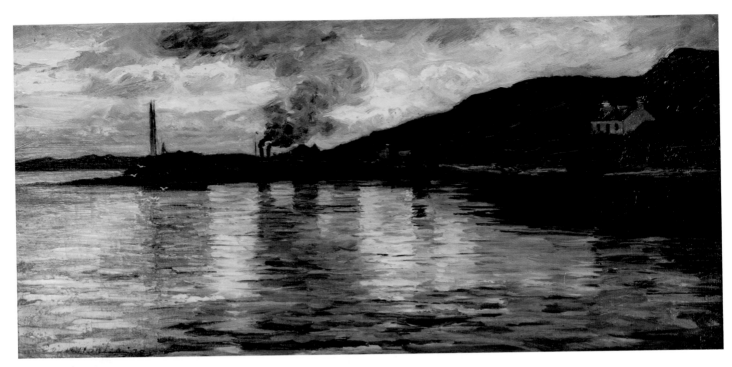

**The Clyde Coast**

1878, oil on canvas, 37 × 75 cm, 14.5" × 29.5"

Signed and dated 'Colin Hunter 78' LL

Private collection

Sold, Bonhams, Edinburgh, 2005

Compare this scene with **A Scottish fishing harbour** 1880 opposite.

At this time, and from now until his death in 1904, Hunter lived at 14 Melbury Road, Kensington, London.

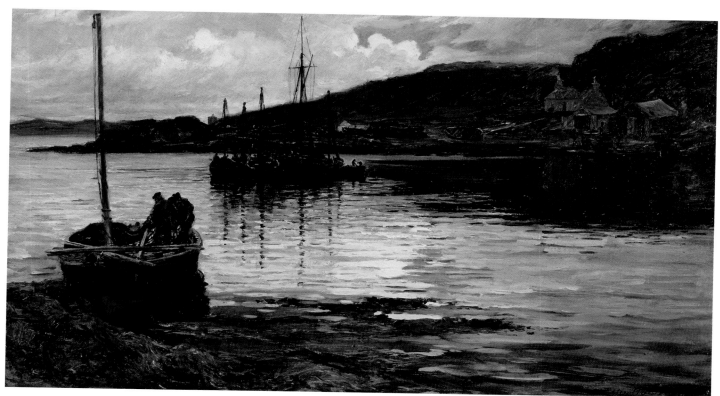

**A Scottish fishing harbour**

1880, oil on canvas, 54.5 × 93 cm, 21.5" × 36.5"

Signed and dated (1880 indistinct)

Possibly the Clyde coast? Compare this scene with **The Clyde Coast** 1878 opposite.

Private collection

Image courtesy of Lyon & Turnbull Fine Art Auctioneers

Sold, Lyon & Turnbull, Edinburgh, 2016

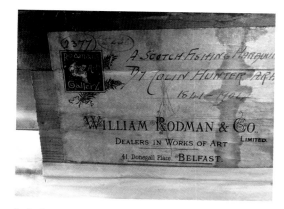

**Label verso A Scottish fishing harbour**

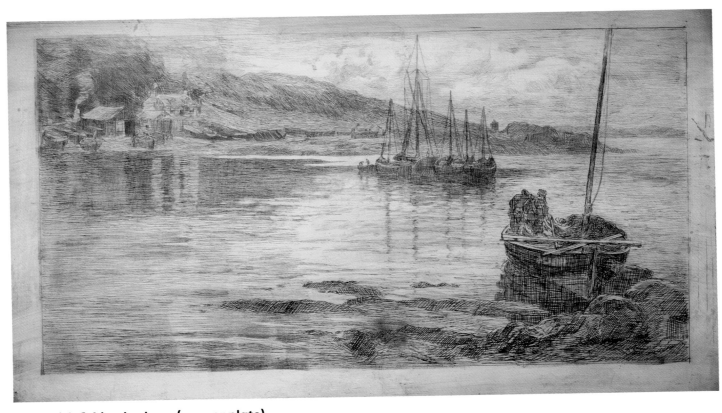

**A Scottish fishing harbour (copper plate)**

1880, original copper plate engraving, 21.6 × 38.1 cm, 8.5" × 15"

© Colin Hunter family estate

**The Lubin**

In her own handwriting, Colin Hunter's granddaughter, Gabrielle Young-Hunter (1905–78 married name Kuster) had written "**The Lubin**" on brown paper wrapped around the plate. It is uncertain what this means or relates to, but a guess is that it might be the name of the boat in the foreground. Although there are some markings on the bow of the boat no name can be clearly made out.

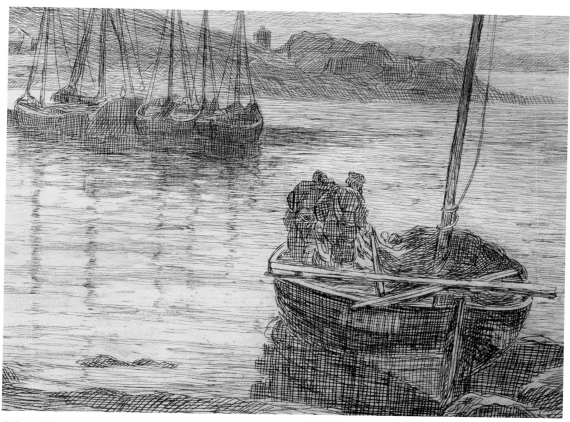

**A Scottish fishing harbour (copper plate detail)**

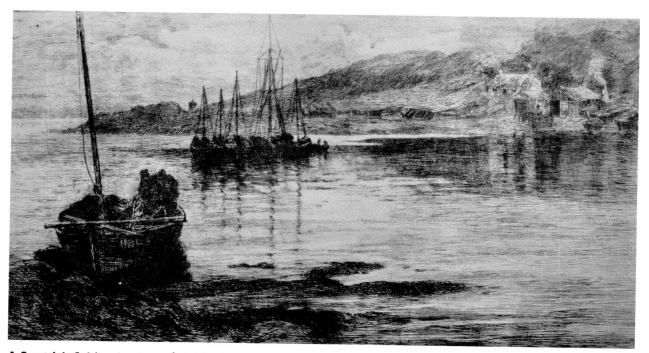

**A Scottish fishing harbour (etching)**

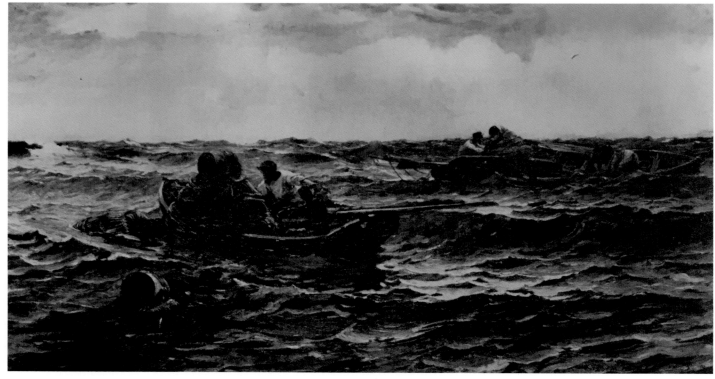

## Lobster fishers (1)

1883, oil on canvas, 67 × 120 cm, 26.5" × 47"

Image courtesy Sotheby's

Exhibited

1883 Royal Academy

1904 Birmingham Municipal Art Gallery Sea Painters Exhibition

**Provenance**
Sold by Hunter, 1883 £500. Today's value £42,500
Possibly the collection of James McGregor (or did he buy the 1893 picture?), 1894
Property of S E Thompson, Belfast, when loaned to the RSA Annual Exhibition, 1926
Sold Sotheby's London (property of Mrs C E (or S E?) Thompson), 1974

Two other pictures entitled **Lobster fishers** were produced later. An etching in 1885 (opposite) and an entirely different picture, also exhibited at the Royal Academy, in 1893 (see page 192).

'This picture was painted from the rocks on the coast of Scotland in a high wind. Two fishing craft in the middle distance, were pitching heavily while the men aboard in their oilskins were hauling in the creels. It was painted with vigour stimulated by a mixture of despair and enjoyment, the colour fresh and clear, and the evident spontaneity of its application denoting his excitement, as well as the combative strain of a fight against the elements. Apparently

this picture was finished on the spot, probably in a few days, for the handling of the thick paint showed no studio reconsideration.'
John Young-Hunter writing on his father's work, from *"Reviewing the Years"*.

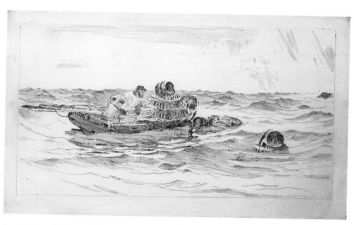

**Lobster fishers (copper plate)**

Original copper plate, 15.2 × 24.1 cm, 6" × 9.5"

© Colin Hunter family estate

Inspired by the oil on canvas of the same name (opposite) but the second boat was omitted.

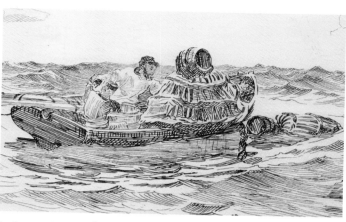

**Lobster fishers (copper plate detail)**

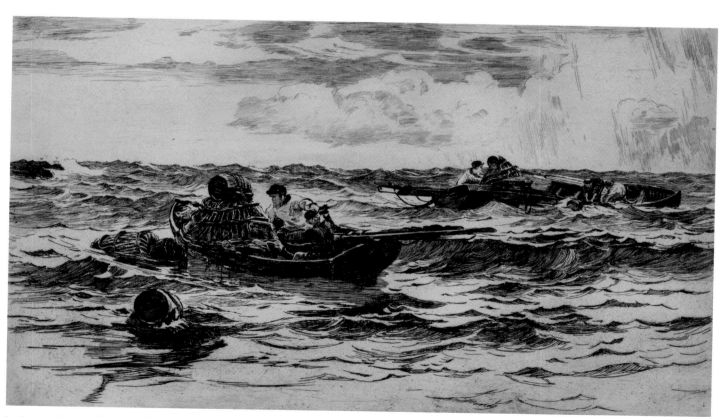

**Lobster fishers (etching)**

Private collection

'One of the greatest qualities of Colin Hunter's marines is his ability to render the mood of the sea. In **Lobster Fishers**, for example, the artist superbly defines wind and wave with bold lines and tonal values. Few etchers of Colin Hunter's time could create such a fine composition with such masterful simplicity.'

Paul Gilbert Hamerton 'Landscape', 1885

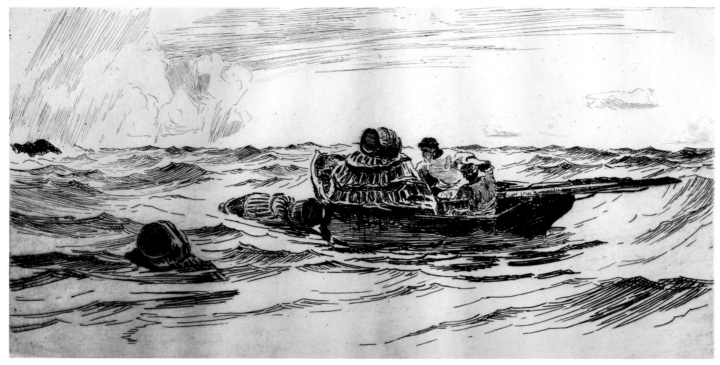

## Lobster Fishers (2)

1885, etching & drypoint engraving, 11 × 21 cm, 4.3" × 8.3"

Private collection (England). Another etching of **Lobster Fishers** was offered for sale in The Estate of a Charleston, South Carolina Art Dealer/Gallery Owner, USA, May 2017.

There are two other pictures with the same name, **Lobster fishers**. This etching in 1885, an oil on canvas in 1883 exhibited in the Royal Academy (see page 148) and an entirely different picture, also exhibited at the Royal Academy, in 1893 (see page 192). The 1883 and 1885 pictures are similar but not identical. In this etching there is not a second boat behind them in the distance.

This etching was published in 1885 in *Landscape* by Philip Gilbert Hamerton, a writer who promoted etching as a fine art form. His first book *Etching and Etchers* was published in 1868 and this attracted many artists, including Colin Hunter, to try out the etching needle. Colin Hunter did so well with the medium that Hamerton invited him to submit this work for his second publication.

'An interesting note might be written on the occupation of these lobster fishers; but such things lie out of the range of the present volume. We need only observe, in this place, that the baskets and nets used to catch lobsters are most valuable objects in a premier plan of sea waves, and that they save the rowing boats from being isolated by extending the quantity of floating material in less massive forms, all which recommends them most strongly to an artist.

Mr Colin Hunter is a powerful and complete painter, by which I mean that he employs all the resources of texture, colour, tone, and handling. In etching his method is founded on abstraction and simplification, and therefore it does not produce the effect of his pictures, but rather that of his pen-sketches and memoranda.

One of the greatest qualities of Colin Hunter's marines is his ability to render the mood of the sea. In **Lobster Fishers** for example, the artist superbly defines wind and wave with bold lines and tonal values. Few etchers of Colin Hunter's time could create such a fine composition with such masterful simplicity.'

P.G. Hamerton '*Landscape*', 1885

'In many ways the **Lobster Fishers** is Mr Hunter's finest work. It has an amount of vigour and coherence, of life and movement, that is hardly to be equalled by any other study of sea I can call to mind. It is fine in colour, but makes a splendid etching. Like many more of his best things it has been etched by Mr Hunter himself and the plate is perhaps as successful as any attempt to so deal with the waves can be. For the genius of the sea and the genius of etching are not to be completely reconciled. The organic line of the etcher, sensitive to his every thought, betraying every passing gust of feeling, is too much controlled by the infinite sameness in variety of the sea. But in spite this the **Lobster Fishers** is a noble plate, and full of that rarest of artistic beauties felicitous selection.'

*The Art Journal*, April 1885

See also **Lobster Fishers 1883** (page 148) and **Lobster Fishers 1893** (page 192).

# Cornwall

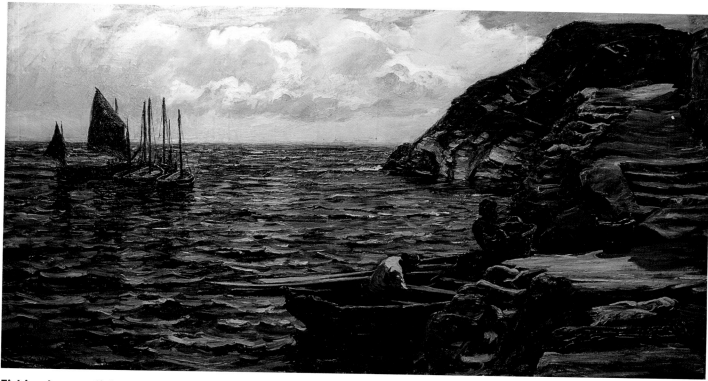

## Fishing boats off the coast of Cornwall

1883, oil on canvas, 56 × 102 cm, 22" × 40.5"

Signed and dated '83

Private Collection

Lot not sold, Bukowskis, Stockholm, Sweden, 2013

Sold, Lyon & Turnbull, 2016

At some point, it appears that an earlier owner of this painting attached a note on the reverse. In his or her own handwriting. It read: *Fishing boats off the coast of Cornwall.*

And (see below) *Cornish Fishing boats by Colin Hunter ARA. Exhibited at the Royal Academy and at Paris 1884*. However, there is no record of either **Fishing boats off the coast of Cornwall**, or **Cornish fishing boats** being exhibited at the Royal Academy in 1884 or in any other year. Nor has it been possible in research to date, to verify the claim that it hung in a Parisian exhibition.

Despite not finding what Hunter exhibited in Paris, apparently he certainly did so. *The Morning News*, Belfast, on February 1st, 1884, reported that "Hunter has exhibited every year [at the Royal Academy] since 1870 and last year his pictures were seen in Paris."

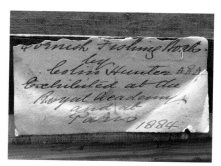

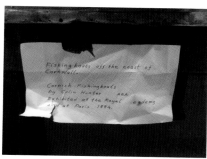

**Labels verso Fishing boats off the coast of Cornwall, 1883**

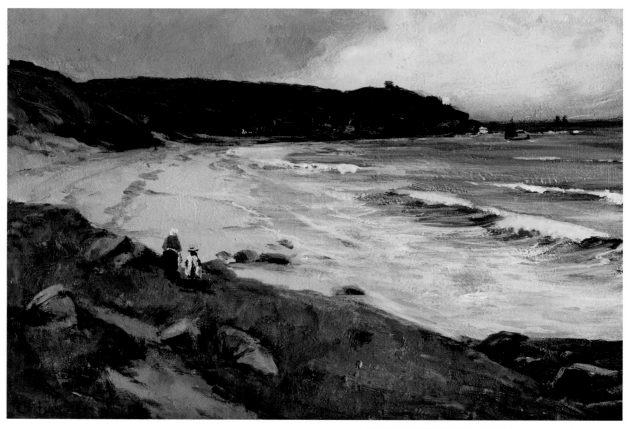

## A coastal walk

Undated, oil on board, 23.5 × 48.2 cm, 9.3" × 13"

Signed C Hunter

Private collection

Sold by auction, Swan & Turner, Jedburgh, Scotland, 2015

Compare with painting opposite.

Verso, indistinct handwriting probably reads Sennen Cove[84] –
which is in Cornwall, where Hunter frequently painted. A similar
scene, possibly painted on the same day, has previously been called
**Figures on the Fife coast** (see opposite) but this title was never
given to it by Hunter himself and is believed to be a mistake.

Handwritten note on reverse of **A coastal walk**.

84 Acknowledgement: Elizabeth Wise

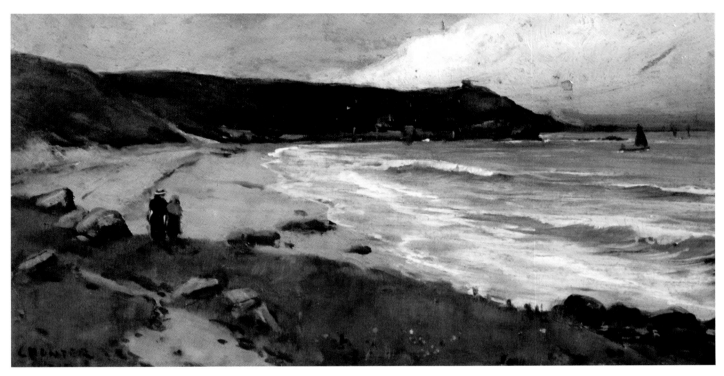

## Sennen Cove, Cornwall

Previously known and sold as **Figures on the Fife coast** but this is
now believed to be a mistake (see opposite).
Undated, oil on board, 20.3 × 36.8 cm, 8" × 14.5"

Image courtesy Gorringe's Auctioneers, Lewes, Sussex

Listed, Gorringe's, Lewes, 2012

Compare with painting opposite.

Same location as **A coastal walk** but notice the two figures have
changed and the painting is smaller. Probably painted the same day.

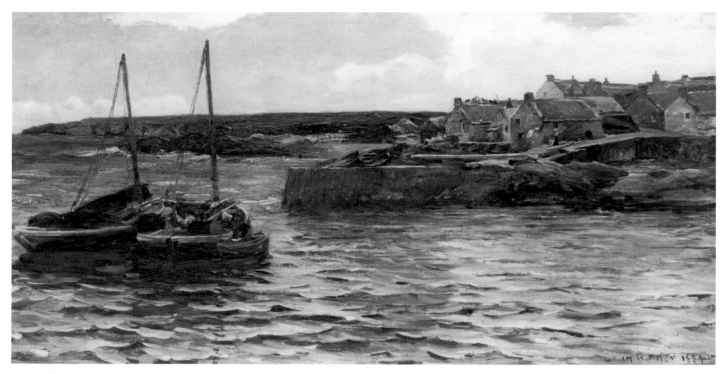

**Cornish harbour**

1884, oil on canvas, 40 × 75 cm, 15.5" × 29.5"

Image: Sotheby's Belgravia 16 Oct 1973

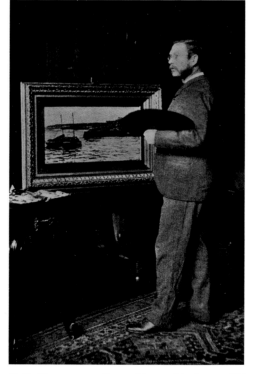

Colin Hunter standing at his easel in front of his work **Cornish harbour**

Photo: *The Windsor Magazine* no. 214, 1912

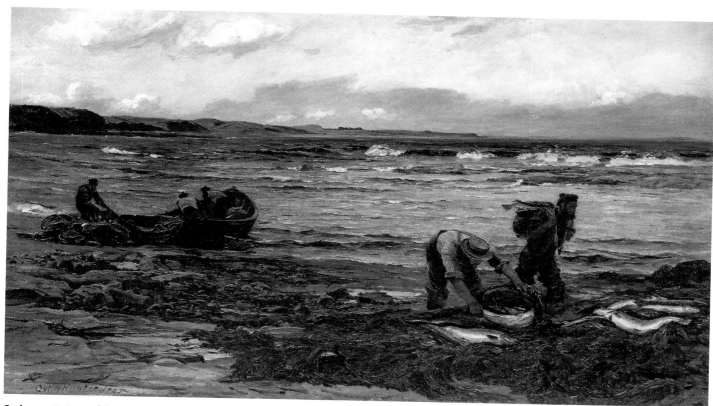

## Salmon fishers (1)

1885, oil on canvas, 71.2 × 122 cm, 28" × 48"

Signed and dated

Reproduced from Christie's auction catalogue

Exhibited Royal Academy 1885

### Provenance

Sold by Hunter for £500 (today's value £45,000), 1885
Anonymous sale; Sotheby's Gleneagles, lot 259, 28 August 1975
Sold, Sotheby's Lot 100 £6,500, 26 Oct 2006

### Literature

*Royal Academy Notes* 1885 no. 1064, p.71
Christopher Wood, *The Dictionary of Victorian Painters*, Vol 2,
Antique Collectors' Club, 1995 p.267

Another painting was also called **Salmon Fishers**. See page 232 for
**Salmon Fishers 1903**.

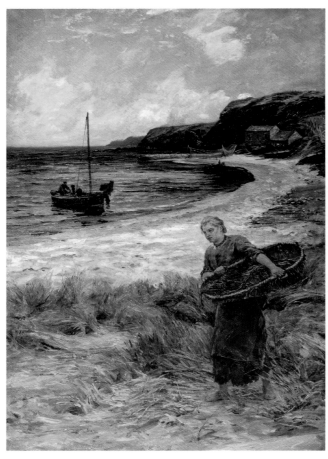

## The lass that baits the line

Originally: **The girl who baits the line**

1885, oil on canvas, 101.6 × 71.1 cm, 40" × 28"

Hand-written label verso *The girl who baits the line.*

© Dundee City Council (Dundee's Art Galleries and Museums)

**Exhibited**
Royal Academy 1885
Fine Art Exhibition Dundee 1885
Victorian Era Exhibition, Earls Court, London 1897

**Provenance**
Sold by Hunter 1885 for £250 (today's value £22,400) (probably
to John Maclauchlan). In 1886 copyright was owned by John
Maclauchlan, the chief librarian and curator of Dundee Art Gallery
& Museum
James Guthrie Orchar (1825–98), a local industrialist, bought the
painting and gifted it to the Dundee collection in 1886. In the
Dundee Museum's Annual Report for 1886 it is listed as **The lass
that baits the line**, valuation £70. It is likely that Orchar changed
the name himself to one with a more poetic Scottish touch.[85]

Another version of this painting, seemingly an almost identical copy,
was sold in Sotheby's London auction 29th November 1999 Lot 10.

---

85 Acknowledgement: Susan Keracher, Art Curator, Dundee's Art
Gallery & Museum

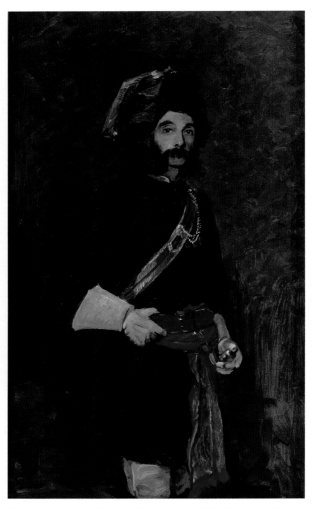

## Surgeon John Henry Sylvester, 11th Bengal Cavalry (Probyn's Horse) c.1865

1885, oil on canvas, 76.2 × 45.7 cm, 30" × 18"

National Army Museum, London/Bridgeman Images

**Provenance**
Purchased by National Army Museum from Miss B A S Hodder via
Whitehead, Fox & Sons, 1987

One of Colin Hunter's few portraits. He probably did this one
simply because in 1885 Sylvester was Hunter's next door neighbour
at 16 Melbury Road.

John Henry Sylvester was born in 1830. After studying anatomy at
the Royal College of Surgeons, he served with the Bombay Medical
Service, participating in the Persian Campaign (1857), the Indian
Mutiny (1857–59) and the Umbeyla Campaign (1863–64). During
the latter expedition he was attached to Probyn's Horse. Sylvester
was later made Deputy Surgeon General in India. He died in 1903 –
a year before Hunter died.

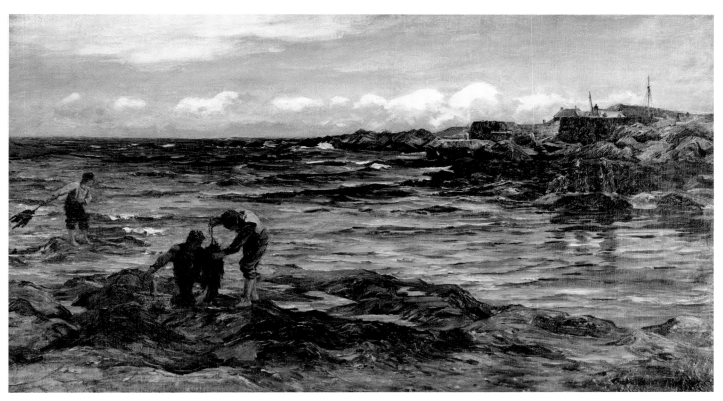

**Crab fishers**

1887, oil on canvas, 51 × 91 cm, 20" × 36"

Signed and dated Colin Hunter 1887

Private collection

**Provenance**

Sold, Lyon & Turnbull, Edinburgh, 2008

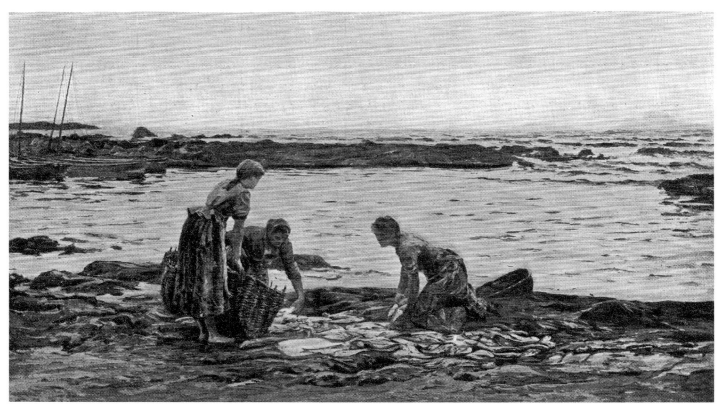

**Their share of the toil**

1887, oil on canvas, 106.7 × 182.9 cm, 42" × 72"

Image reproduced from *The Windsor Magazine* No. 214, 1912

Exhibited Royal Academy 1887

**Provenance**
Sold by Hunter for £150 (today's value £13,750), 1887
Sold by Christie's, London, 13th Nov 1991 for £8,000

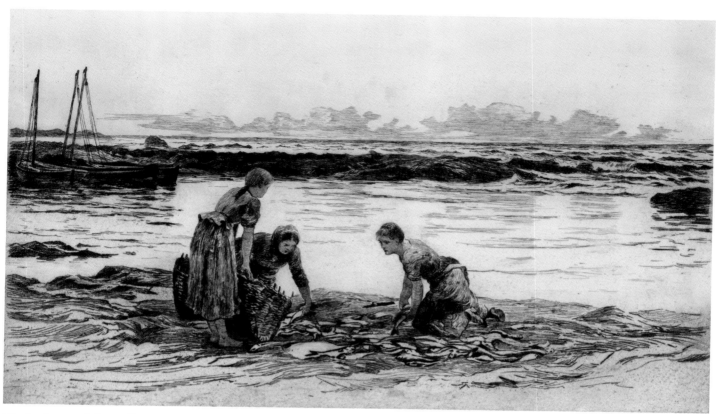

**Their share of the toil**

Also known as **Three women on beach with baskets**
*c.*1887, etching

Image courtesy Kate Rider

Note one difference from the oil on canvas – there is no basket
behind the women on the right.

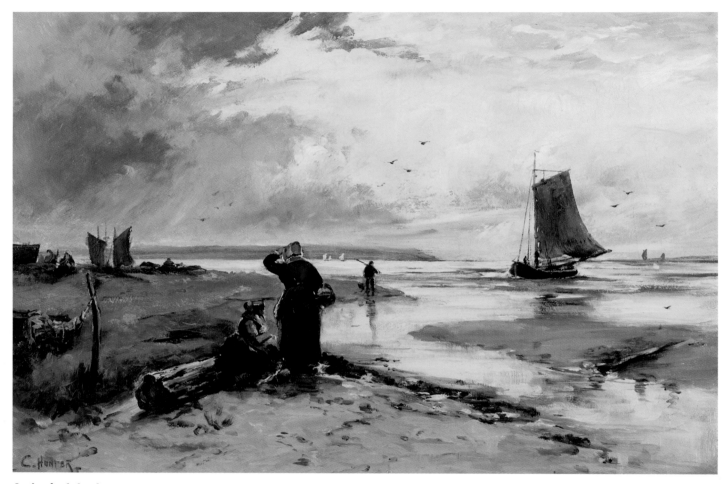

**Arrival of the boats**

Oil on canvas, 35.5 × 50.8 cm, 14" × 20"

Signed C Hunter LL

Courtesy of and © Waddington's Auctioneers and Appraisers,
Toronto, Canada

Listed Waddington's Toronto 15 June 2010 not sold, 2010

**Provenance**

Birchwood Studio, Braemar, Ballater, Aberdeenshire, Scotland
The McEwan Gallery, Glengarden, Ballater, Aberdeenshire

Zurichsee Auctionen, Erlenbach, Switzerland

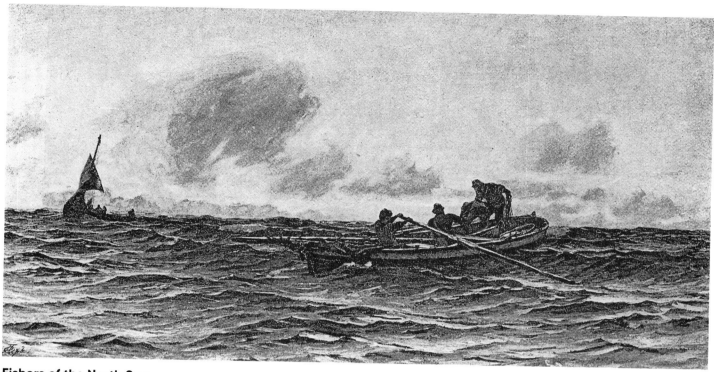

**Fishers of the North Sea**

1888

Reproduced from unidentified magazine but probably *Royal Academy Pictures*

Courtesy Marcia Rider

Also published in *Pall Mall Gazette "Extra" The Pictures of 1888 – Royal Academy*

Exhibited Royal Academy 1888

Exhibited Royal Scottish Academy 1905 (after Hunter's death)

Sold by Hunter 1895 for £500 (today's value £46,000). The buyer was probably F C Stop, Surrey, because he lent it to the RSA to exhibit in 1905.

This painting was shown in John Young-Hunter's water colour of his father's studio at 14 Melbury Road (right, repeated here from Chapter 3). It is seen resting on the floor against an easel.

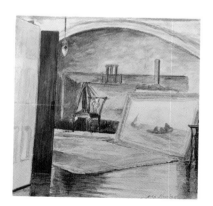

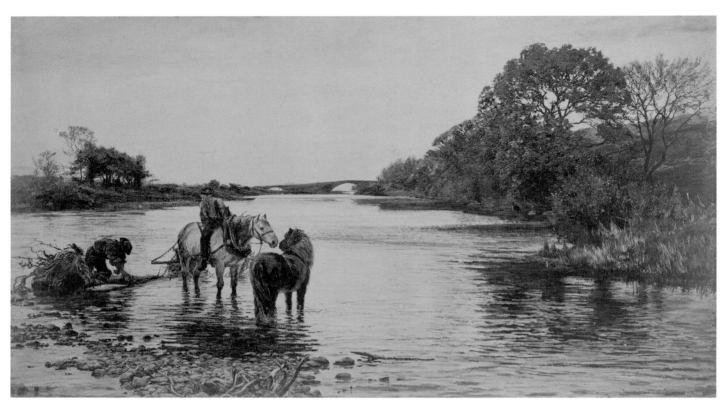

**Dove sfocia il Lugano**

("**Where it flows [leads] into Lugano**")

1887, oil on canvas, 90 × 153 cm, 35.5" × 60"

Signed and dated LR

Image courtesy Kate Rider

2015 Listed Il Ponte Casa D'aste Sri, Milan, Italy

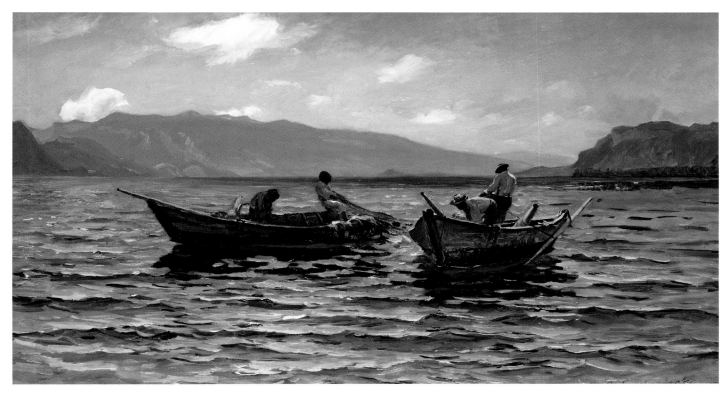

## Lac du Bourget

(aka **Fishermen, Lac du Bourget**)
1888, oil on canvas, 51 × 91 cm, 20" × 36"

Signed and dated

Image courtesy of Lyon & Turnbull Fine Art Auctioneers

**Provenance**
Sold by Hunter to Lady Seton in for £200 (today's value £18,000),
1888
Sold, Lyon & Turnbull, 2013

Another painting of the same name and year was sold to Dr Moore
for £150.

A painting entitled **Lac Du Bourget, Savoie**, was exhibited in the
Royal Academy in 1888.

It is not known whether this painting is the same as that exhibited
in the RA. The one above was called **Fishermen, Lac du Bourget**,
while the RA one omitted the word Fishermen.

And in Hunter's accounts for the fiscal year 1887–88 he lists two
paintings of the same name, simply, **Lac du Bourget**. One sold for
£50 less than the other which suggests a second painting was done,
but perhaps a smaller size.

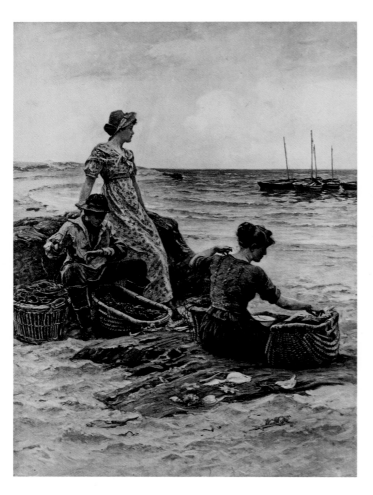

## Baiters

(Hunter called it **The woman's bait**)

1889, oil on canvas, 167.6 × 124.5 cm, 66" × 49"

Image courtesy Kate Rider

Exhibited Royal Academy 1889

Published *The Pictures of 1889, Royal Academy, Pall Mall Gazette*
*"Extra"*

Etching of this work published as the frontispiece in *The British Seas*,
London, 1892 (see page 10)

### Provenance

Sold by Hunter to Watson for £700 (today's value £62,800), 1889
Sold, Sotheby's New York for £7,500, 1991

'**The Baiters** of Mr Colin Hunter is a comparatively new departure
since it is more a figure picture than a "marine". In colour it is
rich, effective and carefully studied, and the drawing of the figures
shows that there is no reason why the painter should always confine
himself to waves and rocks. Mr Hunter, indeed, is this year taking
up figure painting with some seriousness, and in the third room we
have a portrait by him of **Mr Oscar Leslie Stephen.**'[86]

   *The Times*, 22 May 1889 writing about the RA exhibition 1889

'... The most picturesque figures all along the coast are the bait-
gatherers. In the early morning stillness, when one, after bathing,
is resting behind the shadow of a rock, the air is broken by distant
voices sounding like sea-birds; the sounds come nearer – you make
them out to be human voices by the peculiar sharp click; afar off are
troops of figures rapidly approaching in the sands articulate into
words, and the baiters pass with steady swinging pace that would do
any man credit. They are going for lugworm bait for white fishing
which lasts till September (clam bait is only got in May) ...

... The spade the bait-gatherers use is small, and the fishing-girls
apply it deftly with their hands ... Much skill and quickness are
necessary otherwise the worm would swiftly elude the gatherers.
Only those trained from their childhood can ever hope to earn a
living by the work, or to bring home a sufficient supply in their
pitchers. The troops of women in early morning or late evening, on
the wide sands against the expanse of sky and sea are a sight not
readily forgotten.

... They are suitably attired in unison with their open-air
surroundings – sometimes bareheaded and invariably barefooted ...
their hair is often concealed by coloured kerchiefs ...'

   *The British Seas*, W Clark Russell,
   Seeley London 1892

---

86  Oscar Leslie Stephen 1819–98

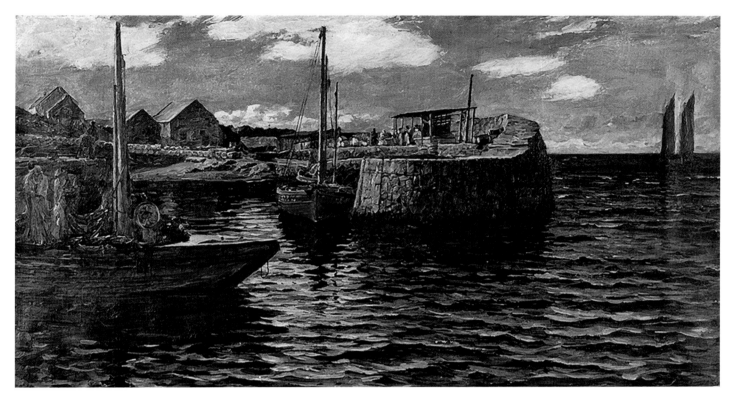

## The first arrivals

1884, oil on canvas, 55 × 101 cm, 21.7" × 39.8"

Indistinctly signed and dated 1884 LR

Titled on a handwritten label verso

Image courtesy of McTear's, Glasgow

Exhibited at the Royal Academy 1884

**Provenance**
Sold to Agnew by Hunter for £200. Today's value £23,200, 1884
Sold, McTear's, Glasgow, 2014

## White Hills, Aberdeenshire

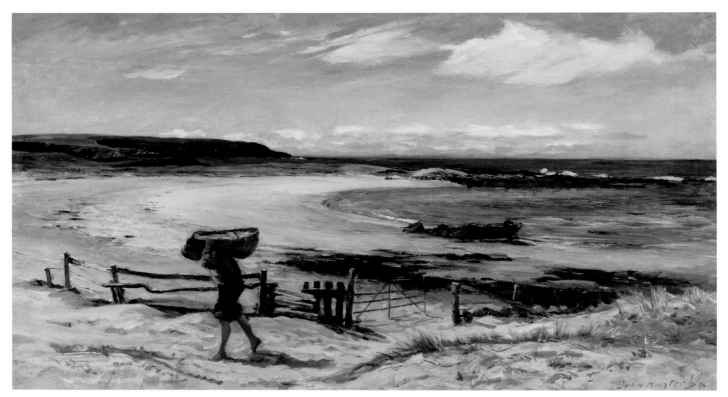

**On the east coast of Scotland**

(possibly **The Sands of White Hills**?)

1888, oil on canvas, 49.5 × 88.9 cm, 19.5" × 35"

© Dundee City Council (Dundee's Art Galleries and Museums)

**Provenance**
Presented to Dundee from collection of James Guthrie Orchar, 1987

This appears to be painted at the same location as **The Sands of White Hills 1889**, opposite.

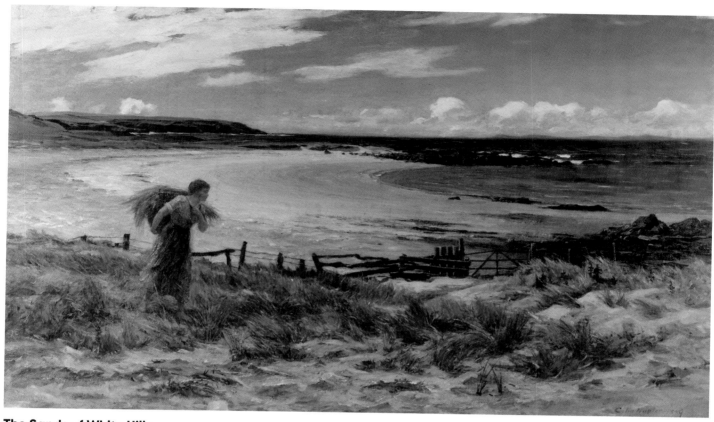

## The Sands of White Hills

1889, oil on canvas, 91.4 × 153 cm, 36" × 60.2"

© Dundee City Council (Dundee's Art Galleries and Museums)

**Provenance**
Bequeathed by Miss H M Cox Alyth, 1965
Sold by Hunter at the Dundee Exhibition for £380 (today's value £34,000), 1889

This was painted at the same location as **On the East Coast of Scotland 1888**, shown opposite.

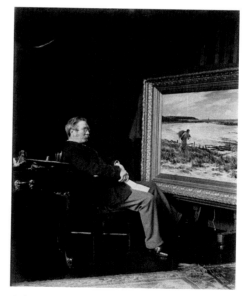

Colin Hunter in his studio 14 Melbury Road viewing his painting **The Sands of White Hills 1889** (above)

Photograph, Crown copyright. Courtesy The National Archives

Photo by Ralph Winwood Robinson, published by C Whittingham & Co

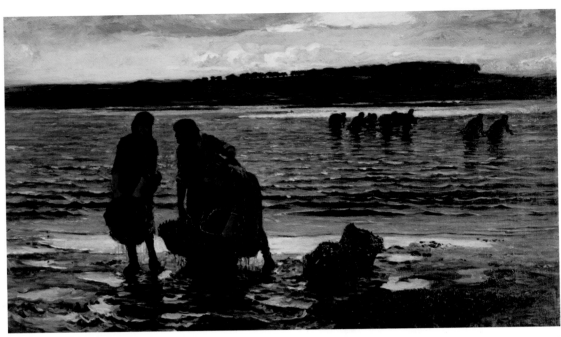

## Kelp (Mussel) Gatherers

(incorrectly named as **Kelp Gatherers**) See the etching opposite,
**The Mussel Gatherers 1881**

1881, oil on canvas, 50 × 90 cm, 19.7" × 35.4"

© The Burton Art Gallery and Museum, Bideford, Devon

1951 Bequeathed from the Hubert Coop Collection

Exhibited Royal Academy 1881 as **Mussel Gatherers**.

Hunter etched **The Mussel Gatherers** for *The Art Journal* in 1881
(opposite).

'... *a better sample of one section of our school*[87] *could scarcely be found ...*'
*The Art Journal*, April 1885

It is believed that at some point this painting was mistakenly
entitled Kelp Gatherers.

It was definitely exhibited in the Royal Academy as Mussel
Gatherers but it was eventually bequeathed to the Burton Art
Gallery as Kelp Gatherers

The Collections and Exhibitions Officer of the Burton Art Gallery,
Warren Collum, confirms his belief that the picture was mistakenly
titled. He says, "I am not sure how it got the name Kelp Gatherers
as it is very clear from the picture that the women are collecting
mussels in baskets at low tide. Something you don't do if you are
collecting kelp!"

According to his accounts, in 1876 Hunter sold another painting
called Gathering Mussels but no image of that earlier work has been
found.

Various images of this picture, from different sources (e.g. heritage-
images.com), also as an etching, are entitled The Mussel Gatherers
which confirms the original oil painting (above) should not have
assumed the name of Kelp Gatherers.

**The Mussel Gatherers** was destined to introduce Hunter to
Germany. Hunter sold it to Mr G C Schwabe (see below). It formed
part of Schwabe's collection that Schwabe later presented to his
home town of Hamburg.[88]

Hunter's 1880–81 accounts (written in his own hand) show he sold
**The Mussel Gatherers** for £800. Today's value £68,000.

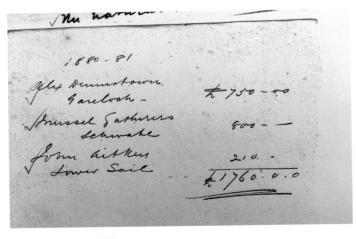

Courtesy Marcia Rider

---

87  The Scottish school of painters in 1885

88  *The Art Journal*, April 1885

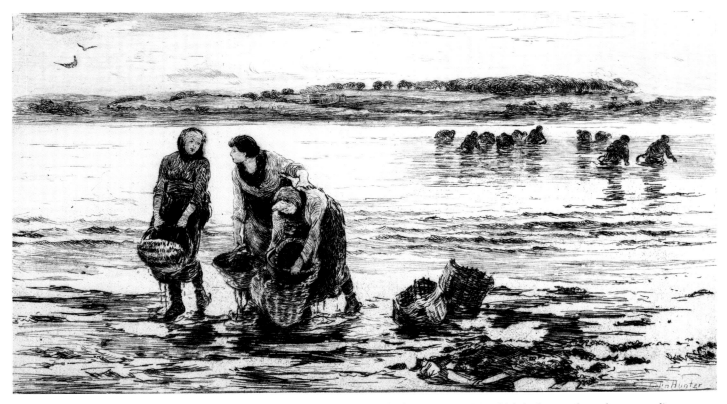

## The Mussel Gatherers

1881, drawn and etched by Colin Hunter, original etching (limited edition of 500 impressions), 17.8 × 27.9 cm, 7" × 11"

Source: *Fifty Choice Examples of Modern Etching*

Private Collection

Once described as **pen and ink drawing of cocklers**

See the painting (opposite), **Kelp Gatherers**. It appears that the most obvious difference between the etching and the oil on canvas is the addition of seagulls in the sky (upper left).

The limited edition run of this etching is recorded as *c.*1890 but the original etching appears in *The Illustrated London News* 1881.

The etching also appeared in *The Art Journal*, London, July 1881, pp 200–206. The copy held in the British Library is very fragile. The etching itself is held by the National Gallery of Scotland:

For the first time, we believe, since the foundation of this Journal – now over forty years ago – we are able to give, thanks to the assistance of the artist and the more rapid method of reproduction now employed, an etching of a picture at present on exhibition at the Royal Academy. Although permanently settled in London, Mr Hunter does not forget his Scottish origin, and with a single exception, **The Harvest of the Sea**, has always gathered his subjects, as in this instance, from the shores of his fatherland.

Whether a recent visit which he has made to the sunny climes of the Eastern Mediterranean may induce him to alter this determination we know not, but we ill spare so truthful, and, at the same time, so poetical an exponent of the luminous atmosphere and lovely colouring of the northern shores of our native isles. The picture of the **Mussel Gatherers** and its companion **In the Gloaming** (page 72) have been cruelly sacrificed in a notoriously badly hung exhibition to the idea that no picture can have a better pendant than its fellow by the same artist. Remembering that Mr Colin Hunter's **Their only harvest** was selected for purchase by the Chantrey Bequest but two years ago, one would be inclined to say the Hanging Committees imagine that they must be cognisant of the good deeds of their predecessors and not repeat them; but this hypothesis is upset by the fact that in the place of honour in the self-same room as that which these pictures are hung are two seascapes (of course pendants to one another) by a young artist whose picture was bought still more recently by the same. The scene of etching is laid at Newburgh, Aberdeenshire.

- *The Art Journal*, London, July 1881

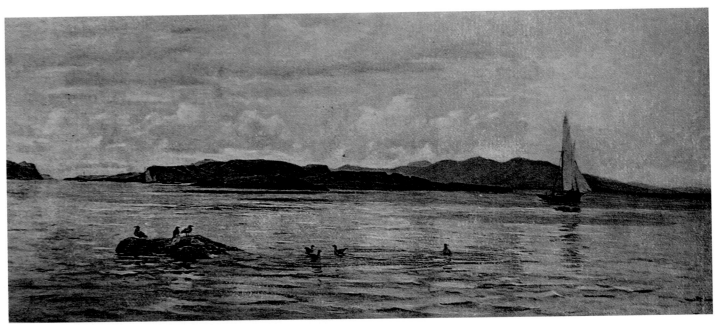

### The morning breeze. Island of Kerrera, Mull Hills in the distance

1889, oil on canvas

Reproduced from *The British Seas*, W Clark Russell, Seeley London 1892

Exhibited Royal Academy 1889

Sold by Hunter 1889 for £500 (today's value £45,000).

There is another picture called **The morning breeze**, an etching (see opposite).

Note similar location of this painting with the following three images.

'... This island of Kerrera ... protecting the bay of Oban from the westerly winds, in which Mr Colin Hunter has found a subject, is probably little different in aspect from what it was some six centuries and a half ago, when Alexander II of Scotland died there. Possibly these gulls that are in the foreground are vexed somewhat by the idle sport by which the Englishman gratifies the national passion for slaughter; but they are the descendants of tribes which have dwelt on these rocks for more centuries than one can count. Here, in this almost nameless island, we find, as so often in these regions, places that are now, so to speak, left high and dry, but were once in the full stream of history. This rugged little Kerrera, for instance, reminds us of all the interesting story of the rise and fall of the Norse dominion in the Western Isles.'

*The British Seas*, W Clark Russell,
Seeley London, 1892

'Those glorious summers always ended at Oban on the north west coast of Scotland with the annual regatta, the final event of the Scottish social season ... Enclosing the bay is the green island of Kerrera and beyond is the Island of Mull with its blue mountains ...'
*Reviewing the Years*, John Young-Hunter, 1963

'At Mr Colin Hunter's yesterday everyone was delighted with the two large marine pieces, **The Morning Breeze** and **Baiters**, the former of Oban Bay, with the green slopes of Kerrera to the left, and further away the blue heights of Mull. These and a smaller canvas painted off the Banff coast go to the Academy, while another Banff seascape (with a sky of the most [?illegible] turquoise-green rather turquoise-blue) goes to the Grosvenor, and to the New Gallery, a Perthshire landscape entitled **The Mill**.'
*The Dundee Evening Telegraph* Monday 08 April 1889
(presumably on a party hosted by Colin Hunter
show-casing the pictures due for exhibition)

'... few will deny that Hunter's best picture is that called **The Morning Breeze**, a delicate and delightful study of the colours of the western Scottish sea in one of its rare intervals of fine weather. Next to the celebrated **Herring Market At Sea** this picture pleases us most of any that have come from Mr Colin Hunter's hand ...'
*The Times*, 22 May 1889 (on the
Royal Academy Exhibition)

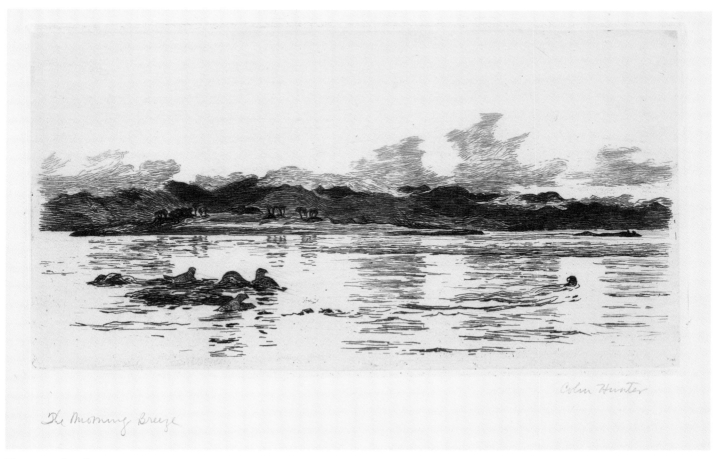

The morning breeze

The morning breeze

*c.*1890, etching, 3.9 × 25.1 cm, 5.5" × 9.9"

Fine Arts Museums of San Francisco

**Provenance**
Acquired by Achenbach Foundation for Graphic Arts, 1963

There is another picture also called **The morning breeze** (see opposite).

Compare this picture with **The Hills of Morven 1890** on page 170 and **The Morven Hills from Lismore 1891** on page 171. It is difficult to distinguish the difference in the picture between the etching above and the oil on canvas exhibited in the Royal Academy in 1890. But the etching has been given an entirely different title.

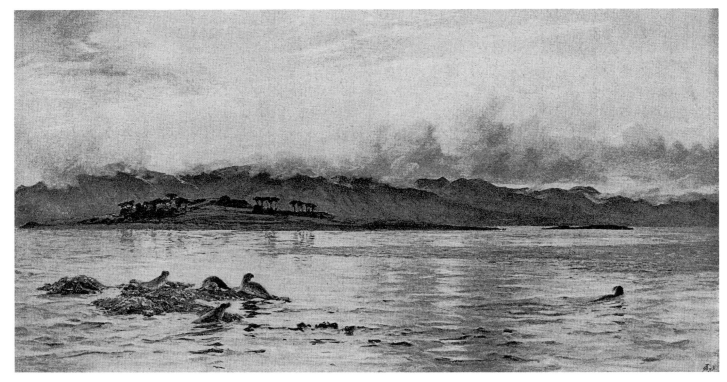

## The Hills of Morven (or Morvern)

Also known as **Morven Hills**

1890, oil on canvas

Reproduced from *Supplement to The Graphic* May 12 1890

Exhibited Royal Academy 1890

Published as an etching in *The British Seas*, W Clarke Russell, Seeley London 1892

'... I hope that the seals which Mr Colin Hunter has put in the foreground of his picture, will never become as mythical as Ossian's heroes. They are certainly rarer in these parts than they were some years ago; in fact they have many enemies.'

*The British Seas*, W Clark Russell,
Seeley, London, 1892

Morven is the historic spelling of Morvern.

Sold by Hunter in 1890 for £525 (today's value £47,000).

In the following year, 1891, Hunter painted another picture similar to this one called **The Morven Hills from Lismore**. One of the variations is that the seal on the right of this picture was omitted. See opposite.

An etching of virtually the same scene (see page 169) but with an entirely different name **The morning breeze**, is in the San Francisco Arts Museums.

Note the similar location of this painting with the previous and following images.

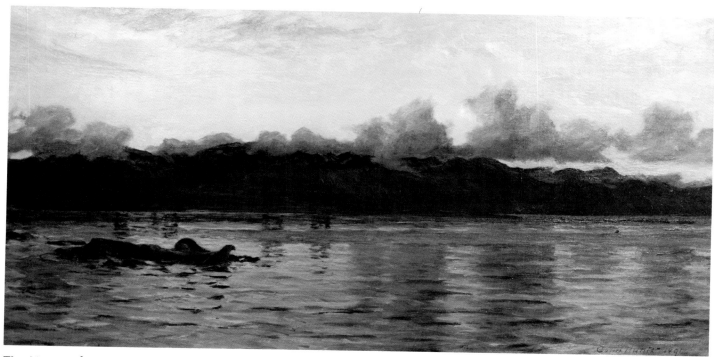

## The Morven (or Morvern) Hills from Lismore

1891, oil on canvas, 44.5 × 90 cm, 17.5" × 35.5"

Signed and dated

Today, Morven is usually spelt Morvern.

Lismore means in Gaelic, "big garden".

Private collection

Sold, Lyon & Turnbull, Edinburgh, 2010

Compare this painting with that opposite. There is very little difference but a few seals have vanished.

One year Hunter rented a house at the north end of the Island of Lismore in Loch Linnhe, opposite Appin (made famous by Robert Louis Stevenson in "Kidnapped") and with the Hills of Morven fringing the loch on the northwest.

A ferry was available between the end of the Island and Appin and seals frequently accompanied the row boat. Once Colin asked his son John to shoot a seal so he could have it stuffed and use it as a model in his studio in Melbury Road.[89]

Note the similar location of this painting with the previous images.

89 *Reviewing the Years*, John Young-Hunter

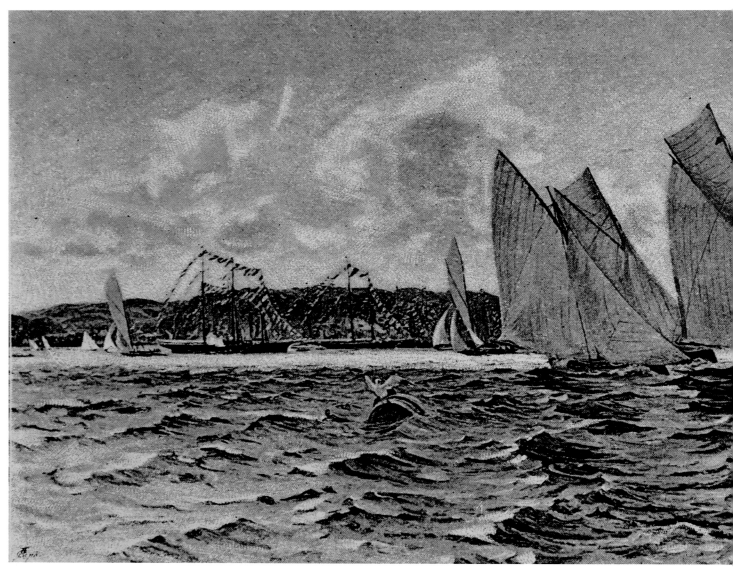

## Oban regatta 1890

1890, oil on canvas, 75 × 152 cm, 30" × 60"
Reproduced from *Royal Academy Pictures 1891*.

Sold, Sotheby's, London, 1998
Sold, Lyon & Turnbull, Edinburgh, 2006

**Provenance**
The Royal Highland Yacht Club

**Exhibited**
Royal Academy 1891, no. 438
Royal Institute, Glasgow 1892, no. 194
West Ham, Free Exhibition, Easter 1897
Melbourne International Exhibition 1902

**Literature**
*Art Journal* 1891, illus p.211
*Royal Academy Pictures 1891*, Cassell & Co, illus. p.16

'Hunter and his family spent their summers on the north west coast of Scotland in their yacht *Carissima* and always ended the holiday at Oban.

Enclosing the bay is the green island of Kerrera, and beyond is the Island of Mull with its blue mountains; but both are completely obscured during the time of the regatta, for then the harbour is literally full of yachts. When another one moves in, the question is, "Where can she find anchorage?" Nearly all of the yachts are flying burgees, and we, in the *Carissima*, scan each new arrival through binoculars tp ascertain her identity.'

*Reviewing the Years*, John Young-Hunter, 1963

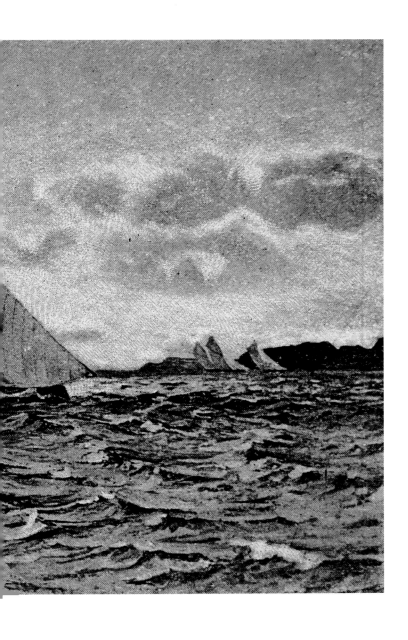

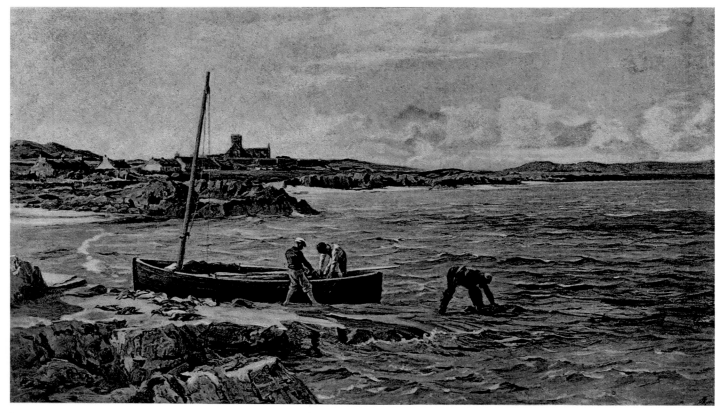

## Iona

1891, oil on canvas

Reproduced from *Royal Academy Pictures 1891*

Exhibited Royal Academy 1891

In the same year, Hunter's **Iona Crofters** was also hung at the RA (opposite).

Sold by Hunter in 1891 for £200 (today's value £17,750).

Another **Iona** was painted in 1879 and sold for £150. In the same year, 1879, Hunter painted **Iona Shore** and sold it for £525. Despite **Iona Shore** being exhibited in the RA in 1880, no images of either of these earlier Iona paintings have been found.

Iona is a small island in the Inner Hebrides off the Ross of Mull on the west coast of Scotland.

Note: Interestingly, directly preceding Hunter's picture above in *Royal Academy Pictures 1891*, was Hunter's neighbour's picture, a portrait *The Lady Catherine Thynne*, by G F Watts RA. Another flag for the Melbury Road Set. G F Watts lived at Little Holland House, 6 Melbury Road.

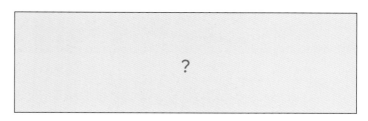

## Iona Shore

1880 (oil) and also 1882 (water colour). No image found of either painting.

Colin Hunter ventured on more brilliant effects of Hebridean waters in his sweep of sea round **Iona Shore** with its change of blue and blue-green and purple flushes, "the peacock's neck in hue".

*The Times*, 18th May 1880

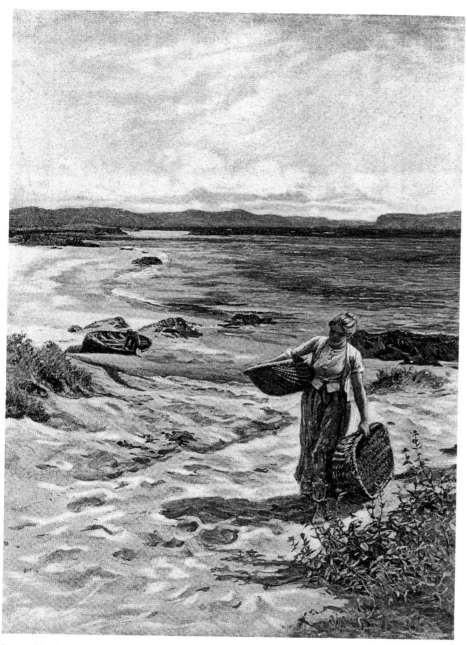

**Iona Crofters**

1891, oil on canvas

Reproduced from *Royal Academy Pictures 1891*

Also published in *Royal Academy Pictures of the Year*, Sep 19, 1891

Exhibited Royal Academy 1891

In the same year, Hunter's **Iona** was also hung at the RA (opposite).

Sold by Hunter 1891 for £235 (today's value £20,800)

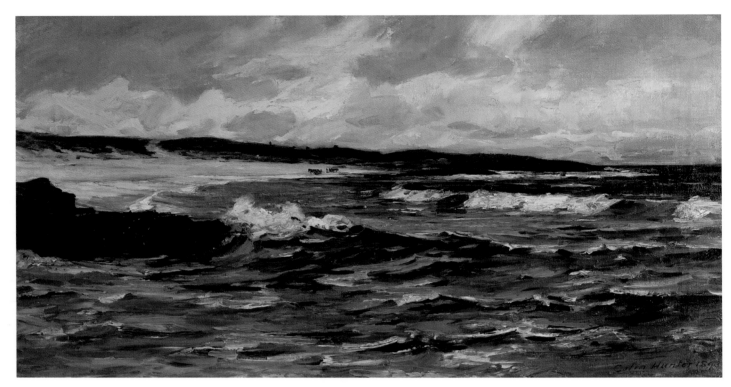

**Waves breaking with figures on the beach**[90]

Also known as **Rocky seascape**

1898, oil on canvas, 39 × 75 cm, 15.3" × 29.5"

Signed and dated

Image courtesy Iona Gallery (Isle of Iona, Inner Hebrides, Scotland)

Location: possibly north Iona.

This scene also reproduced as **Rocky Seascape** and sold commercially as poster/prints by niceartgallery.com and plentyofpaintings.com

2006: Listed as **Rocky Seascape** by Sotheby's Hammersmith London

2008: Listed as **Waves breaking with figures on the beach** by Lyon & Turnbull. Sold to Iona Gallery

2010: Sold to Anthony Woodd Gallery Edinburgh

90  Indistinct. Sometimes sold as dated 1893

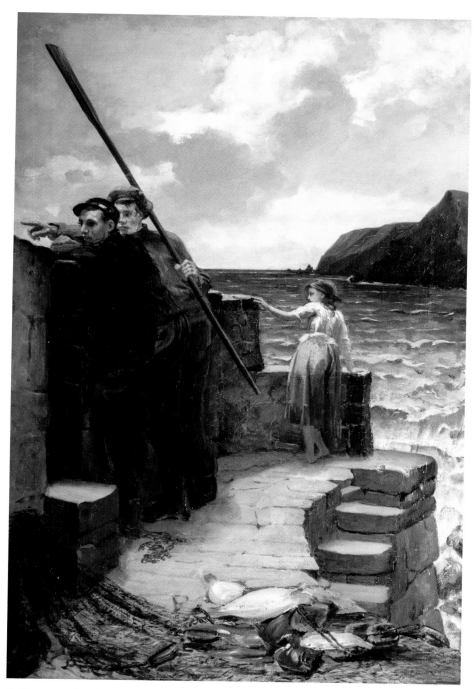

**A Strange Craft**

1891, oil on canvas, 76 × 51 cm, 30" × 20"

Signed and dated Colin Hunter 1891, titled on frame

Private Collection

Sold, Bonhams, Solihull, 2011

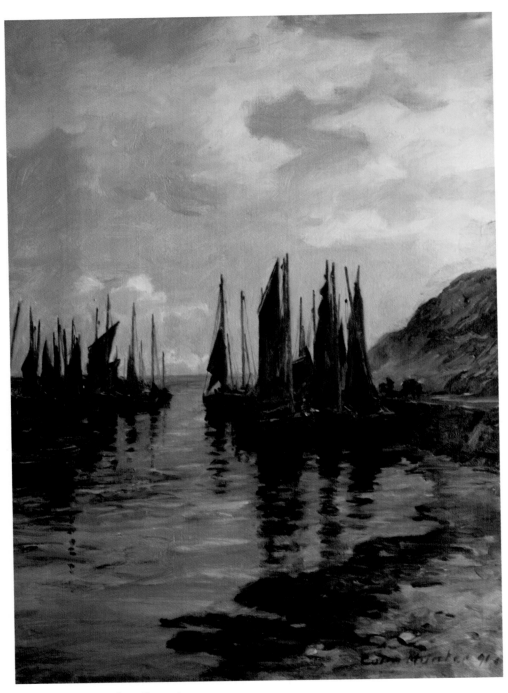

**Fishing boats unloading at a quay**

1891, oil on canvas, 55 × 39 cm, 21" × 15"

Signed and dated 91

Private collection

Sold, Eldreds, Plymouth, 2016

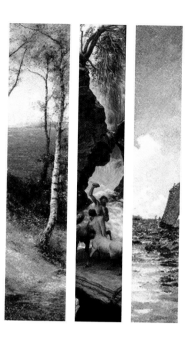

**A fishing boat off the coast** (picture on right)

Also known as **A seascape**, also known as **A sea piece**
probably 1891, oil on canvas, 80.7 × 13.4 cm, 32" × 5"

Sold, Hampton & Sons, London, 1913

Sold, Christie's, London, 2003

Also accompanying paintings:
(centre) **Battle of Centaurs**, 1891 by James Archer
(left) **Silver Birches**, by John MacWhirter

A very unusual painting because of its dimensions. It was painted specifically for Alma-Tadema's house at 17 Grove End Road, St John's Wood, London.

Lawrence Alma-Tadema (1836–1912) was a Dutch painter who settled in England in 1870 and spent the rest of his life here (although he died in Germany). It is likely that Alma-Tadema commissioned Hunter to paint this panel for the hall in his home, as he did two other Scottish painters MacWhirter (1839–1911) and James Archer (1823–1904).

Hunter's picture was placed two to the right of MacWhirter's *Silver Birches*, with James Archer's *Centaurs* in between.

'Those who care for Mr Colin Hunter's work, will easily recognise his characteristic sea piece, in which the sea is painted with his masterful knowledge of its ever-varying moods.'

> R de Cordova, *'The Panels in Sir Lawrence Alma-Tadema's Hall'*,
> *Strand Magazine*, vol XXIV no. 144, December 1902 p 623,
> illustrated as *A seascape*.

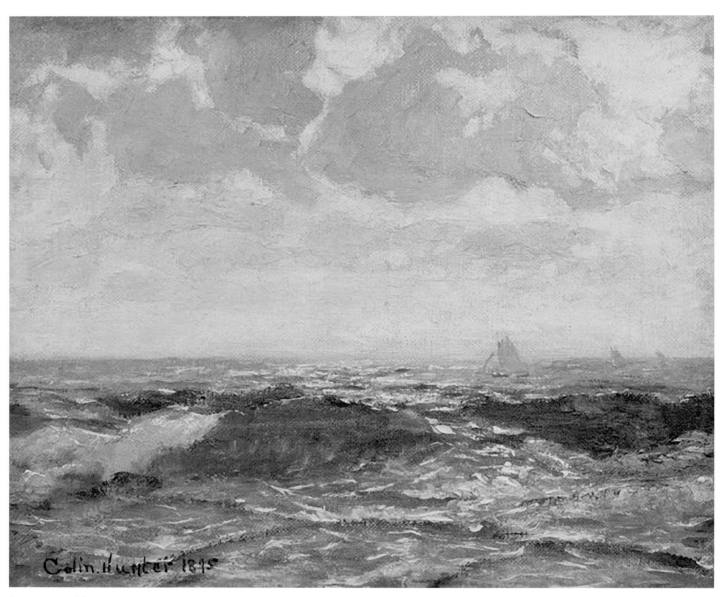

**Seascape (1)**

1895, oil on board, 29 × 34.5 cm, 11.4" × 13.6"

Signed and dated

Image courtesy of McTear's Gallery, Glasgow

11th October 2017, sold The Pictures Auction, McTear's

Devon

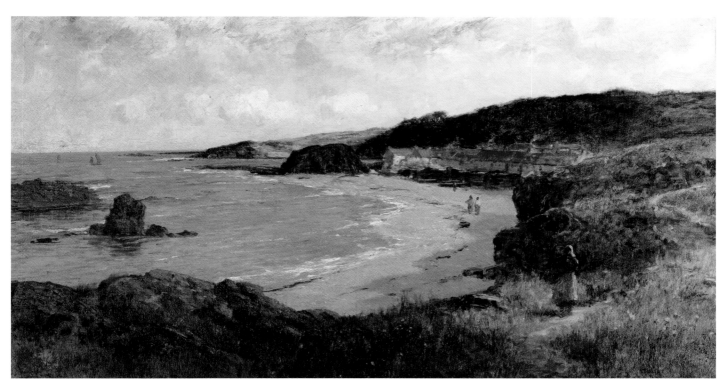

## The coast of Devon

1891 (or 1894), oil on canvas, 45.7 × 83.8 cm, 18" × 33"

Signed and dated indistinctly 'Colin Hunter 189*' (1891 or 1894) LR

Private collection

Sold, Christie's, London, 2010

Right: One of Colin Hunter's more unusual signatures – in block capitals, so perfect the letters appear almost as if they were stencilled.

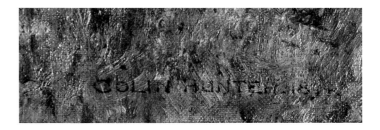

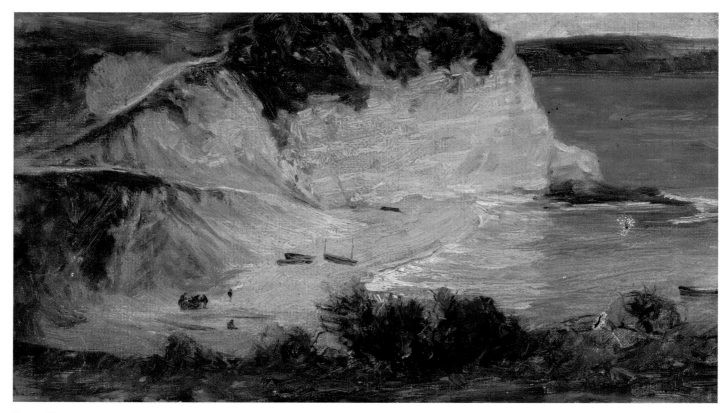

**Beer, Devon**

Possibly *c.*1879, oil on canvas, 20.5 × 35.7 cm, 8.1" × 14.1"

Signed Colin Hunter

Courtesy Royal Albert Memorial Museum, Exeter

Verso: ink stamp: 'Soho Square, London Newman'.

**Provenance**
Bequeathed to Royal Albert Memorial Museum by Mr Roland and
Mrs Gertrude McAlpine Woods, 1949

The top cliff path in the painting leads to Seaton.[91]

91 Acknowledgement: Selwyn Channon

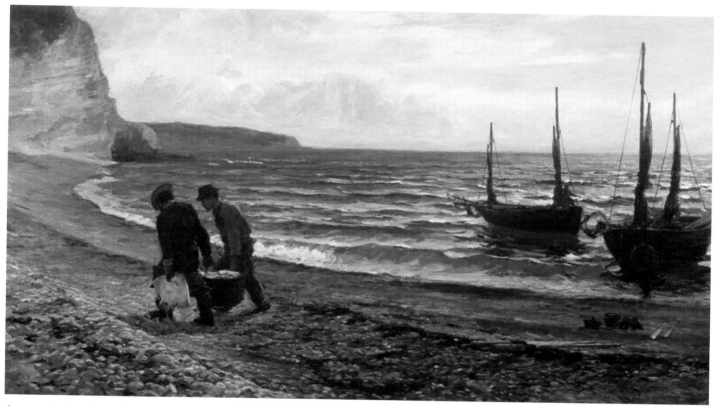

**A sea view – Beer, Devon**

1879, oil on canvas, 50 × 86 cm, 19.5" × 33.8"

City of London Corporation, Guildhall Art Gallery

© London Metropolitan Archives

**Provenance**
Presented to Guildhall Art Galley by Sir Marcus Samuel (Lord Bearsted), 1919

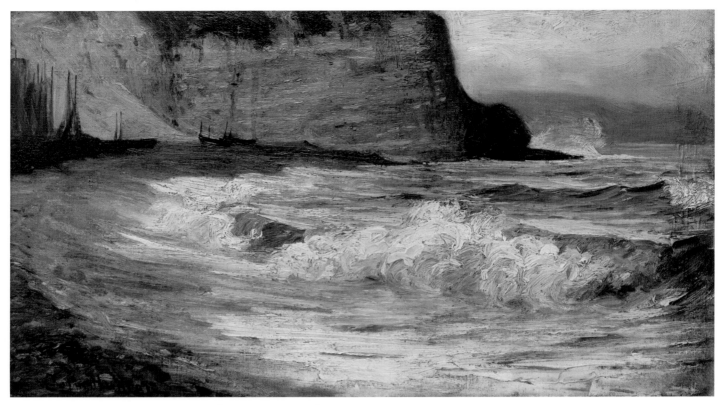

**Safely back under the white cliffs (possibly Devon)**

Also known as **Fishing boats under the white cliffs**
oil on canvas, 35.5 × 61 cm, 14" × 24"

Signed

Private collection

Sold, Murray's Fine Art Auctioneers, Douglas, Isle of Man, 2018

Restored, Fine Art Restoration Co., London, 2018

Compare this picture with the picture opposite. Possibly the same location.

# Kent – or Devon?

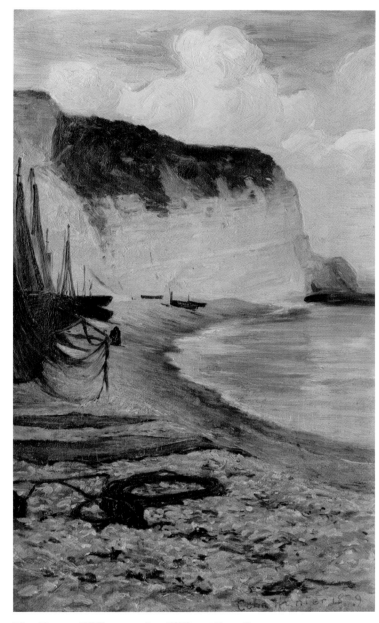

## The Dover Cliffs – or the Cliffs at Beer?

1879, oil on canvas, 51 × 30.5 cm, 20" × 12"

Signed and dated

Ross's Auctioneers, Belfast, Northern Ireland, 2015

The Old Courthouse, Greyabbey, Northern Ireland, 2017

Private collection, England, 2018

Despite being sold and entitled on frame as Dover Cliffs, there is an argument for believing these cliffs are in fact at or near Beer, Devon. Compare this painting with other Beer paintings (see pages 182 and 183). Indeed, a local resident has said, "This is definitely Beer."

There is no evidence that Hunter himself named this painting as Cliffs of Dover and no other pictures that we know of prove Hunter ever painted in Kent. But he frequently painted in Devon. It is more likely that someone later on believed they looked like the White Cliffs of Dover and promptly named the painting as such. A name that has stuck. It is also worth noting that clearly it was framed and titled long after Hunter painted it. It quotes Hunter as "ARA" but he did not become an Associate of the Royal Academy until 1884 and the painting was dated 1879.

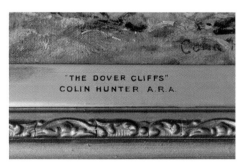

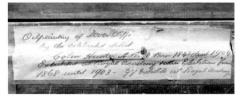

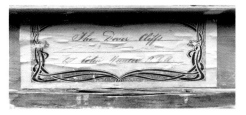

# Sutherland, Scotland

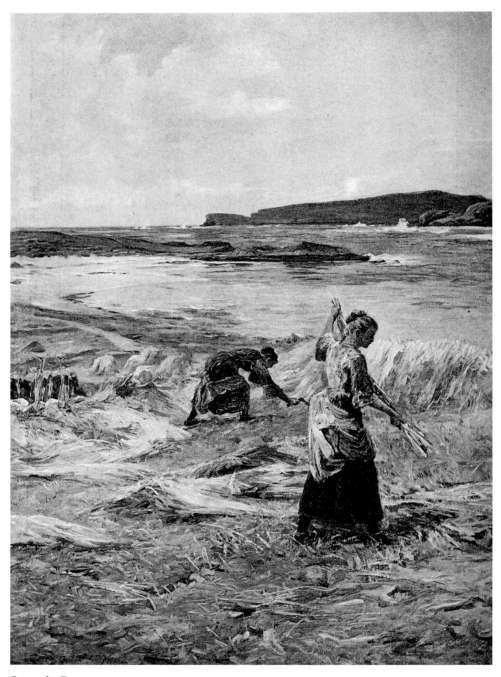

**Scourie Bay**

1892, oil on canvas, 121.9 × 101.6 cm, 48" × 40"

Reproduced from *Royal Academy Pictures* 1892

Exhibited Royal Academy, 1892

Sold by Hunter in 1892 to Stuart Hall, for £250 (today's value £22,200)

Scourie Bay is in Sutherland, north west Scotland

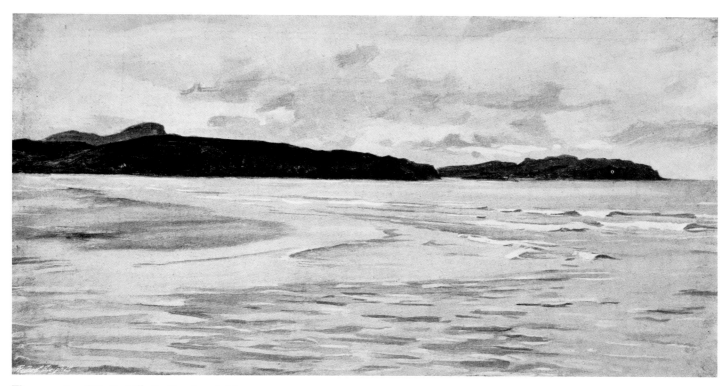

**The sands of Bettyhill, Sutherlandshire**

Also known as **Coastal view**

1902, oil on canvas, 40.6 × 76.2 cm, 16" × 30"

Reproduced from *Royal Academy Pictures* 1902

Exhibited Royal Academy 1902

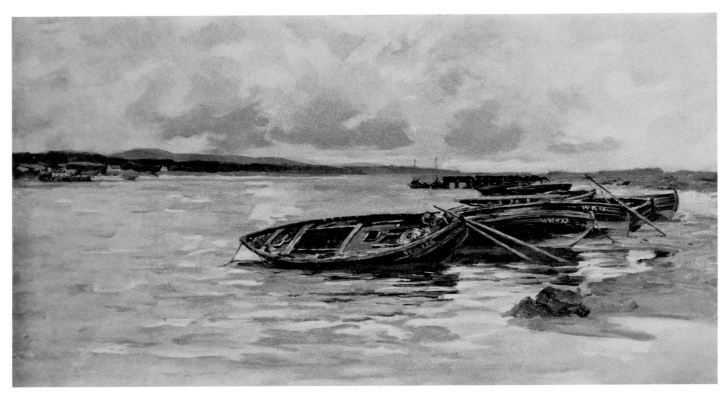

**The Little Ferry**

Also known as **The day of rest**
1897, oil on canvas, 50.8 × 91.4 cm, 20" × 36"

Reproduced from *Royal Academy Pictures* 1897 as **The day of rest**

Image also published elsewhere in unidentified magazine as **The Little Ferry, Dornoch**.

Dornoch is in the county of Sutherland in the highlands of Scotland.

Exhibited Royal Academy 1897

This is a puzzle as Hunter himself called this picture **Little Ferry** in his 1897–98 accounts. But it was exhibited in the Royal Academy as **Day of rest**.

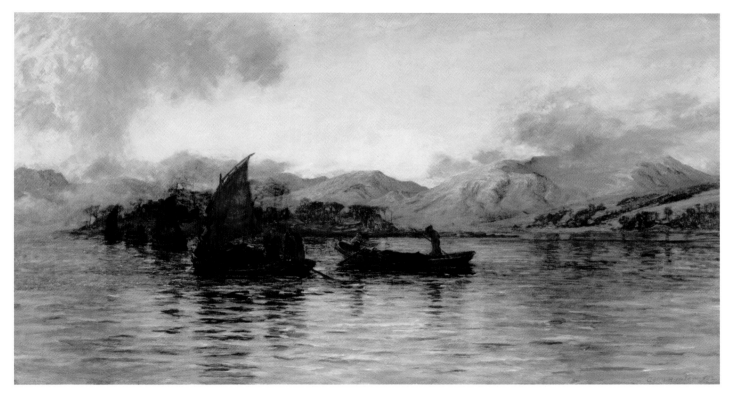

**The burial of the MacDonalds of Glencoe on St Munda Island, Loch Level, 1692**

1892, oil on canvas, 116.5 × 212.1 cm, 46" × 84"

Image: Perth Museum & Art Gallery, Perth & Kinross Council

Exhibited Royal Academy 1892

**Provenance**
Sold by Hunter to James Reid for £487 (today's value £43,250), 1892
Gifted to Perth & Kinross Council by Sir Douglas Reid, 1931

This provenance suggests that the painting stayed in the Reid family until it was gifted to Perth & Kinross Council in 1941.

Hunter's picture drew much sympathy from those viewers who could recall the account of the massacre of the clan by Campbell of Glenlyon at Glencoe, and the complicity in it of William III. But the scene as Colin Hunter painted it – the taking of the bodies across the gloomy loch by the few survivors of the clan, chiefly women – has in it an innate suggestion of tragedy.[92]

---

92  The Art of Colin Hunter, R C Trafford, *The Windsor Magazine*, 1912

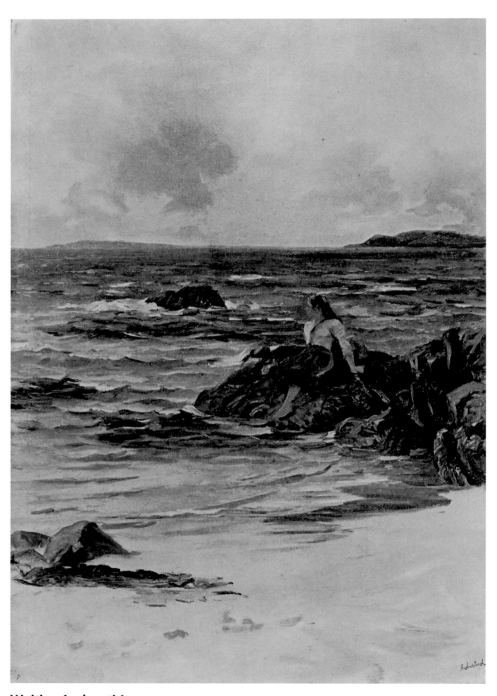

**Waiting for low tide**

1893, oil on canvas, 71.1 × 50.8 cm, 28" × 20"

Reproduced from *Royal Academy Pictures 1893*

Also published in *The Illustrated London News,* May 6, 1893

Exhibited Royal Academy 1893

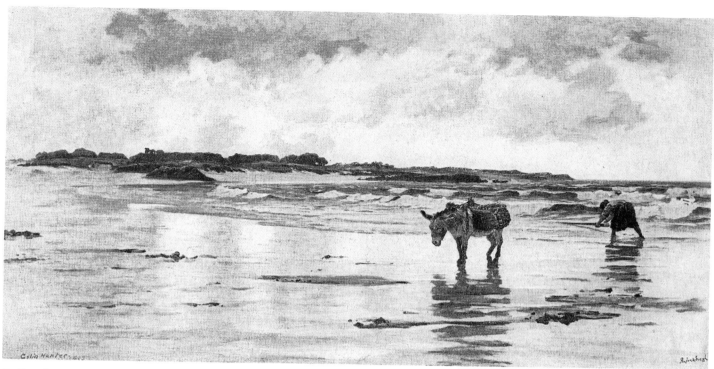

## Reflections

1893, oil on canvas, 99.1 × 182.9 cm, 39" × 72"

Reproduced from *Royal Academy Pictures 1893*

Also published in *Special Number of The Graphic*, May 1, 1893

Exhibited Royal Academy 1893

A second painting of the same scene was painted but called **Donkey in a marsh landscape**. However, this painting is smaller than the Royal Academy picture above.

'Mr Colin Hunter's picture, punningly named **Reflections**, shows us a wide stretch of shore with a very meditative donkey standing in the midst, while its mistress is gathering seaweed or bits of wreckage brought up by the waves. The donkey is very well, but the real motive of the picture is the expanse of wet sand with its reflections of the sky; and here, as in the larger picture in the seventh room [of the Academy exhibition halls], **Ireland**, Mr Hunter has, not for the first time, proved himself to be the most dexterous of those who paint "the melancholy ocean" and its barren shores.'

*The Times*, May 6, 1893 on the
Royal Academy Pictures 1893

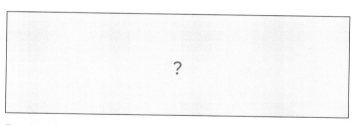

## Donkey in a marsh landscape

No image found

Oil on canvas, 71.1 × 141 cm, 28" × 55.5"

Estate of Maria B Saraczynski

Listed William Doyle New York auctioneers 18 February 2015

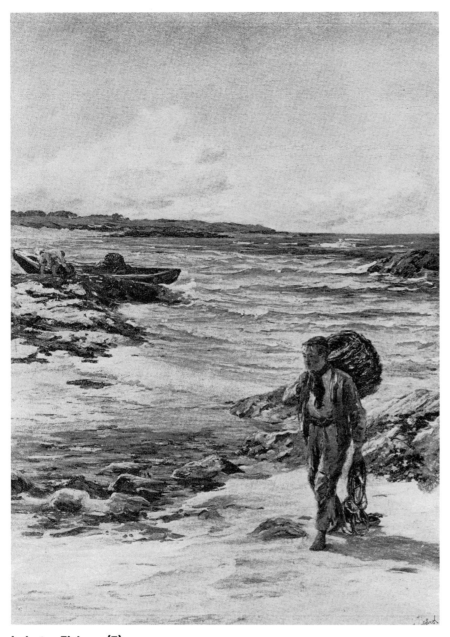

### Lobster Fishers (3)

1893, oil on canvas, 101.6 × 71.1 cm, 40" × 28"

Reproduced from *Royal Academy Pictures 1893*

Exhibited Royal Academy 1893

This is Colin Hunter's third **Lobster Fishers**. The first, an entirely different picture, was exhibited in the Royal Academy ten years earlier in 1883. The second was an etching done in 1885.

See also **Lobster Fishers 1883** (page 148) and **Lobster Fishers 1885 (**page 150**)**.

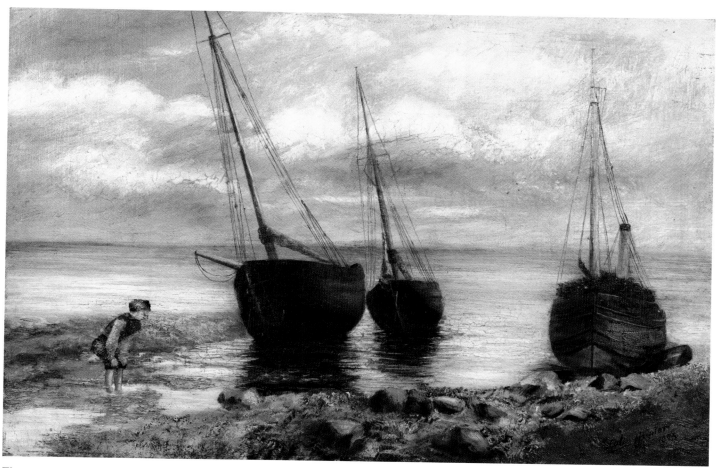

**The young explorer**

1893, oil on canvas, 29.5 × 45 cm, 11.6" × 17.7"

Signed and dated

Private collection

Sold, John Swan Auctions, Melrose, Scotland, 2015

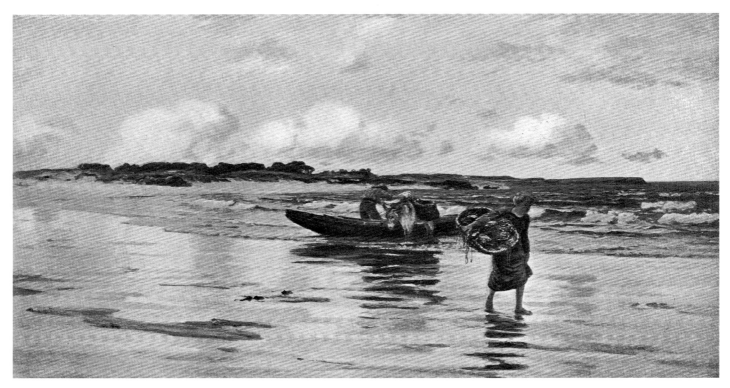

**Wet sands**

1894, oil on canvas, 99.1 × 182.9 cm, 39" × 72"

Exhibited Royal Academy 1894

Reproduced from *The Windsor Magazine* No. 214, 1912

**Published**
*Royal Academy Pictures*, 1894
Royal Academy Supplement of *The Magazine of Art*, 1894

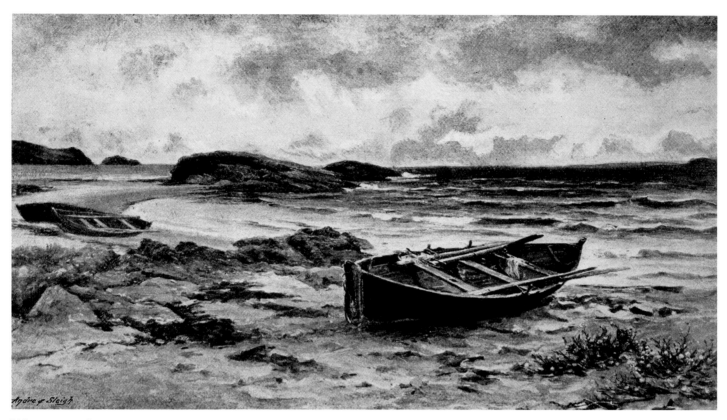

**Wintry weather**

1894, oil on canvas, 66 × 111.8 cm, 26" × 44"

Reproduced from *Royal Academy Pictures 1894*

Exhibited Royal Academy 1894

Sold to Sir Julius (?) Goldsmid in 1894 for £250 (today's value £22,800).

This picture was mistakenly entitled **Wet Sands** in *The Illustrated London News* May 12, 1894. **Wet Sands** was also exhibited in the Royal Academy 1894. See opposite.

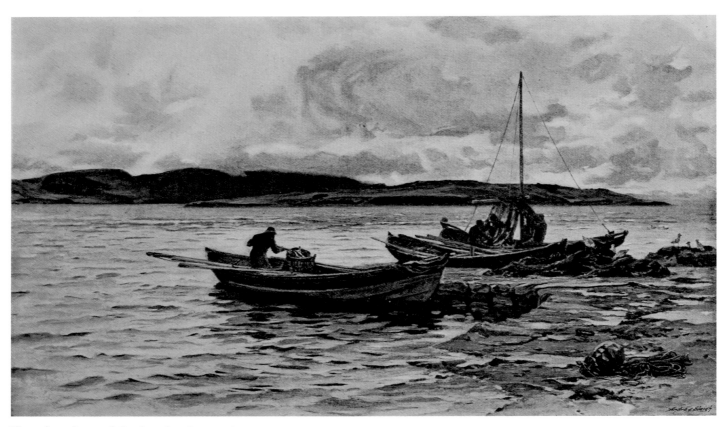

### The gleanings of the herring harvest

1894, oil on canvas 106.7 × 182.9 cm, 42" × 72"

Reproduced from *Royal Academy Pictures 1894*

Also published in the *Royal Academy Supplement of "The Magazine of Art"* 1894

Also published in *The Illustrated London News*, May 12th 1894

Exhibited Royal Academy 1894

Sold by Hunter 1894 for £700 (today's value £63,600)

This scene is reminiscent of Scalloway for there, after the fleet of herring-boats has departed, the village fishers go over the waters with small nets and sometimes glean a whole winter's supply.

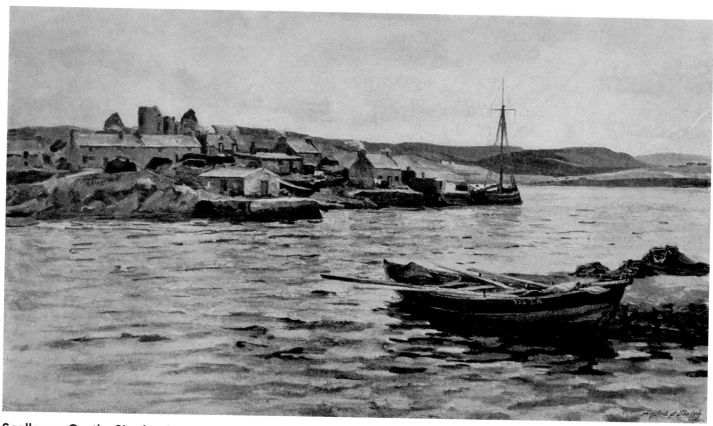

**Scalloway Castle, Shetland**

1894, oil on canvas, 45.7 × 76.2 cm, 18" × 30"

Reproduced from *Royal Academy Pictures 1904*

Also published in the *Royal Academy Supplement of "The Magazine of Art"* 1894

Also published in *The Illustrated London News* May 12th 1894

Exhibited Royal Academy 1894

# Skye

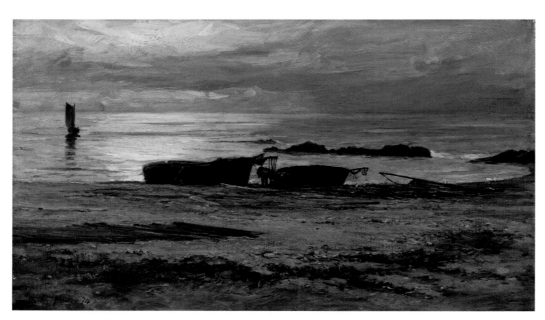

## Good night to Skye

1895, oil on canvas, 101.6 × 182.9 cm, 40" × 72"

© CSG CIC Glasgow Museums Collection

**Exhibited**
London Royal Academy, 1895
London Franco-British Exhibition, 1908
Bath, Victoria Art Gallery, 1908–09
Nottingham City Art Gallery, 1909
Stirling Fine Art Exhibition, 1921

Personal letter written by Hunter from Castlebay Hotel, Barra, by Oban.

Dated 20th July 1895:
By the request of the Lord Provost I am sending to your care at the close of the Royal Academy my picture **Good night to Skye** – that the fine art committee may see it. A purchaser has come forward for the one I had in the Guildhall Exhibition. In the event of which the Lord Provost kindly said I might submit the other. Since you saw the Skye picture I have greatly improved it – and I include it among my best works and should be pleased to be represented by it in Glasgow.

One summer Hunter rented "The Manse" just beyond Jeantown on Loch Carron. Due west is the Island of Skye, only a mile across at the Kyle of Lochalsh and from the mainland, the Cuillin Hills are an impressive sight. Hunter painted this picture of the mountains of Skye at Reraig opposite the village of Plockton. His son recalls that his father's health was beginning to fail about this time and John personally never considered this picture as representative of his father's best works.[93]

**Letter written by Colin Hunter on 30th October 1895**

Image credit: Glasgow Museums Photo Library.

Hunter sold **Good night to Skye** to the Glasgow Corporation for £500 (as shown in his handwritten accounts for 1895–1896). Today's value £62,000.

The letter shows a good image of Colin Hunter's signature. Note the address.

---

93 *Reviewing the Years*, John Young-Hunter

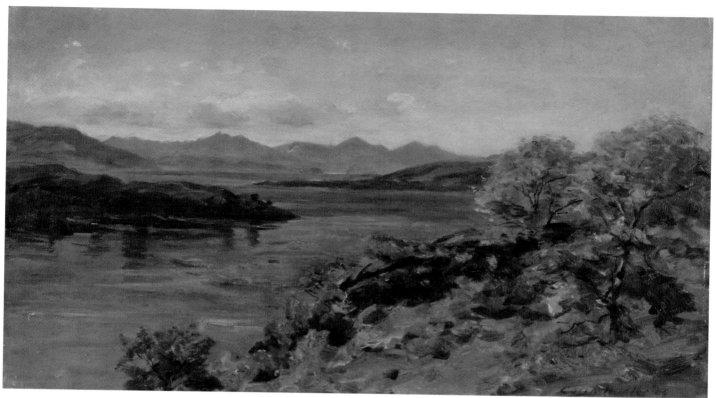

## The hills of Skye from Loch Duich

1898, oil on canvas, 35.5 × 61 cm, 14" × 24"

Image courtesy Brian Searby, Sloans & Kenyon, Auctioneers & Appraisers, Chevy Chase, Maryland, USA.

Auctioned in the USA in 2006 and 2014. From auction catalogue: *Signed and dated '98 lower right; also signed and titled on label affixed to stretcher*

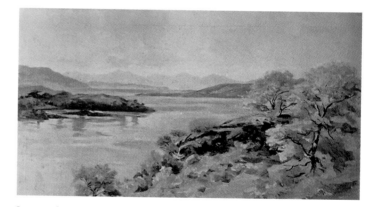

Image photographed from *Royal Academy Pictures 1898*

Exhibited Royal Academy 1898

Colour image of original above.

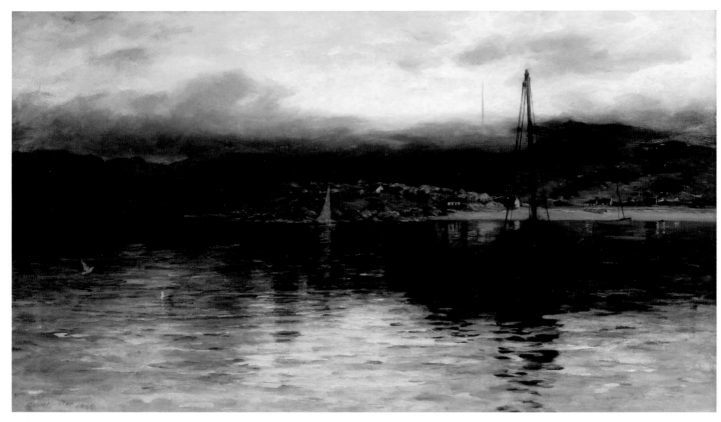

## Kyles of Skye

Also known as **View of the Scottish coast**

1899, oil on canvas, 91.5 × 152.4 cm, 36" × 60"

Private collection. Photograph courtesy of Sotheby's, New York

Published in *Black & White Handbook to the Royal Academy & New Gallery* 1899

Also published in *The Illustrated London News* May 6th 1899

Exhibited Royal Academy 1899

Sold, Sotheby's, New York 21st June 2005, Lot 156

Niceartgallery.com reproduced this painting for commercial reasons (posters/prints) and named it **View of the Scottish coast**.

Kyle is a Scottish word meaning narrow sea channel.

Hunter's 1899–1900 accounts (written in his own hand) show he sold **Kyles of Skye** to Dumfries Council for £135 (today's value £12,100). Despite research Dumfries Council found no record of it. There was a fire at the Dumfries Town Hall in 1928 but the newspaper report said that paintings were removed to safety. An audit of the Council Offices in 1980 does not list anything likely.[94] As the apparently same painting turned up for sale at Sotheby's New York in 2005 perhaps Dumfries Council never had it or promptly sold it.

94  Acknowledgement: Joanne Turner, Dumfries Museums Officer

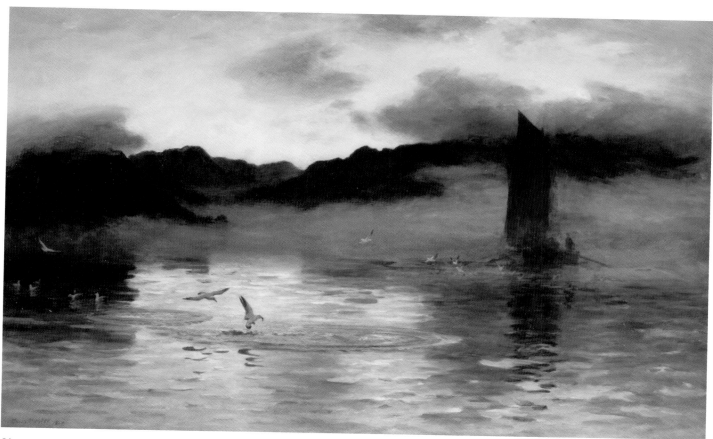

**Signs of herring**

1899, oil on canvas, 101.5 × 183 cm, 40" × 72"

Harris Museum and Art Gallery, Preston, Lancashire/Bridgeman Images

Exhibited Royal Academy 1899

"one of Hunter's finest works"

Wikisource Hunter, Colin (DNB12)

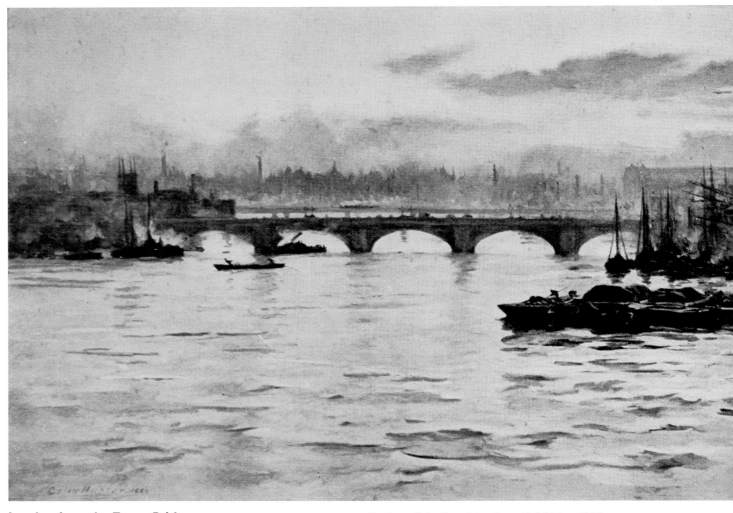

## London from the Tower Bridge

1900, oil on canvas, 91.4 × 274.3 cm, 36" × 108"

Reproduced from *Royal Academy Pictures 1900*

Also published in:
*The Illustrated London News*, June 2, 1900
*The Black & White Handbook to the Royal Academy and New Gallery*, 1900

Exhibited Royal Academy 1900

Original bought by Sir Donald Currie (1825–1909)

According to the Benezit Dictionary of British Artists (Oxford University Press USA 2012) this work "is owned or held in Bristol". However, Bristol Museum & Art Gallery have clarified that it is not in their collection. Research to date has failed to find any Bristol connection.

Review of the Royal Academy Exhibition 1900:
'Mr Colin Hunter has deserted the Highlands in his principal work and painted London from the Tower Bridge. Perhaps this work is the pleasantest of all the landscapes to be seen this year. It is a long, narrow canvas, with St Paul's forming the principal point of the composition. The whole picture is extremely harmonious, the sky and river being in complete sympathy. Probably the greatest compliment that can be paid to the work is to confess that it is most difficult to write about it, as it is impossible to single out any part to praise more than the whole. The illusive colour is very beautiful, and the pale rose and yellow sky and the opalescent water are such as only a fine colourist could achieve.'

*The Spectator*, 12 May 1900 p 18

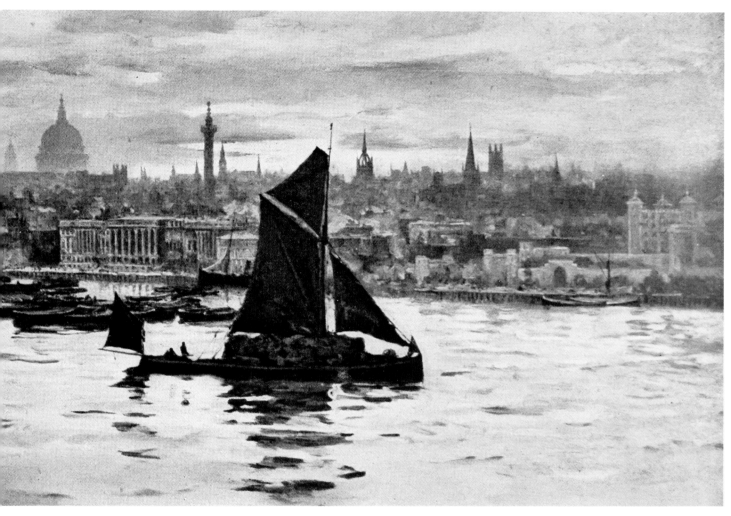

1902 calendar in Sydney:

'Messrs Alex Cowan and Sons Ltd, auctioneers, whose Sydney headquarters are in Wynyard Square, send us their calendar for the forthcoming year. These calendars are always welcomed by everyone who may have the privilege of receiving one because they are framed and introduce principal works of leading artists. So that after the calendar for the year has served its purpose, the picture remains ... For the year about to close the picture is **London from the Tower Bridge** by Colin Hunter ARA – a work the varied charms of which appeal to everyone.'

*The Sydney Morning Herald*, 5 Dec 1902

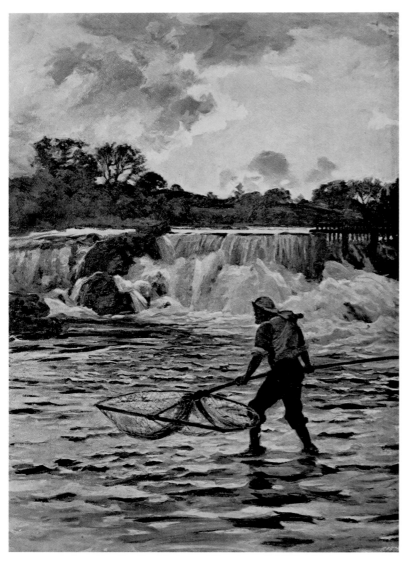

**Salmon fishing on the Dee, Kirkcudbright – the shoulder net**

Also known as **The Shoulder Net**
1895, oil on canvas, 101.6 × 73.7 cm, 40" × 29"

Reproduced from *Royal Academy Pictures 1895*

Exhibited Royal Academy 1895
In the same exhibition (and in many others) Colin Hunter's neighbour Luke Fildes – right across the road from No. 14 – also hung three works: another renowned painter in the Melbury Road Set.

Sold after Hunter's death at his studio sale, Christie's London 8th April 1905, for £68.5s (today's value £8,500) to (surname) Sampson.

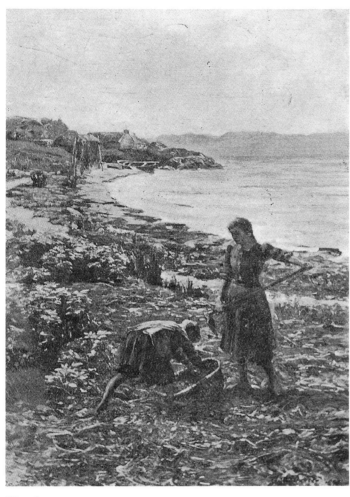

## Digging potatoes

1895

It appears to have been re-named **Potato-gatherers** in Christie's estate sale 1905

Reproduced from *The Album* July 29, 1895. Courtesy Marcia Rider

**Exhibited**
1895 New Gallery[95] Eighth Summer Exhibition
1901 Royal Glasgow Institute of Fine Arts

Photo (right) shows Colin Hunter sitting in front of this painting at his home 14 Melbury Road.

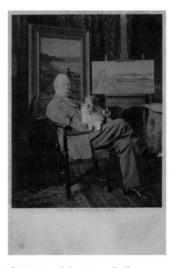

© National Portrait Gallery, London

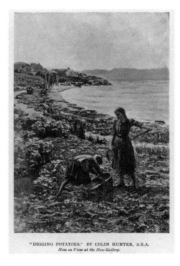

From *The Album* July 29 1895. Courtesy The British Library

95  The New Gallery was an art gallery at 121 Regent Street, London from 1888–1910.

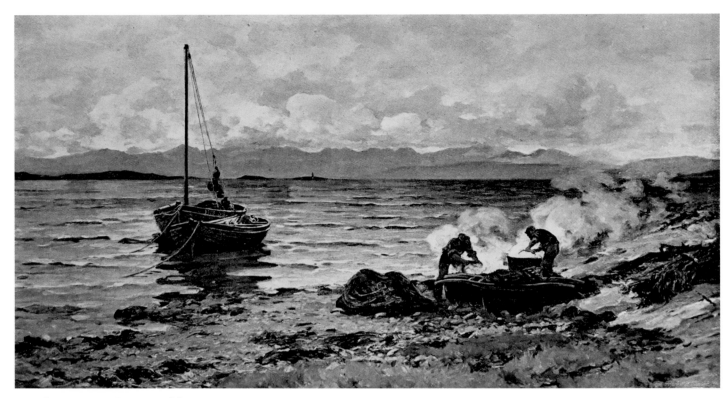

**Tanning the herring nets (1)**

Also known as **Fishermen tanning the herring nets**

Oil on canvas, 101 × 182 cm, 40" × 72"

Reproduced from the *Royal Academy Pictures 1895*

Also published in the *Special Number of the Graphic*, May 6, 1895

Exhibited Royal Academy 1895 no.385

Sold, Christie's, London, 1991

Another painting **Tanning the herring nets 1895** same title, same
year, but smaller, was sold in Sotheby's also in 1991. See opposite.
Although there are variations in the picture such as the addition of
a boat on the far right they are very similar. Another difference is
that in this painting, the figures on the beach are not bent over as
far.

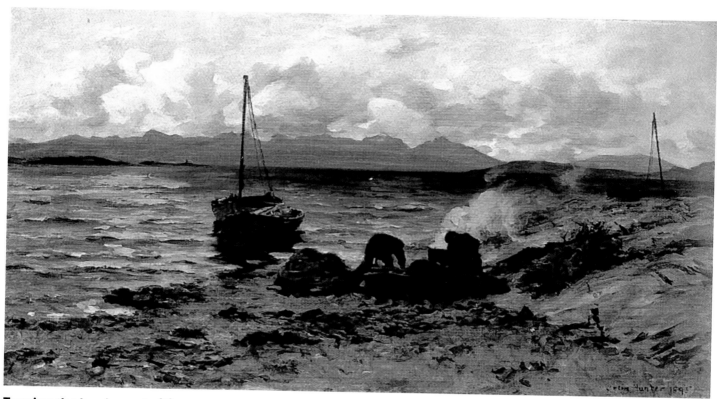

**Tanning the herring nets (2)**

1895, oil on canvas, 51 × 91 cm, 20" × 36"

Sold, Sotheby's, Edinburgh, 1991

Listed, Christie's, London, 2007

Image by permission of Christie's London from their auction catalogue 25 May 2007

Provenance: with William Rodman and Co, Belfast

A second painting **Tanning the herring nets 1895** same title, same year, but larger, was exhibited at the Royal Academy in 1895. The two pictures are similar but not identical. For example, this painting has a boat on the far right which is not in the other painting and the figures on the beach are more bent over. See opposite.

# Firth of Forth?

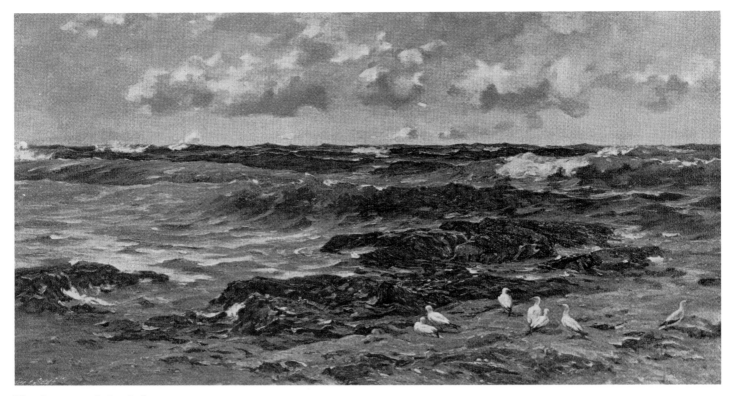

**The haunts of the Solan goose**

1896, oil on canvas, 101.6 × 182.9 cm, 40" × 72"

Reproduced from *Royal Academy Pictures* 1896

Exhibited Royal Academy 1896

The Solan goose is an old name for the Northern gannet.

The picture may be of Bass Rock in the Firth of Forth, which holds the world's largest colony of northern gannets.

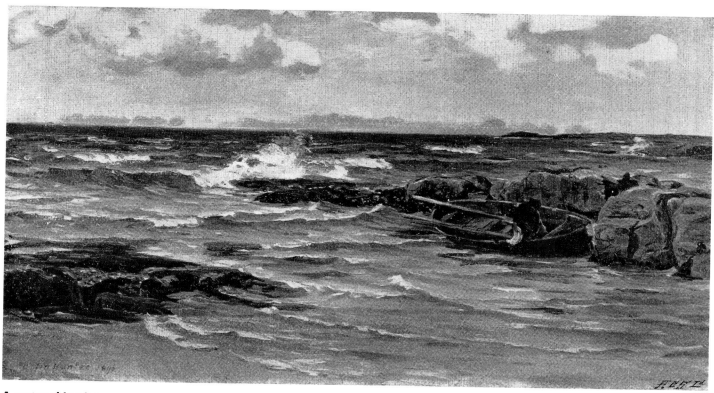

**A natural harbour**

1896, oil on canvas, 40.6 × 91.4 cm, 16" × 36"

Reproduced from *Royal Academy Pictures* 1896

Exhibited Royal Academy 1896

Hunter's 1896–97 accounts (written in his own hand) show he sold
**A Natural Harbour** for £150. Today's value £13,630.

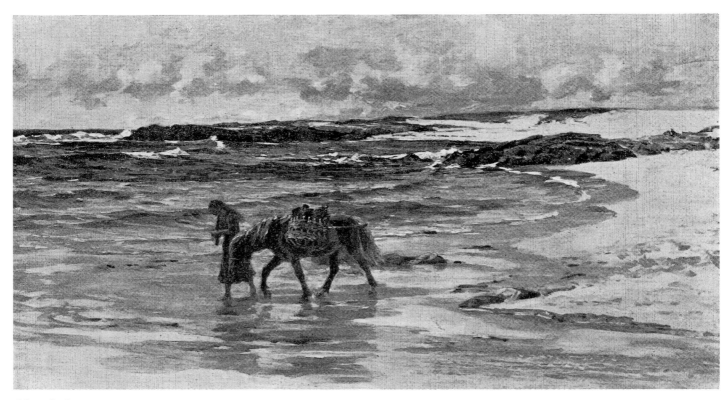

**A load of peat**

1896, oil on canvas, 71.1 × 121.9 cm, 28" × 48"

Reproduced from *Royal Academy Pictures* 1896
Also published in *Special Number of The Graphic* May 4, 1896

Exhibited Royal Academy 1896

Is this the same donkey and its mistress as depicted in **Reflections**?
The latter was painted three years earlier but has Hunter returned
to the same theme?

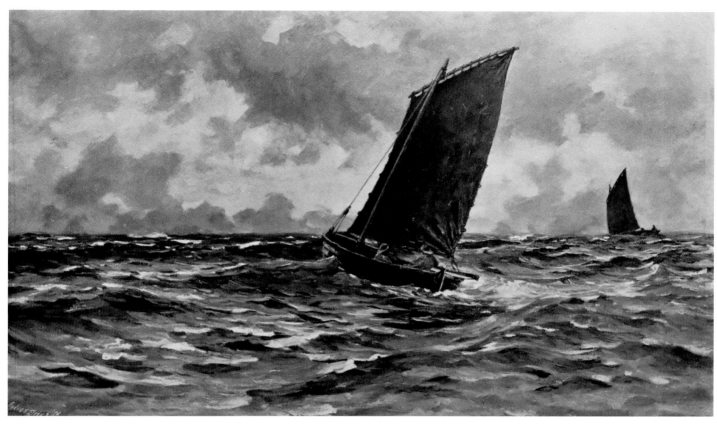

## Haddock boats beating to windward

Also known as **Sailing to windward**
Also known as **Beating to windward** (the simple title that Hunter himself used)
1896, oil on canvas, 91.4 × 152.4 cm, 36" × 60"

Reproduced from *Royal Academy Pictures* 1896
Also published in *Supplement to The Illustrated Sporting and Dramatic News* May 16, 1896

Exhibited Royal Academy 1896

Hunter's 1899–1900 accounts (written in his own hand) show he sold **Beating to Windward** for £100[96] (today's value £8,500).

---

96  However, there is some confusion in Hunter's accounts here, as he lists 5 sales, but only 4 buyers.

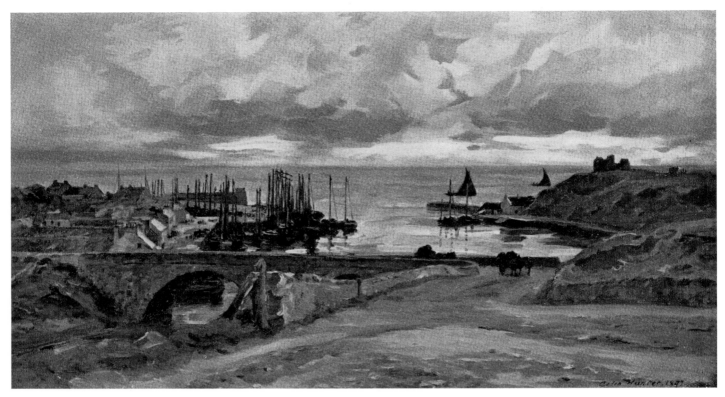

**Helmsdale**

1897, oil on canvas

Reproduced from *The Magazine of Art*.

Exhibited Royal Academy 1897

Although this painting is listed in *The Royal Academy Exhibitors* as being exhibited in 1897, it is not illustrated in the *Royal Academy Pictures 1897* which is highly unusual for a Hunter. Not all exhibited pictures listed in the index or "full catalogue" are included in the illustrated catalogue. Only approximately ten percent of works shown at the exhibitions are selected for the illustrated catalogue. That being so, Hunter was extremely lucky (or deservedly recognised for his talent) to have three or four paintings regularly selected each year for the *Royal Academy Pictures* book. Many artists did not have any of their works shown in this publication.[97]

A second picture also by Colin Hunter, **The pool in the wood Helmsdale** was hung in the same exhibition. See page 216

Note the engraving with the same name as this painting, **Helmsdale** but 1892 and an entirely different picture. See page 215

Note also a very similar picture to the one above, **The mouth of the River Helmsdale** 1898. But the two pictures have different features in the background. See opposite.

97  Acknowledgement: Andrew Potter, Royal Academy library.

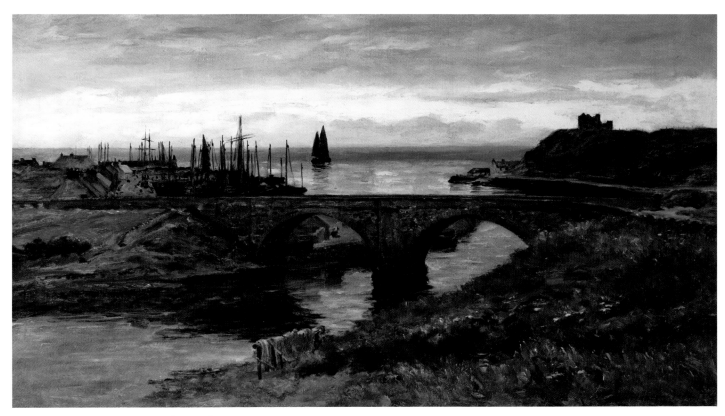

### The mouth of the River Helmsdale

Also known as **The mouth of the Helmsdale**
1898, oil on canvas, 61 × 99 cm, 24" × 39"

Image Victoria Art Gallery, Bath & North East Somerset Council/
Bridgeman Images

2016 on loan to the Guildhall, Bath

**Provenance**
Bequeathed by Miss Alice Dorothea Henderson, 1954.

A similar picture but with a slightly different background called
**Helmsdale** was exhibited in the Royal Academy 1897. See opposite.

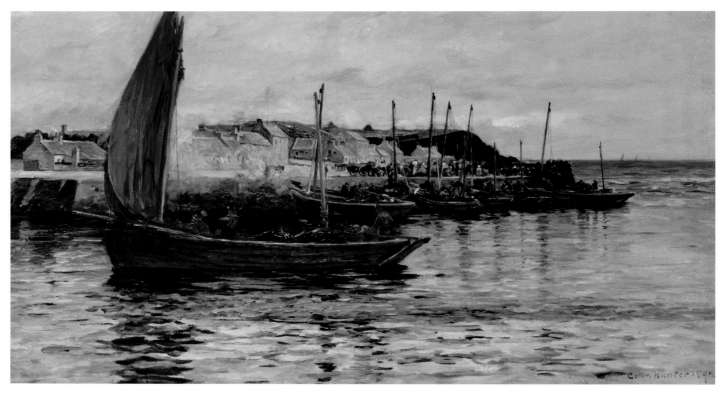

## Helmsdale

(previously incorrectly titled **Shipping in the harbour of Oban 1892**)

1892, oil on canvas, 56 × 102 cm, 22" × 40"

Signed and dated LR

Image courtesy Fiona Menzies, Iona Gallery

This painting has been previously incorrectly titled as it is the identical scene (and date) to the engraving **Helmsdale** (opposite). Moreover, Oban is more than four hours drive away from Helmsdale so it must be a mistake, rather than a confusion of two similar or nearby locations.

Further evidence of an error in its title, lies in Hunter's accounts. Hunter himself named this painting **Helmsdale**. The dimensions he quotes are identical. He sold it in 1896–97 for £157-10s. Today's value £13,630.

Lot not sold, Christie's, Netherlands, 2002
Sold, Christie's, London, 2004

From 1868 fishing boats were required to identify their port of origin. In this painting, the boat shows a Lerwick (Shetland) registered boat, 200 miles from its home port.[98]

---

98 *Painting Labour in Scotland*, John Morrison: assumed this painting to be entitled correctly as Oban. The mileage from Lerwick has been recalculated to Helmsdale.

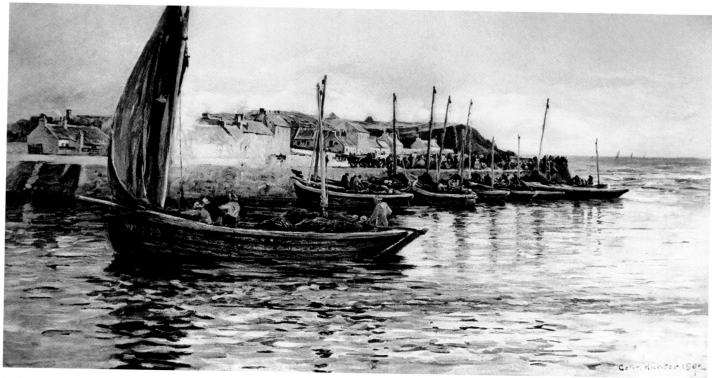

## Helmsdale

1892, engraving. Image in book, 9.5 × 17.5 cm (original plate dimensions unknown)

Reproduced from Plate 3 *The Album of the Scottish Artists Club* 1892

This same scene, an oil on canvas, was sold by Christies, London, in 2004 with the title **Shipping in the Harbour of Oban**, also dated 1892. See opposite. As this scene above was called **Helmsdale** in the publication of the same date, it would indicate that the Oban title is incorrect.

There are five Helmsdale pictures:
1. Helmsdale 1892 (oil on canvas)
2. Helmsdale 1892 (engraving) (above)
3. Helmsdale 1897 exhibited in the Royal Academy 1897 (page 212)
4. Pool in the wood Helmsdale 1897 exhibited in the Royal Academy 1897 now Walker Art Gallery, Liverpool (page 216)
5. The mouth of the River Helmsdale 1898 owned by the Victoria Art Gallery in Bath (page 213)

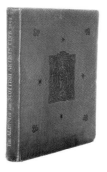
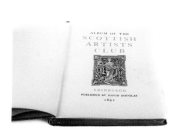

The Album of the Scottish Artists Club 1892

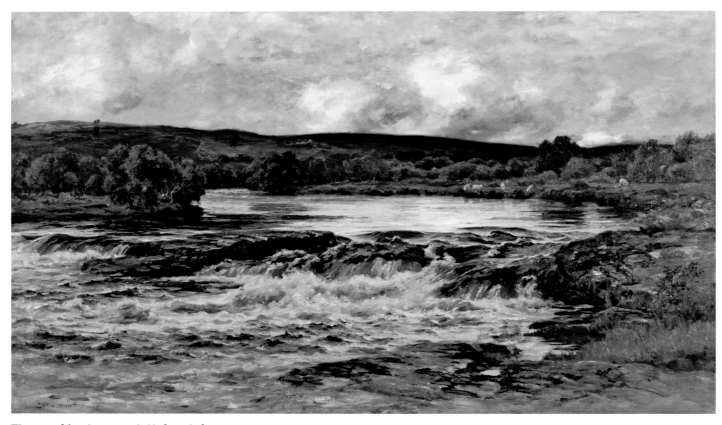

## The pool in the wood, Helmsdale

1897, oil on canvas, 108 × 183.5 cm, 42" × 72"

See also **Highland Waterfall 1898**

Courtesy Walker Art Gallery, Liverpool

**Published**
*Special Number of The Graphic* May 3, 1897
*The Illustrated London News* May 8, 1897

Exhibited Royal Academy 1897

**Provenance**
Purchased by Liverpool 1897
Despite Liverpool purchasing this in 1897, Hunter's 1896–97
accounts (written in his own hand) show he sold **Pool in the Wood**
to Drew (possibly Mrs Drew – a long standing client) for £400
(today's value £36,350). It may have been a different painting or
Drew sold it to Liverpool shortly afterwards.

Another painting of the same scene is known as **Highland
Waterfall 1898** but it is a different size 52 × 89 cm. Apart from
date and size it is hard to spot any differences. See opposite.

Royal Academy Pictures 1897
'Mr Colin Hunter, whose **Their Only Harvest** was one of the first
of the Chantrey selections, has lately been devoting some of his time
to portrait-painting, but his large picture **The Pool in the Wood** is
worthy of his best time, of the time when he painted **Waiting for
the Homeward Bound**, and the **Herring Market at Sea**.'

*The Guardian*, 19 May 1897

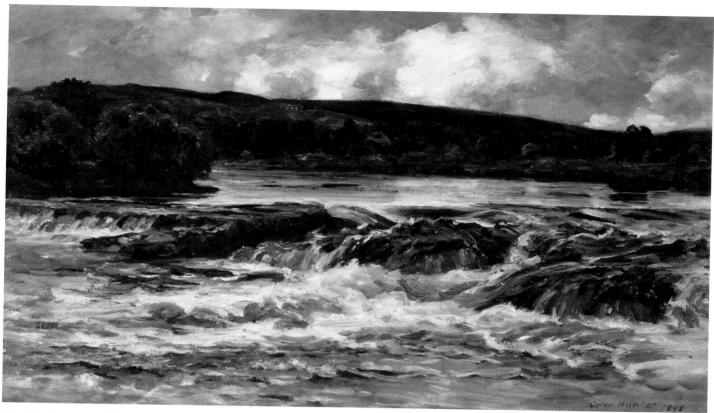

## Highland waterfall

Aka **Helmsdale**

1898, oil on canvas, 52.1 × 89 cm, 20.5" × 35"

See also **The pool in the wood Helmsdale 1897**

By permission of Fife Cultural Trust Kirkcaldy Galleries on behalf of
Fife Council

**Provenance**

Bequeathed to Kirkcaldy Galleries by E B Malcolm in memory of
Charles Henry McEuen, 1966

According to Hunter's accounts of 1898–99 this painting may have
been called **Helmsdale**. Hunter quoted the size as 53.3 × 91.4 cm,
21" × 36" – and this is the nearest canvas size to that of the several
paintings called **Helmsdale** or similar. If this is the same painting,
Hunter sold it to Miss Radcliffe for £200. Today's value £18,000.

Another painting of the same scene is known as **Pool in the Wood
Helmsdale 1897** but it is a different size. See opposite. Apart from
size and date it is hard to spot any differences.

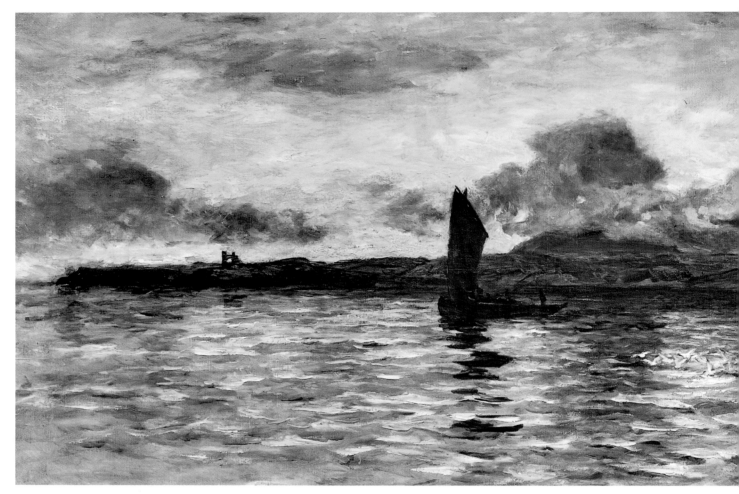

## Herring fishers (or fishing) off Kildonan Castle, Isle of Arran

Also known simply as **Kildonan Castle** (according to Hunter's own notes)
1897, oil on canvas, 89 × 278 cm, 35" × 109"

Image courtesy of Lyon & Turnbull Fine Art Auctioneers

### Published

*Black and White Handbook to the Royal Academy and New Gallery*, December 1901
*The Illustrated Sporting and Dramatic News*, May 18, 1901
*The Art Journal*

Exhibited at Royal Academy 1901. Loaned by Sir Donald Currie. This is only the third time in thirty years when Hunter exhibited just one work at the RA. In 1901 he was already in declining health and perhaps he asked Currie if he would loan the picture. Hunter's 1899–1900 accounts (written in his own hand) show he sold **Kildonan Castle** to D Currie for £300. Today's value £25,750.

Exhibited after Hunter's death at Nottingham City, Nottingham Castle Art Gallery, 1909

Sold, Lyon & Turnbull, 2017

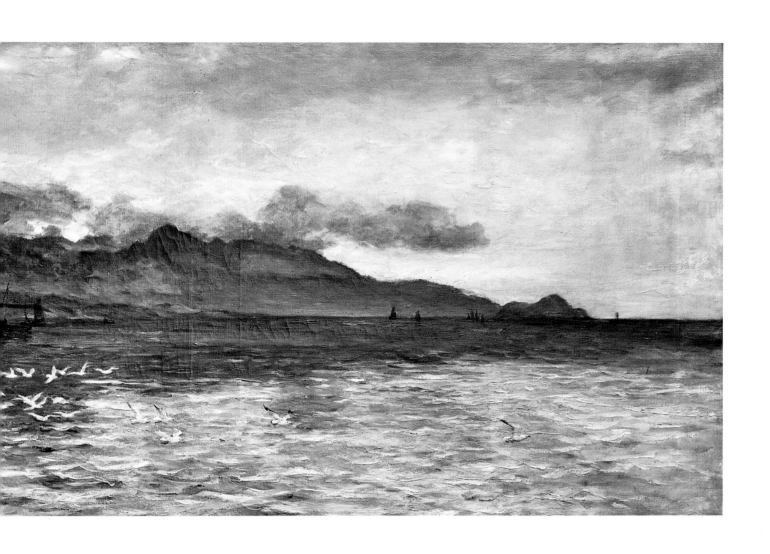

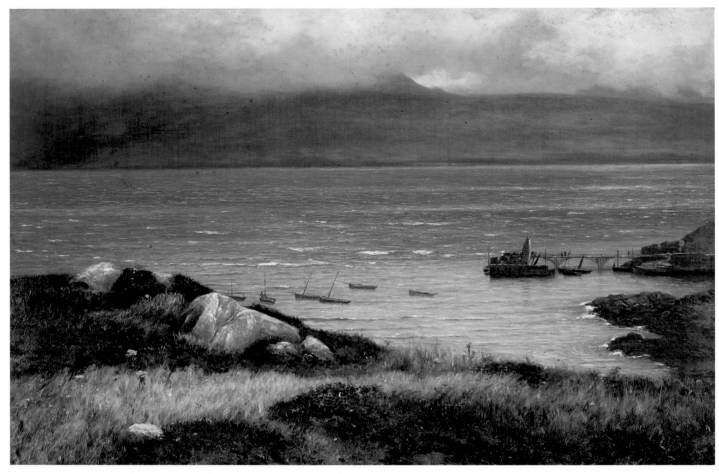

**View from Lamlash (Isle of Arran)**

1882, oil on canvas, 67.3 × 99.1 cm, 26.5" × 39"

© Christie's/Bridgeman Images

Private collection

Sold, Christie's, Glasgow, 2000

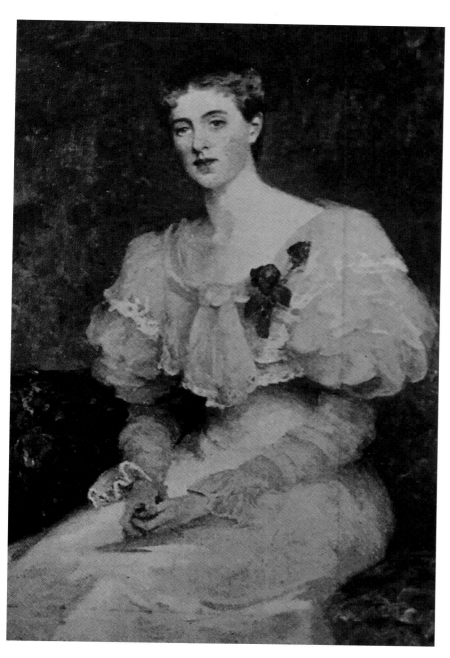

**Miss Isobel Donaldson**

1897, oil on canvas, 121.9 × 81.3 cm, 48" × 32"

Photographed from *Royal Academy Pictures 1897*

Exhibited Royal Academy 1897

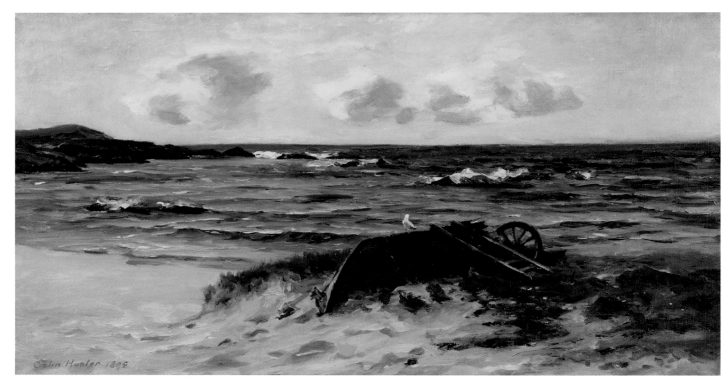

## Voices of the Sea (1)

1898, oil on canvas, 40.6 × 76.2 cm, 16" × 30"

Signed and dated LL

Titled on gallery label verso

Image courtesy and © of Waddington's Auctioneers and Appraisers, Toronto, Canada

Sold by Waddington's, Toronto, 2012

**Provenance**

Walter Klinkhoff Gallery, Montreal

This is the first painting with the title **Voices of the Sea**. An entirely different picture but with the same name was painted four years later which was exhibited in the Royal Academy (see page 230).

Because of the significant difference between this **Voices of the sea 1898** and **Voices of the sea 1902**, and also because the title seems strangely unconnected to the scene above, there may be doubt whether this is the correct original title. In Hunter's personal handwritten accounts which appeared to include his major works over many years, neither **Voices of the sea** is listed. But his personal note accounts stopped before 1902, probably because of his ailing health.

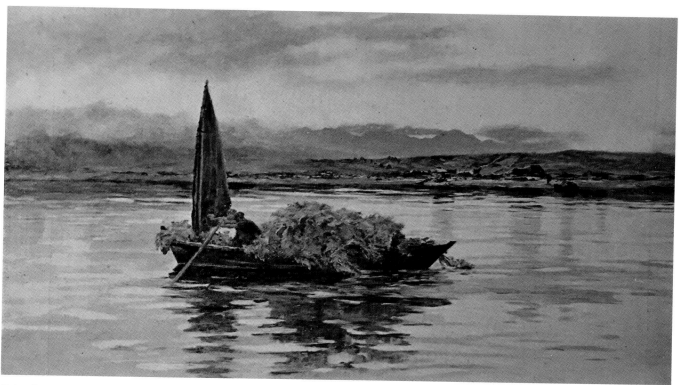

## Bringing home the bracken

Also known as **Taking home the bracken**

1898, oil on canvas, 106.7 × 182.9 cm, 42" × 72"

Image photographed from *Royal Academy Pictures 1898*

Also published in:

*The Illustrated London News*, May 7, 1898
*Special Number of The Graphic*, May 2, 1898
*The New York Times*, July 24th 1898 under *"Noted pictures of the year at The Royal Academy, London"* and entitling it Taking Home the Bracken.

Exhibited Royal Academy 1898

Hunter's 1898–99 accounts (written in his own hand) show he sold **Bringing home the bracken** for £300. Today's value £25,750.

'**Taking Home the Bracken** shows a modernness not often seen in the somewhat older [Academicians]. Mr Hunter is a Glasgow Scot and shows the strong colour sense of the still younger band of painters who are nicknamed the Glasgow School, among whom, in fact, he is often counted. He is an ardent yachtsman, fisherman, golfer and shot. In **Taking Home the Bracken** he has brought out by free brushwork the rich colours that lurk in Scottish bough and moor, colours reproduced in stronger tones in the sail and cargo of the barge, filled with the coarse bracken of the moors, which is used as bedding for the cattle. The sombre, uncultivated shore carries the eye onward to a range of hills whose low crests are wreathed in mists. The colour scheme is rich but mournful, and the two oarsmen have the look of conspirators, as if the bracken concealed a cargo of proscribed men, fleeing from pursuit with a price on their heads.

Mr Hunter has painted sailors and the sea with a very decided love for such subjects. **Herring Boats at Sea** was in the Academy in 1884; one of his earliest sendings was **Trawlers Waiting for Darkness** shown in 1873; other notable paintings are **Waiting for the Homeward Bound**, **Their Only Harvest** and **Salmon Stake Nets**. He has a feeling for sentiment expressed by landscape and seascape and is able to translate that sentiment into colour.'

*The New York Times*, Sunday 24th July 1898

'When Hunter painted a hillside of grey rock and green brae and purple peak, lying under a quiet but rather sullen grey sky, reflected in deeper tones in the still loch across whose unrippled surface ... a load of bracken, which cast a long quivering shadow of tarnished gold, was being slowly rowed home, a glamour seemed to lie upon the land. One felt the air pregnant with a suggestion of mystery and knew that the silences were unbroken save by the bleat of sheep, the crying of sea birds, or the rare pulsation of distant oars.'

*Scottish Painting, Past and Present, 1620–1908*,
James Lewis Caw, 1908

Curiously, the review above is almost identical to that given to **Changing pastures 1898** apart from the change of a few words. See page 225

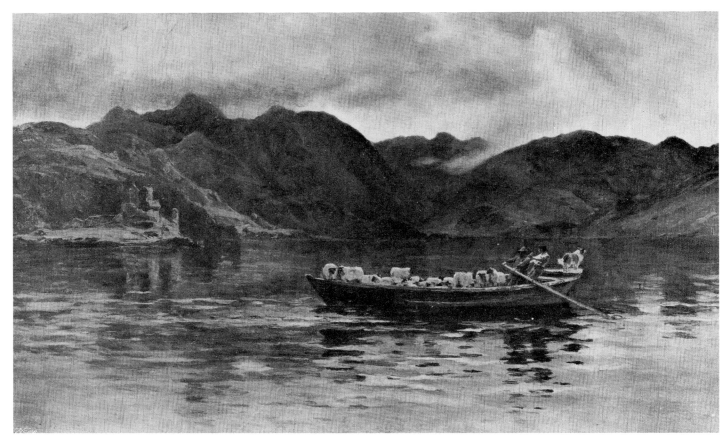

## Changing pasture (1)

1898, oil on canvas, 91.4 × 152.4 cm, 36" × 60"

Image photographed from *Royal Academy Pictures 1898*

Exhibited Royal Academy 1898

A different picture with the same boat but different background,
and the same size, called **Changing Pastures No. 2** (note the plural
of pasture) was also painted in 1898. See opposite.

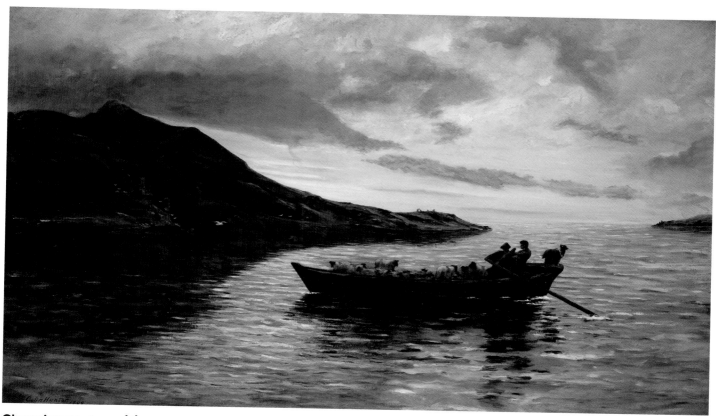

## Changing pastures (2)

1898, oil on canvas, 90.2 × 152.4 cm, 35.5" × 60"

Image courtesy Sotheby's

Signed, titled and inscribed on an old label attached to the stretcher:
*Colin Hunter, 14 Melbury Road, London, Changing Pastures No. 2*

Sold, Sotheby's, London, 2009

This picture had almost the same name (note the plural of
"pastures") as another picture painted in the same year and on
the same size canvas. The boat is the same but the background is
different. See opposite.

'When Hunter painted a hillside of grey rock and green brae and
purple peak, lying under a quiet but rather sullen grey sky, reflected
in deeper tones in the still loch across whose unrippled surface
<u>sheep were being ferried in a clumsy boat</u> ... a glamour seemed to
lie upon the land. One felt the air pregnant with a suggestion of
mystery and knew that the silences were unbroken save by the bleat
of sheep, the crying of sea birds, or the rare pulsation of distant
oars.'

*Scottish Painting, Past and Present, 1620–1908,*
James Lewis Caw, 1908

Curiously, the review above is almost identical to that given to
**Bringing home the bracken 1898** apart from the change of a few
words. See page 223

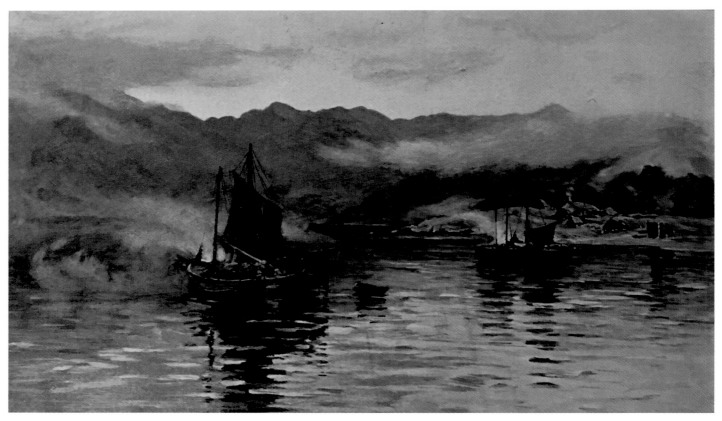

**Still evening**

1898, oil on canvas, 71.1 × 121.9 cm, 28" × 48"

Image photographed from *Royal Academy Pictures 1898*

Exhibited Royal Academy 1898

A painting called **A still evening No. 3** also 1898 and same dimensions was sold by Sotheby's Chicago USA in 2000. It is not known what the significance of "No. 3" is or if it was this painting.

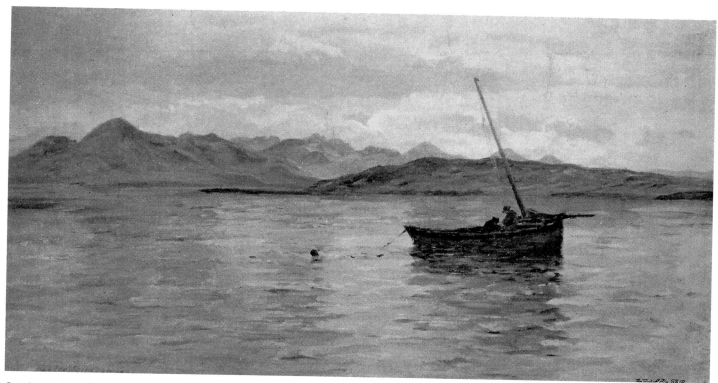

**Anchored to the nets**

1900

Reproduced from unidentified magazine but probably *Royal Academy Pictures*

Courtesy of Marcia Rider

Exhibited Royal Academy 1900

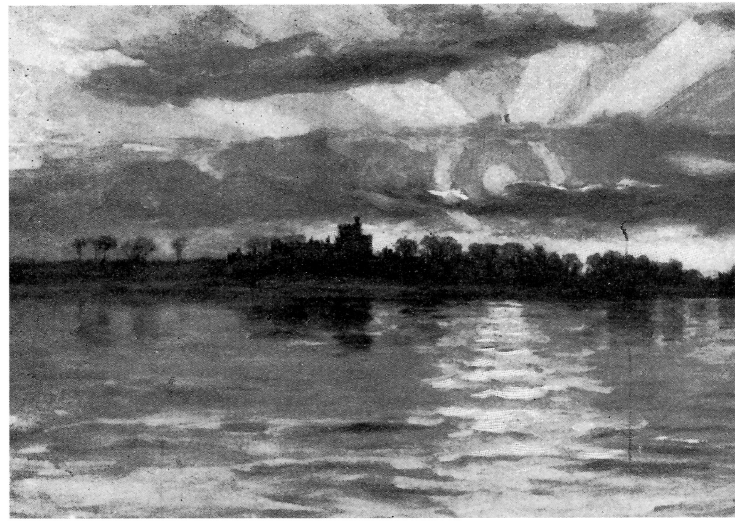

### The "Victory" off Walmer Castle 1805 after the Battle of Trafalgar

1901, oil on canvas

Reproduced from *The Sketch* May 5, 1901

Exhibited Royal Academy 1903, the last year Hunter exhibited at the RA.

Unusually, this picture was painted in 1901 but not exhibited in the Royal Academy until 1903 – two years after he had sold it to Sir Donald Currie. Hunter was ill by then and he died just a year later so it would not be surprising if he had ceased painting new works. It would appear that once again he asked Currie if he would loan one of his Hunters to the RA to exhibit (as he did with **Herring fishers off Kildonan Castle** in 1901 see page 218). In any event, this picture marks a divergence from his typical themes of fisher folk on the Scottish coastlines, although Hunter rarely escapes from his love for the sea or water in his subjects.

Walmer Castle is in Kent.

Hunter's 1900–01 accounts (written in his own hand) show he sold **Walmer Castle** to D Currie for £300. Today's value £25,750.

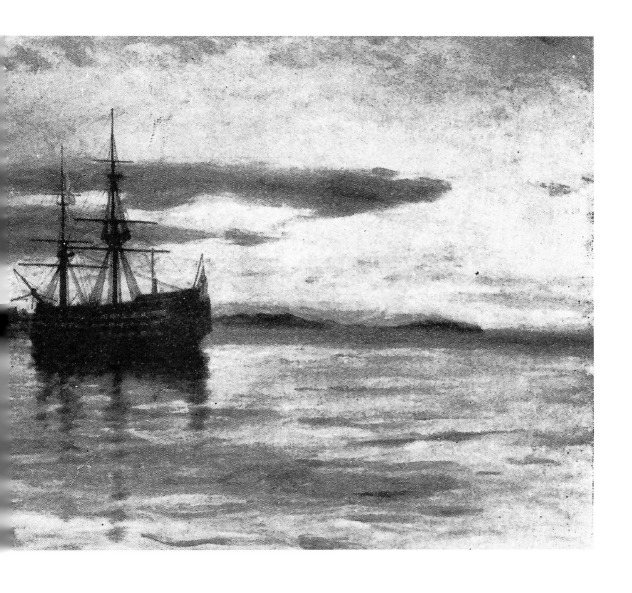

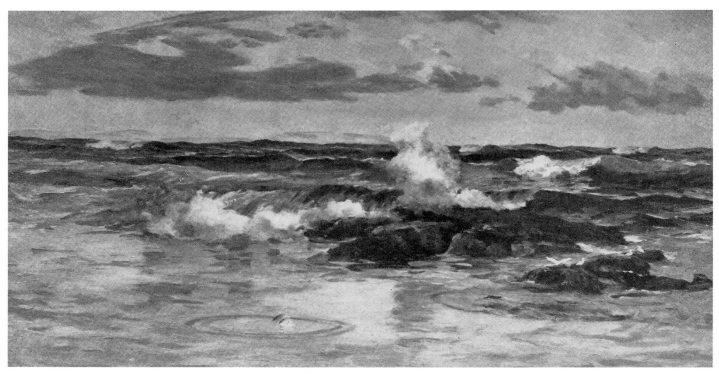

## Voices of the sea (2)

1902, oil on canvas, 101.5 × 182.8 cm, 40" × 72"

Reproduced from *Royal Academy Pictures* 1902

**Also published**
*The Illustrated Sporting & Dramatic News*, May 17, 1902
*Supplement to the Illustrated London News*, May 10, 1902

**Exhibited**
Royal Academy, 1902
St Louis Exhibition, 1904

See page 222 for an earlier picture with the same name but an entirely different picture.

Sold after Hunter's death in studio sale held at Christies (then Messrs. Christie, Manson & Woods), 8 King St, St James's Square, London SW on 8th April 1905
Consignors were John Young-Hunter of Giffords Hall, Wickhambrook, Suffolk and Miss C I Hunter (Colina Isabella) of 14 Melbury Road.
Sold for £199.10s (today's value £23,097) to (surname) Sampson

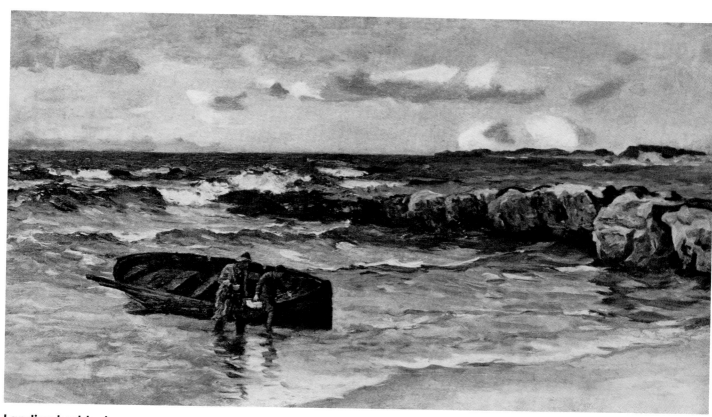

**Landing haddock**

1902, oil on canvas, 70 × 122 cm, 27.5" × 48"

Exhibited Royal Academy 1902

Reproduced from *Royal Academy Pictures* 1902.
This year Hunter's painting was selected for one of the rare colour plates included in the illustrated catalogue.

Also published in *The Illustrated Sporting and Dramatic News*, 17 May 1902

Sold after Hunter's death in his studio sale held at Christie's London, 8th April 1905.

Sold for £147 (today's value £17,000) to (surname) Mullins (indistinct).

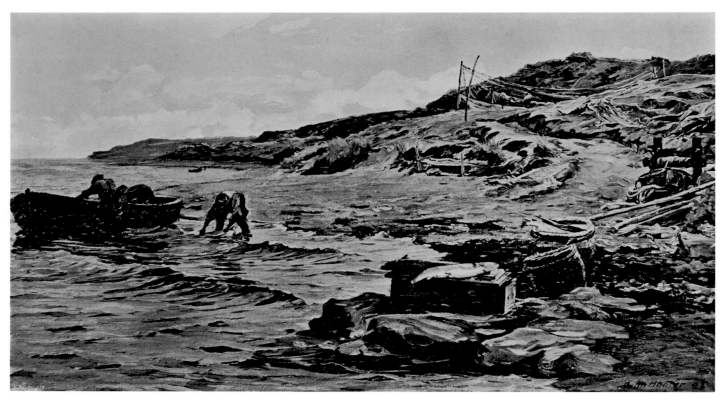

**Salmon fishers (2)**

1903, oil on canvas, 50.8 × 91.4 cm, 20" × 36"

Reproduced from *Royal Academy Pictures* 1903

Exhibited Royal Academy 1903
(Hunter's last RA exhibition. He died the following year.)

In 1885 another painting was also called **Salmon Fishers**. See page
153.

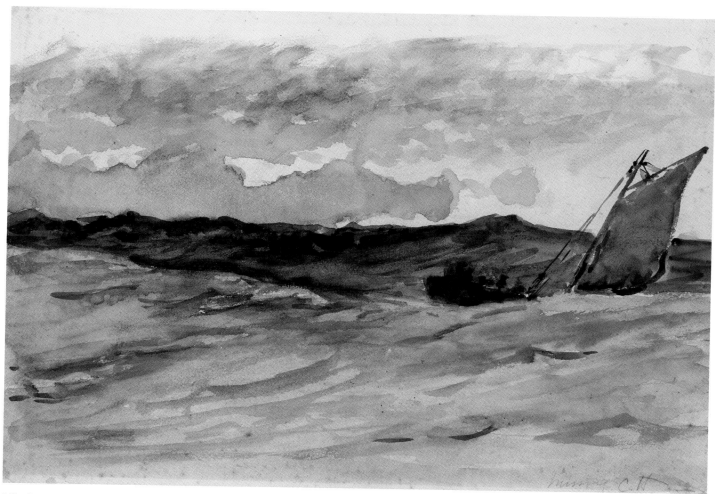

**Missing**

Undated, water colour 36 × 51 cm, 14" × 20"

Signed C H

**Provenance**
Estate of the artist
Family by descent

Courtesy Kate Rider

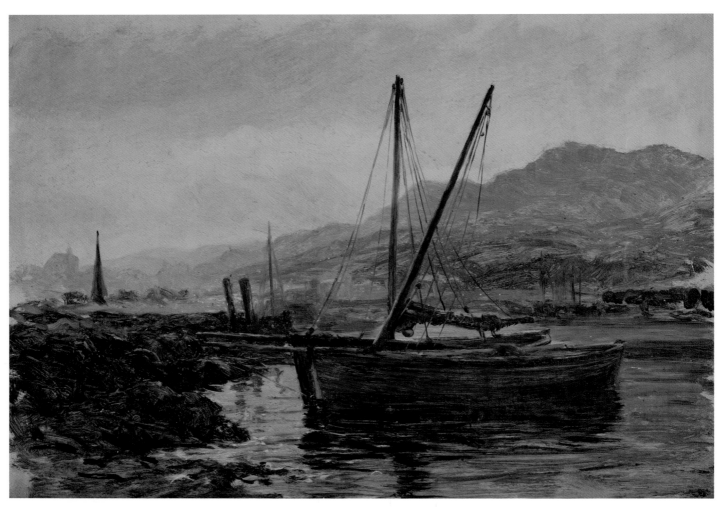

**Moored boats in harbour**

Undated, oil on canvas, 25.7 × 35.5 cm, 10" × 14"

Unsigned

**Provenance**
Estate of the artist
Family by descent

Courtesy Kate Rider

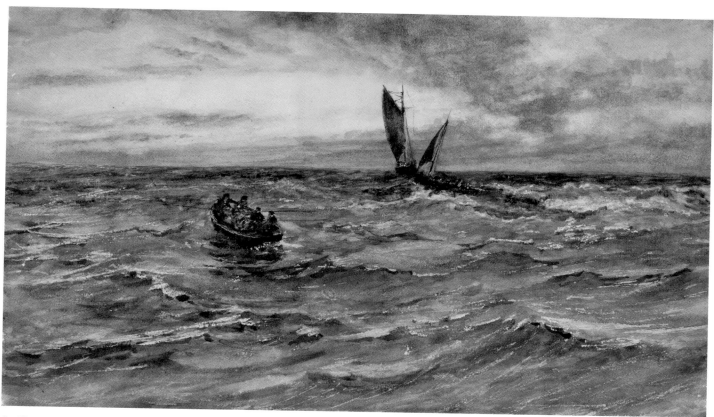

**Sailing and rowing**

Undated, water colour (with tempera?), 31 × 51.5 cm, 12" × 20"

Unsigned

**Provenance**
Estate of the artist
Family by descent

Courtesy Kate Rider

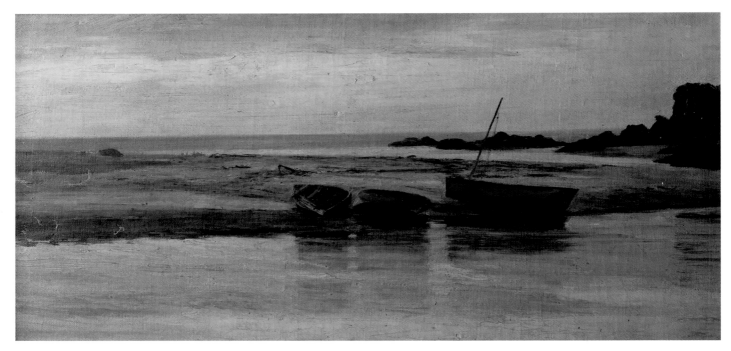

## Beached boats

Undated, oil on panel, 47.5 × 84.5 cm, 18" × 33"

Unsigned

Photo credit: Scott Kuster

Private collection

**Provenance**
Family inheritance
Shipped to Gabrielle Young Kuster (nee Young-Hunter) in the USA
after Colina Hunter's death in Kent England in 1972, thence by
descent.

Although this work was unsigned and undated and therefore its
authenticity could be queried, with this shipment were many of
Colina's father's art works and memorabilia including photographs,
prints and scrapbook collections.

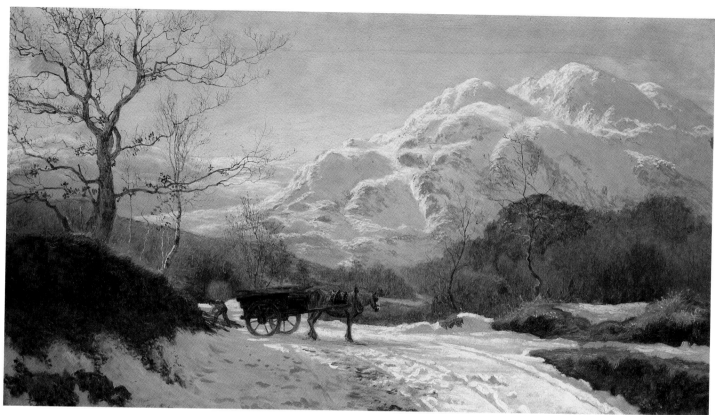

**Gathering wood in an alpine landscape**

Also known as **Winter landscape**
Also known as **Figure with horse and cart on snowy road**
1886, oil on canvas, 44 × 76 cm, 17" × 30"

Private collection
© Christie's Images/Bridgeman Images

Location: Possibly Ben Venue, Trossachs National Park. This is only just over an hour's drive from Hunter's home town of Helensburgh.

Ritchie's, Toronto, sold as **Figure with horse and cart on snowy road**, 1999
Christie's, London, sold as **Gathering wood in an alpine landscape**, 2000
McTear's, Glasgow, sold as **Winter landscape**, 2012

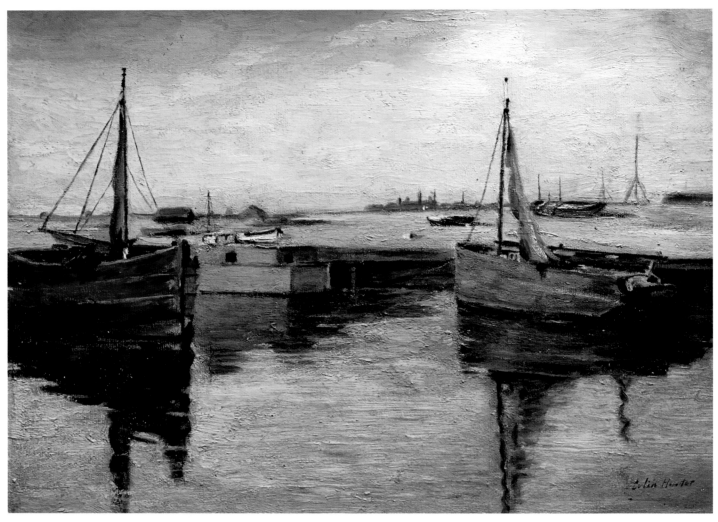

**Harbour scene with blue boat**

Undated, oil on board, 30 × 40cm, 11" × 15"

Signed

Private collection

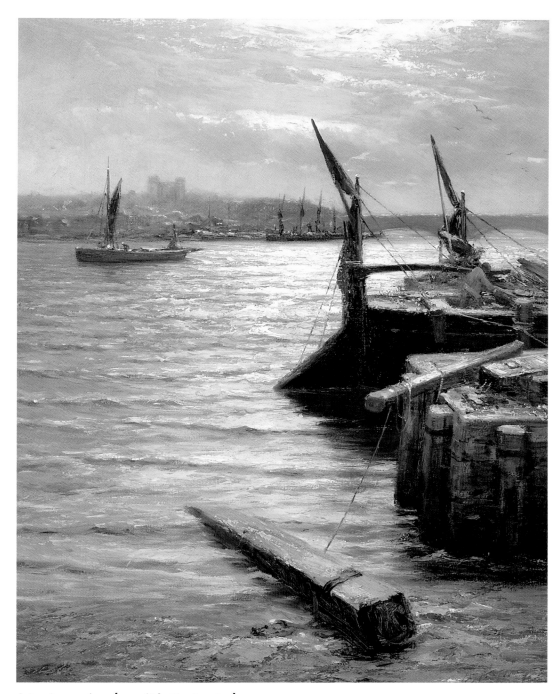

**A harbour view (possibly Rochester)**

Also known as **Barges moored by the riverbank**
Also known as **Estuary view**
Oil on canvas, 58.5 × 46 cm, 23" × 18"

Photo © Christie's Images/Bridgeman Library

Not sold, Christie's, 2001
Sold, Bonhams, 2004

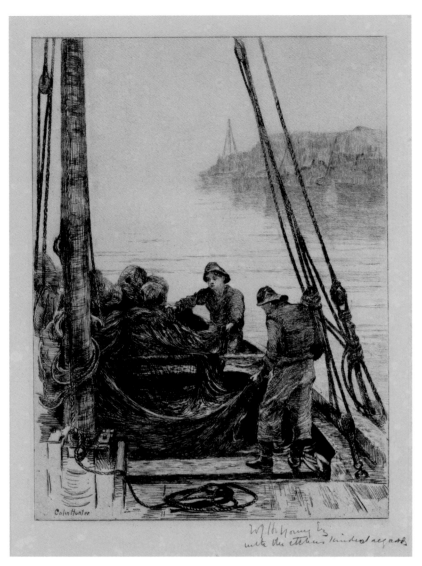

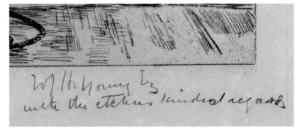

## Shaking the nets

Undated but before 1887, etching plate, 27.9 × 19.7 cm, 11" × 7.8"

Signed in plate LL

**Published in:**

c.1887 *A Score of Etchings* by Roger Riordan published Dodd, Mead & Co, New York

1892 *The British Seas*, W Clark Russell, Seeley London

Image: courtesy Kate Rider. Inscription on mount: "To J H Young[99] Esq, with the etcher's kindest regards"

One of the etchings of **Shaking the nets** is also held in the Bristol Museum & Art Gallery.

Sir Hubert von Herkomer RA, a fellow artist, observed Hunter's power as an etcher. In c.1888, the critic says of **Shaking the nets**: "We are not at all surprised to learn that Mr Hunter has already, after but little practice, acquired a strong liking for the etching needle."

---

99  J H Young, John Hamilton Young, Hunter's father-in-law

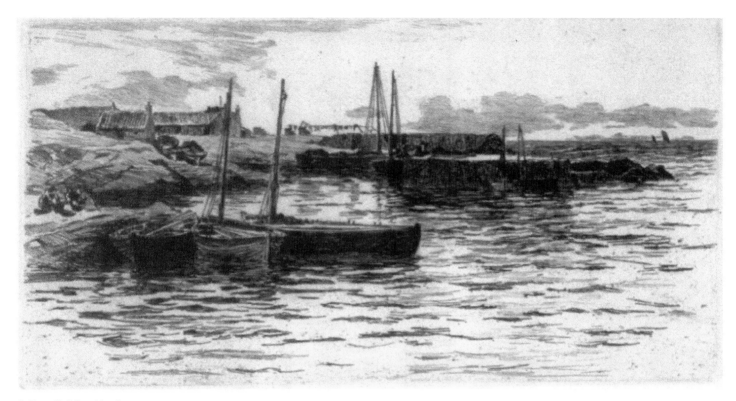

**A Banffshire Harbour**

Etching, 12.5 × 22.6 cm, 5" × 9"

Recorded at Fine Arts Museums of San Francisco as **Ba... Harbour**, presumably because originally the title was missing or indistinct.

Fine Arts Museums of San Francisco

**Provenance**
Acquired by Achenbach Foundation for Graphic Arts 1963

Another etching of this picture was sold through Toovey's Auctions, Washington (UK) 2011

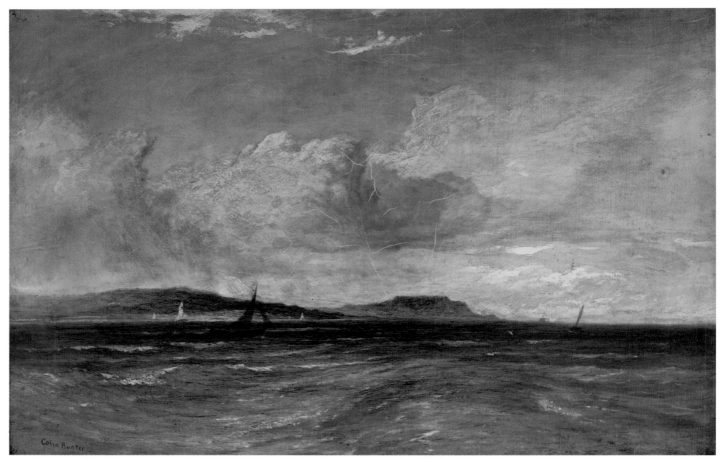

**On the coast of Scotland**

Undated, oil on canvas, 36 × 53 cm, 14" × 21"

Signed

Private collection

**Provenance**
Sold, Ross's Auctioneers, Belfast, Northern Ireland (Consigned
for auction from private collection, Co Down, Estate of the late
E Falloon), 2017

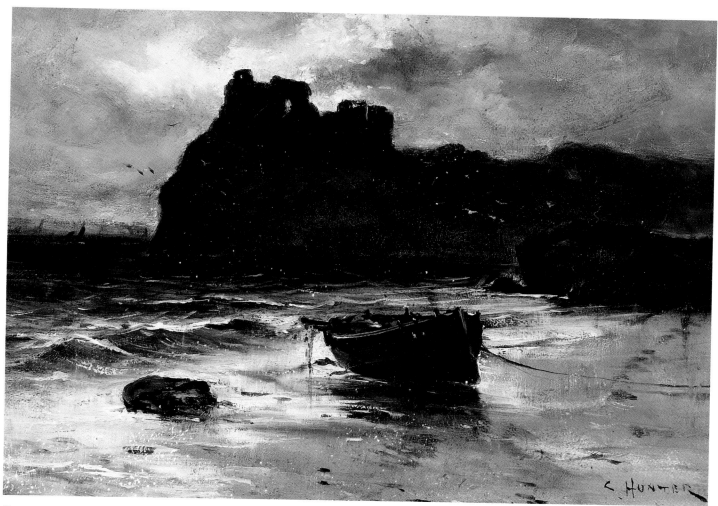

**Seascape with a castle**

Undated, oil on board, 35.4 × 44.8 cm, 14" × 17.5"

Aberdeen Art Gallery and Museums Collections

**Provenance**
Bequeathed to Aberdeen Art Gallery by Duncan Wright, 2003

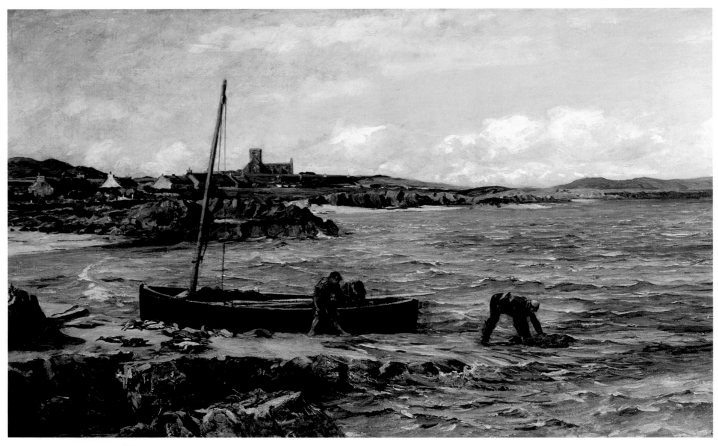

## Landing the catch (1)

Image courtesy Iona Gallery.

**Provenance**

Fiona Menzies of Iona Gallery, understands that this painting had been bought in the UK c.2002 by Canadian visitors. They sent her a print of it (above) saying that the "painting had crossed the Atlantic OK". Nothing more is known about the painting.

There is another painting with the same name but entirely different scene **Landing the catch (2)**. See page 266.

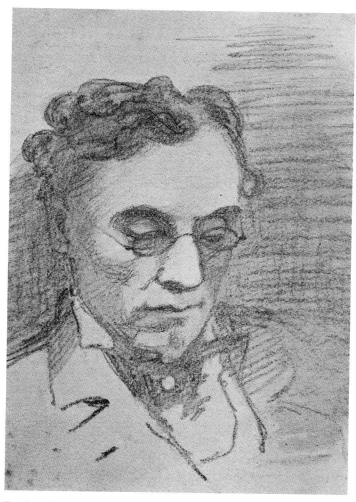

**Dr Charles Blatherwick**

Undated but before 1895, pencil sketch

Reproduced from *Black and White Handbook to the Royal Academy and New Gallery*, 28 Sep 1895

'Dr Charles Blatherwick RSW (1867–95) whose sudden death while he was on a holiday at Kirkcudbright has cast a profound gloom over Scottish art circles, was versatile as genial. He painted, wrote, composed, played and sang, all with uncommon skills; and he was an able lecturer and a clever after-dinner speaker. For many years he discharged the duties of Government Inspector of Alkali Factories in Scotland, and he was a member of the medical profession.'

*Black and White Handbook to the Royal Academy and New Gallery*, 28 Sep 1895

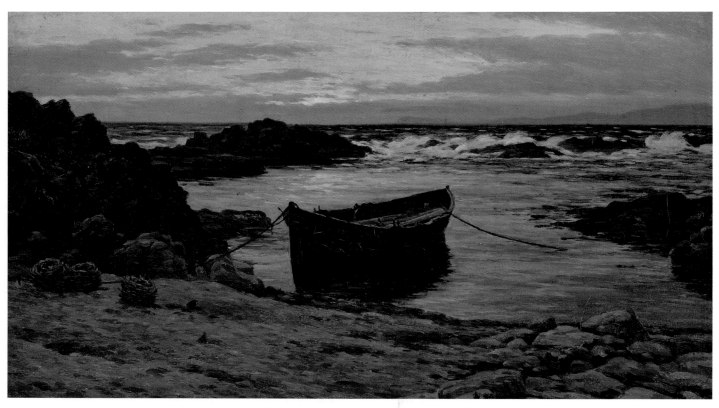

**Sunset over the coast**

Undated, oil on canvas, 36 × 61 cm, 14" × 24"

Photo © Christie's Images/Bridgeman Images

Private collection

Sold, Christie's, London, 2001

Scene also reproduced as poster/print for commercial reasons by
plentyofpaintings.com

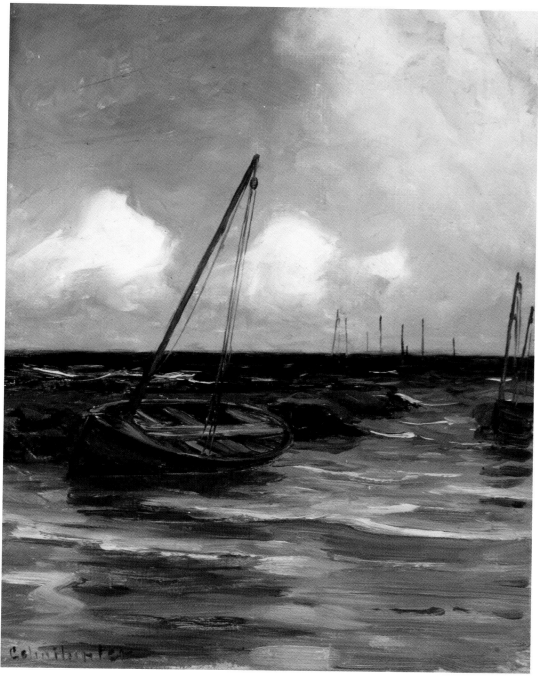

**At rest**

Undated, oil on board, 24 × 19 cm, 9.4" × 7.5"

© Dundee City Council (Dundee's Art Galleries and Museums)

**Provenance**

Purchased from James Guthrie Orchar's niece, Miss A M Douglas, 1924

Presented to Dundee Art Galleries, 1987

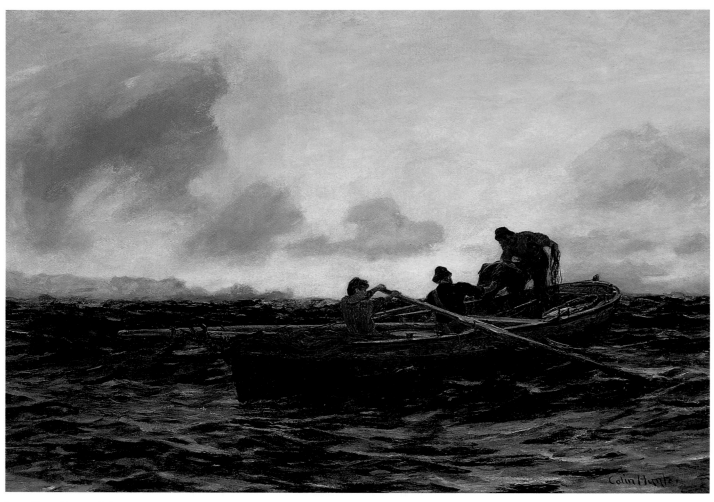

**Loading the catch**

Oil on canvas, 81.2 × 114.3 cm, 32" × 45"

Signed LR

Private collection. Photo © Christie's Images/Bridgeman Images

Sold, Christie's, South Kensington, 13 March 2005

Provenance: With the Cooling Galleries, London

Exhibited: Corporation of London, Guildhall Exhibition 1895

The copper plate and etching inspired by this painting are shown opposite.

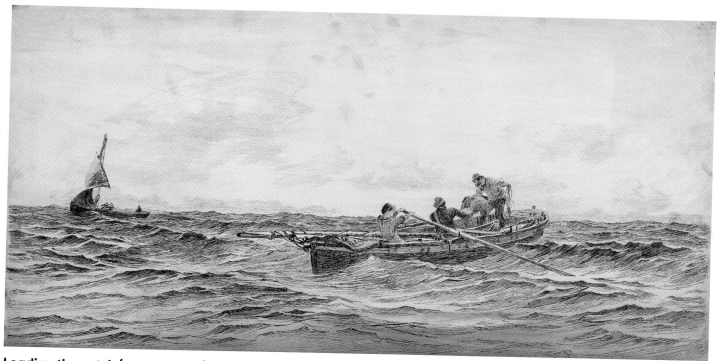

**Loading the catch (copper plate)**

Plate size 30.5 × 59.7 cm, 12" × 23.5"
© Colin Hunter family estate

Hunter expanded the oil on canvas scene by adding
a boat in the distance in the etching.

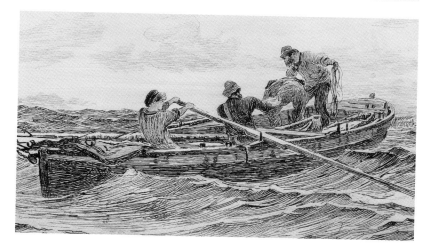

**Loading the catch (copper plate detail)**

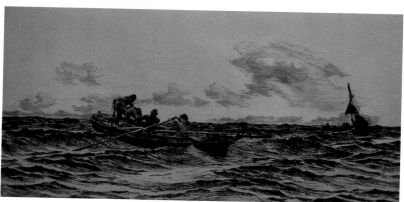

**Loading the catch (etching)**

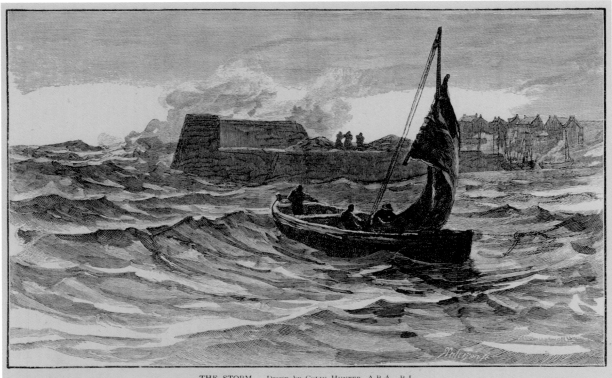

THE STORM.  Drawn by COLIN HUNTER, A.R.A., R.I.

".  .  .  the dark brown sails of the fishermen's fleet,
As they make for the harbour bar."                    *See Poem on page* 110

## The Storm

Undated but after 1884, drawing

Reproduced from *Essays for Young Men* p.105

Courtesy Kate Rider

The picture is known to be drawn after 1884 because it was published with the caption "by Colin Hunter ARA RI". Hunter was elected to the RI in 1882 and to the RA (Associate) in 1884.

"... the dark brown sails of the fishermen's fleet,
As they make for the harbour bar."

It would seem that Hunter was illustrating a poem published in *Essays for Young Men* on p.110 but unfortunately neither the publication nor the full poem has been found.

*Essays for Young Men* is presumed to be a journal or periodical with a compilation of essays, book excerpts, pictures, poetry and so on. It was definitely published after 1889.[100]

### Provenance of original
Estate of the artist
Family by descent

100  Acknowledgement: Parie Watterson, Reference Specialist (Rare Books) British Library.

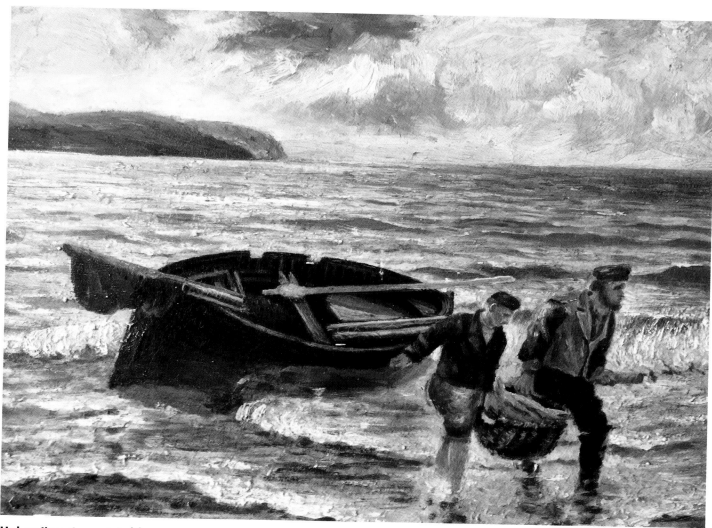

## Unloading the catch (1)

Undated, oil on canvas, 22 × 30 cm, 8.7" × 11.8"

Inscribed Colin Hunter on rear of frame.

**Auctioneer's description**
A fisherman and a boy carrying a basket of fish from their rowing boat on the beach.

Sold, Maillard & Son Auctions, Jersey, Channel Islands (business since sold), 1996
Sold, Stroud Auction Rooms, Gloucestershire, 2016

Private collection

There is another **Unloading the catch** but an entirely different scene. See page 263.

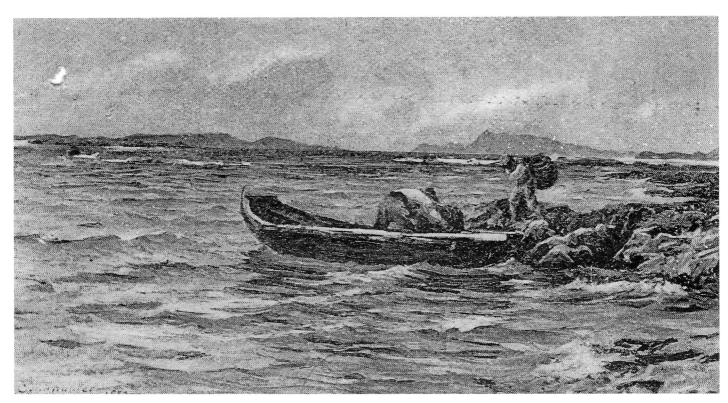

**Atlantic islands**

Undated but probably 1893

Reproduced from unidentified magazine

Courtesy of Marcia Rider

According to Hunter's own accounts, this painting was sold in 1892 or 1893 to Dyce Brown for £150 (today's value £13,500). Of course Hunter may have painted it earlier but 1892 is a believable painted date.

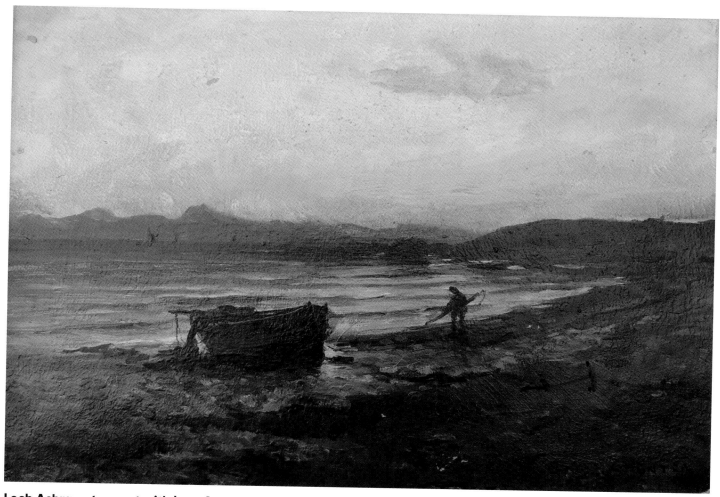

**Loch Achray at sunset with lone figure and beached sailing vessel**

Undated, oil on board, 25 × 34 cm, 9.8" × 13.8"

Signed C Hunter

Private collection

(Image has been slightly cropped due to damage on perimeter from earlier framing.)

Sold by auction Mallams, Oxford, 2015

Loch Achray is about 40 miles from Hunter's home in Helensburgh.

Note similarity of this painting and location with the following two images.

A similar painting **Loch Achray** (without a lone figure) was sold by Bonhams in 2006. The fact that the two pictures are both oil on board, the same size, appear to be painted at the same time of day and from the same viewpoint, suggests they were painted on the same date. See page 254.

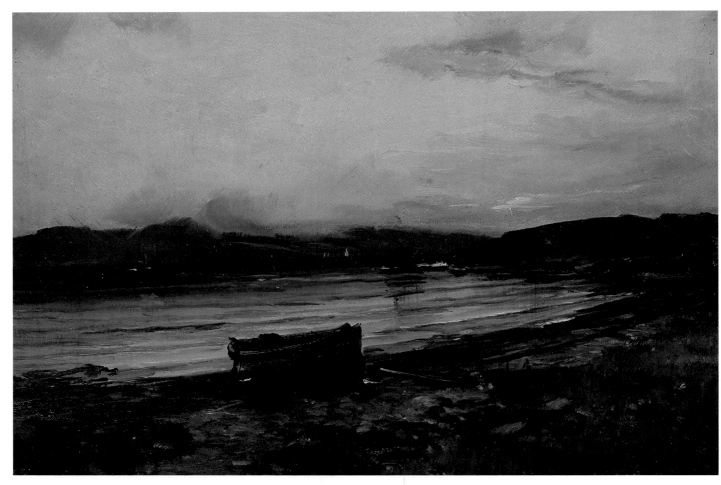

**Loch Achray**

Also known as **Beached fishing boat Loch Achray**
Undated possibly 1866, oil on board, 25 × 34 cm, 9.8" × 13.8"

Signed

Image courtesy Bonhams International Auctioneers and Valuers

A painting called **Loch Achray** was exhibited at the Royal Scottish
Academy in 1866 but the RSA could not provide an image of it.
That it is this painting must remain only a possibility.

Private collection

Sold, Richardson & Smith, Whitby, 2001
Sold, Bonhams, London, 2006

A similar painting **Loch Achray at sunset with lone figure and
beached sailing vessel** was sold by Mallams in 2015. The fact that
the two pictures are both oil on board, the same size, appear to
be painted at the same time of day and from the same viewpoint,
suggests they were painted on the same date, i.e. possibly 1866. See
page 253.

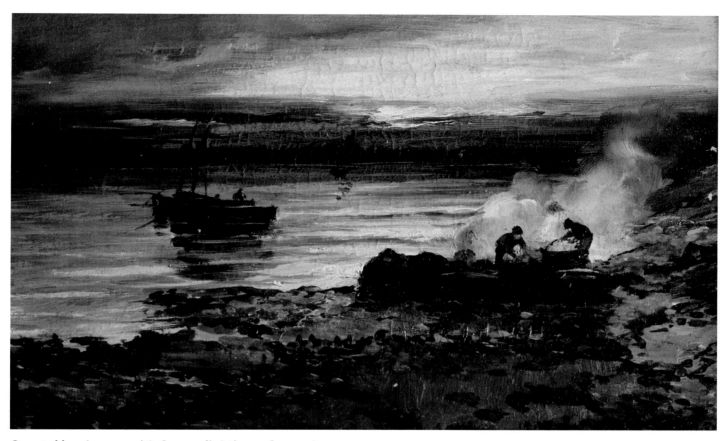

**Coastal landscape with figures lighting a fire and moored fishing boats**

Possibly Loch Achray

Undated, oil on canvas, 15.2 × 25.4 cm, 6" × 10"

Private collection

Sold, Gorringes Auctioneers, 2015

Note similarity of this painting and location with previous two images. Arguably, it is also Loch Achray. See pages 253 & 254.

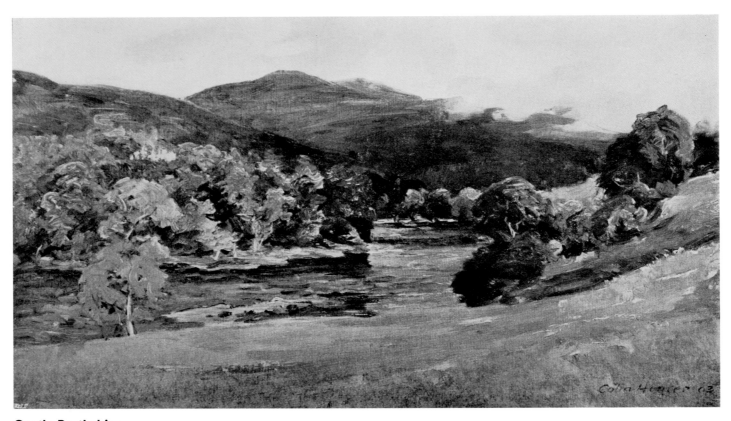

**Garth, Perthshire**

1903, oil on canvas, 33 × 58.4 cm, 13" × 23"

Reproduced from *Royal Academy Pictures* 1903

Exhibited Royal Academy 1903
(Hunter's last RA exhibition. He died the following year.)

A rare landscape from Hunter in the last year of his life. He painted landscapes (as opposed to seascapes) most regularly as a young man, in the 1860s and 1870s, before his passion for the sea and working fisher folk consumed him.

It was not possible to track down the owners of many Colin Hunter works to request permission to publish or to obtain quality images suitable for the best reproduction. These images are predominantly small thumbnail website files, presented here for reference only and to make the catalogue of all Hunter works as comprehensive as possible. Some images are reproduced from old auction catalogues.

If you are the owner of any of these paintings or if you know where the originals may be located, please contact the publisher.

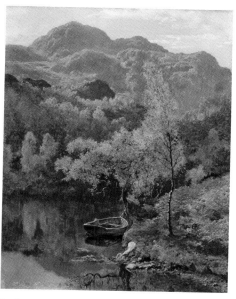

**Lake scene with boat**

(Probably Ben Venue in the Trossachs)
Oil on canvas, 38.5 × 29 cm, 15.3" × 11.5"

Signed

Image courtesy Peter Wilson, Fine Art Auctioneers, Nantwich, Cheshire

Sold, Peter Wilson auctioneers, Nantwich, Feb 2017

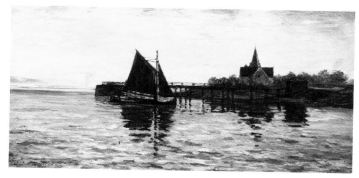

**Coastal view with sailing vessel moored at a jetty, a church beyond**

Oil on canvas approx. 35.6 × 73.7 cm, 14" × 29"

Sold, Toovey's, Washington, West Sussex, Lot 101, 30 November 2011

Image courtesy of Toovey's Fine Art Auctioneers, Washington, West Sussex

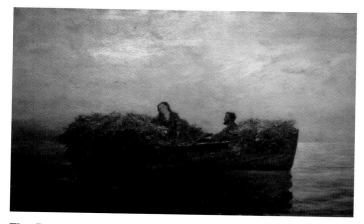

**The Return Home**

1871 or 1891 (indistinct), oil on canvas, 44.5 × 75 cm, 17.5" × 29.5"

Atmospheric dusk scene, couple drifting in the boat home

Image courtesy of Lawrences Auctioneers, Bletchingley, Surrey

Listed Catherine Southon Auctioneers & Valuers, Bromley, Kent, Feb 2017 ("dated 1871")

Sold, Lawrences of Bletchingley auctioneers, 25 April 2017 ("dated 1891")

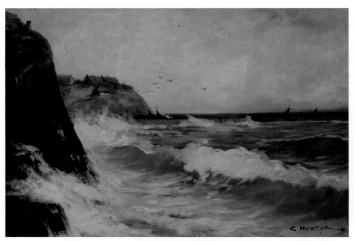

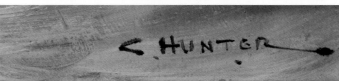

## Rotskust (Rocky coast)

Also known as **Stormy seas**

Oil on board (or oil on canvas according to one source), 34 × 24 cm, 13" × 9.5"

Image courtesy of Venduehuis der Notarissen, The Hague, Netherlands

Sold (no more details known), 2007

Sold in auction at the Venduehuis der Notarissen, The Hague, Netherlands, 2017

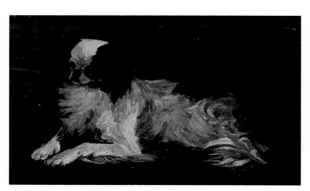

## Portrait of a Cavalier King Charles Spaniel

Signed LL with a canvas stencil from Newman, Soho Square London on the reverse.

Image courtesy of Skinner Inc (USA)  www.skinnerinc.com

Sold in USA, 17 July 2013

Is this the or a Hunter family dog? Note a family dog on Hunter's lap in the photo on page 19

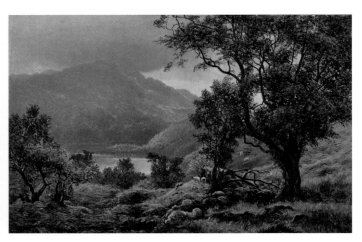

## Ben Venue

Also known as **Lake with mountains in distance**

1865, oil on canvas, 39 × 59 cm, 15" × 23"

Image courtesy of Whyte's Fine Art & Collectibles Auctioneers & Valuers, Dublin Ireland

Exhibited RSA 1865

Ben Venue is a mountain in the Trossachs

Sold, Whyte's, Dublin, 26th Sep 2016

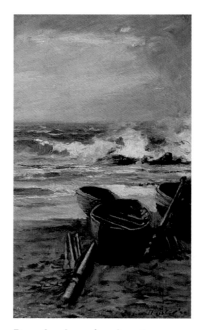

## Beached rowing boats

Oil on canvas, 61 × 35.6 cm, 24" × 14"

Sold, Lyon & Turnbull, Edinburgh, 2006

*Owner not traced; image not found at auctioneers*
*This low resolution image: mutualart.com*

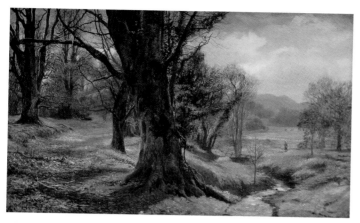

**Figur i hostlandskap (Figure in autumn landscape)**

Oil on canvas, 37 × 60 cm, 14.5" × 23.5"

Signed verso Colin Hunter

Image courtesy Uppsala Auktionskammare, Sweden

Sold, Uppsala Auktionskammare, Sweden, 2010

Re-sold, Uppsala Auktionskammare, Sweden, 2015

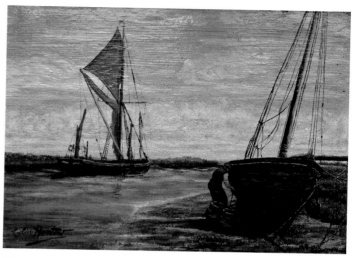

**River scene with a Norfolk wherry\***

(* incorrectly titled by one auction house or owner as 'weir')
Also known as **Moored fishing boats**
Oil on board, 24 × 32.5 cm, 9.5" × 11"

A wherry is a type of boat that was traditionally used for carrying cargo or passengers on rivers and canals in England and is particularly associated with the River Thames and the River Cam. They were also used on the Broadland rivers of Norfolk and Suffolk.

Private collection

Sold, Eastbourne Auctions, Feb 2018

Sold, Lawrences of Bletchingley, Surrey, Apr 2018

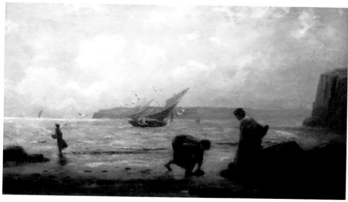

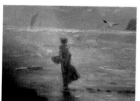 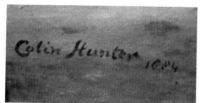

**A Victorian beachcombing scene with sailing boats in background**

1884, oil on canvas

Signed

Image courtesy Dukes Auctions Dorchester, Dorset

Sold, Duke's Avenue Auctions, Dorchester, 2017

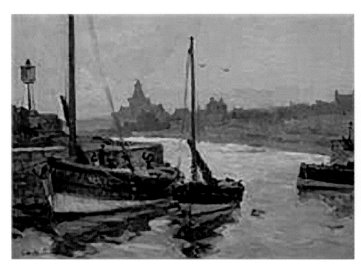

## Pittenweem, Fifeshire

1899, oil on canvas/board (?), 29.2 × 39.3 cm, 11.5" × 15.5"

Previously mistakenly entitled **Pennyween**

Pittenweem is a small fishing village on the east coast of Scotland

Sold, Gorringes, Sussex, 2004

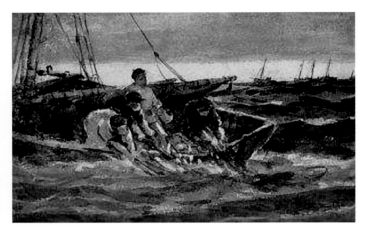

## Fishing boats in rough sea

1867, watercolour & gouache, 32 × 47 cm, 12.6" × 18.5"

Sold, Horner's, Acle, Norwich, 2010

*Owner not traced; image not found at auctioneers*
*This low resolution image: arcadja.com*

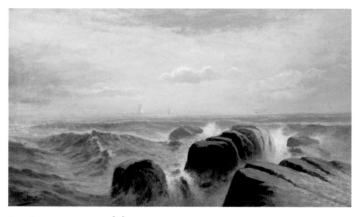

## Rocky seascape (2)

Oil on canvas, 45.7 × 76.2 cm, 18" × 30"

(another Hunter was given an alternative name of **Rocky seascape** see page 176)

Signed Colin Hunter RA (sic) LL. See signatures section.

Possibly circa 1876? Possibly USA location?

Image courtesy Heritage Auctions, Dallas, Texas HA.com

Sold, Heritage Auctions, Texas, 6 December 2007

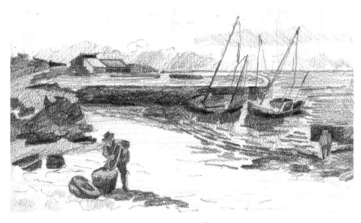

## Pecheur au travail sur la plage (Fisherman working on the beach)

Oil on canvas, 64 × 188 cm, 25.2" × 74"

Signed and dated

Sold, Bernaerts Veilinghuis, Antwerp, Belgium

*Owner not traced; no image available from auctioneers; only a copyright low resolution image found for which permission to use was not obtained. Therefore Leigh Glover did this sketch of the painting so at least it could be identified. Image © Leigh Glover 2018.*

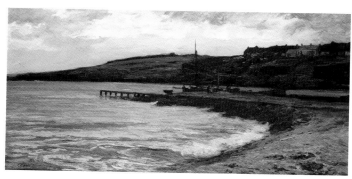

**West coast jetty**

1876, oil on canvas, 38.1 × 76.2 cm, 15" × 30"

Image courtesy Sotheby's

Sold, Sotheby's, London, 2003

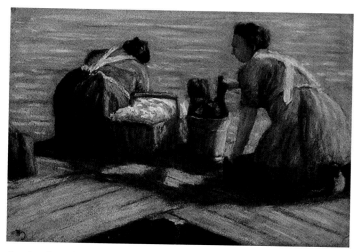

**At the herring market**

Oil on canvas, 21 × 28 cm, 8.3" × 11"

Monogrammed LL

Sold, Zurichsee Auktionen, Erienbach, Switzerland, 22 September 2010

*Owner not traced; Zurichsee auctioneers no longer in business*
*This low resolution image: artnet.com*

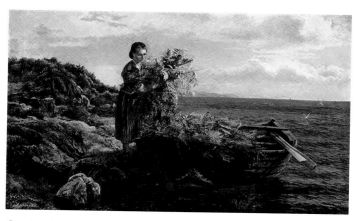

**Gathering bracken**

Also known as **The fern gatherer**
1869?, oil on canvas, 46 × 73 cm, 18" × 28"

Despite the different date, which may be an error, the question is raised whether or not this is the painting that was exhibited at the Royal Scottish Academy in 1868.

Not sold, Sotheby's, Gleneagles, 1998

Sold, Sotheby's, London, 2003

*Owner not traced; image not found at auctioneers*
*This low resolution image: mutualart.com*

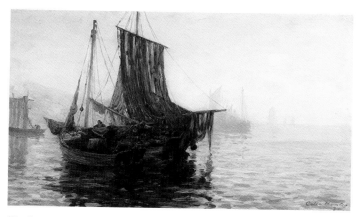

**Harbour scene with fishing boats**

Oil on canvas, 30.5 × 50.8 cm, 12" × 20"

Listed, Bloomsbury Auctions London (now Dreweatts, Newbury, Berkshire), 2008

*Owner not traced; image not found at auctioneers*
*This low resolution image: artnet.com*

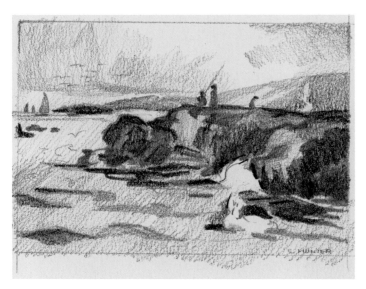

### Figures fishing from the rocks on the coast

Oil on canvas, 22 × 31.8 cm, 8.7" × 12.5"

Listed, Burstow and Hewett, Battle, 2008

*Owner not traced; no image available from auctioneers; only a copyright low resolution image found for which permission to use was not obtained. Therefore Leigh Glover did this sketch of the painting so at least it could be identified. Image © Leigh Glover 2018.*

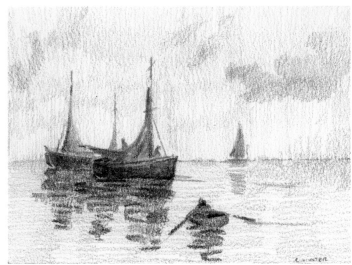

### Untitled

Oil on canvas, 33 × 43 cm, 13" × 16.9"

Listed, Burstow and Hewett, Battle, 2008

*Owner not traced; no image available from auctioneers; only a copyright low resolution image found for which permission to use was not obtained. Therefore Leigh Glover did this sketch of the painting so at least it could be identified. Image © Leigh Glover 2018.*

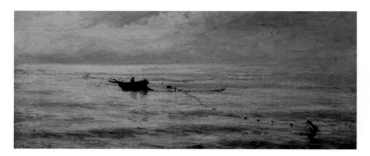

### Fishing boat on a calm sea

Oil on canvas, 33 × 76 cm, 13" × 29.9"

Image courtesy Gorringe's Auctioneers, Lewes, Sussex

Sold, Gorringe's Auctioneers, 2010

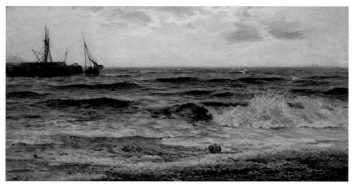

### After the gale

Oil on canvas, 66.5 × 123 cm, 26" × 48"

Listed, Horta Auctions, Brussels, May 2017

From a Belgian private collection

In 1873 a picture called **After a gale** was exhibited in the Royal Academy. No image of that painting has been found, and nor any further reference to it, including dimensions. It is therefore impossible to know if this is the same picture as the one exhibited in the RA. But it may be.

Image courtesy Hotel de Ventes Horta, Brussels

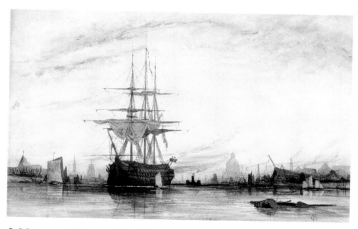

**A Man-o-War on the Thames at sunset with St Paul's in the distance**

Watercolour, 16.5 × 26.5 cm, 6.5" × 10.5"

Sold, Anderson & Garland, Newcastle-upon-Tyne, 2017

Image courtesy Anderson & Garland

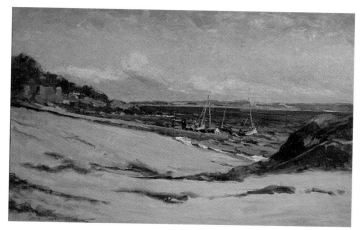

**Unloading the catch (2)**

1903, oil on canvas, 30 × 45 cm, 11.8" × 17.7"

Sold, Lyon & Turnbull, 2006

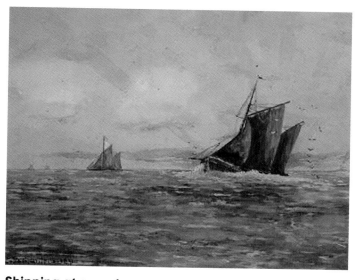

**Shipping at sunset**

1891, watercolour, 21.5 × 28 cm, 8.5" × 11"

Sold, Lyon & Turnbull, 2006

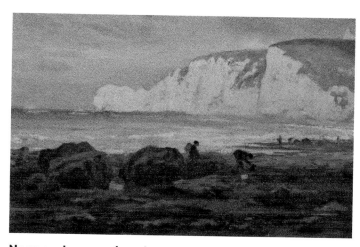

**Normandy mussel gatherers**

Oil on canvas, 40.6 × 61 cm, 16" × 24"

Signed LR Colin Hunter

Image courtesy Kamelot Auction House, Philadelphia, Pennsylvania, USA

Sold, Kamelot Auctions, Philadelphia, USA, 2014

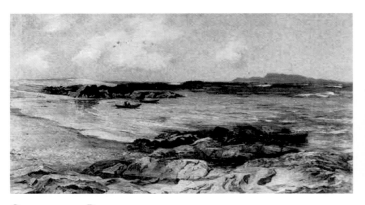

**Connemara Bay**

1894, oil on canvas, 50.8 × 91.4 cm, 20" × 36"

Sold, Sotheby's, London, 1994

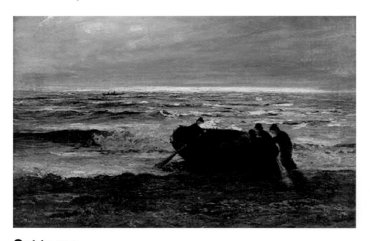

**Out to sea**

Oil on canvas, 75 × 84 cm, 29.5" × 33.1"

Sold, Lyon & Turnbull, 2006

*Owner not traced; image not found at auctioneers*
*This low resolution image: artnet.com*

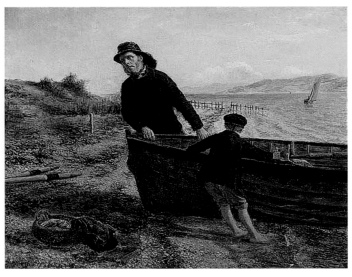

**Bringing in the boat**

1865, oil on canvas, 51 × 61 cm, 20" × 24"

Lot not sold, Sotheby's, London, 2000

*Owner not traced; image not found at auctioneers*
*This low resolution image: arcadja.com*

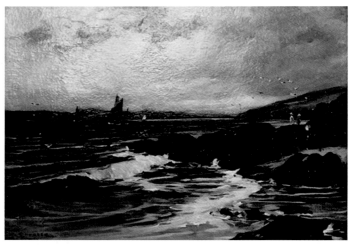

**Seascape (2)**

Oil on canvas, 47 × 56.5 cm, 18.5" × 22.3"

Signed C Hunter l.l. verso note added "Colin Hunter 1841–1904 D 1071" (indistinct)

Sold by EBTH.com, October 2016

*Low resolution image only available, courtesy EBTH.com*

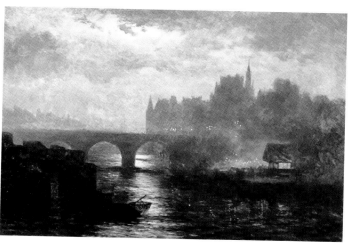

**North Bridge, Edinburgh**

Oil on canvas, 34 × 50 cm, 13.4" × 19.7"

Signed and indistinctly dated

Image courtesy Bellmans Auctions

Sold, Bellmans Auctions, Billingshurst, Sussex, 2018

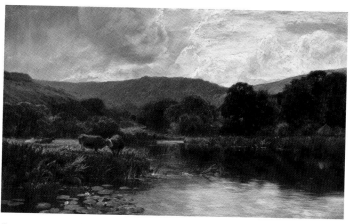

**An wasserstelle weidende kuhherde in sommerlicher (Cattle at water hole in summer)**

Oil on canvas, 41 × 63.5 cm, 16.1" × 25"

Signed

Image courtesy Dr Fischer Auctioneers, Heilbronn, Germany

Listed, not sold, Dr Fischer, 2013

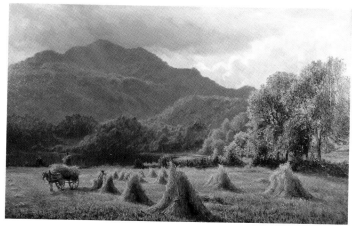

**A figure loading a hay wagon in an extensive wooded landscape**

1865, oil on canvas, 39.4 × 61 cm, 15.5" × 24"

Signed and dated

Image courtesy Halls Fine Art Auctioneers & Valuers, Shrewsbury, Shropshire

Sold, Halls Fine Art, Shrewsbury, 2006

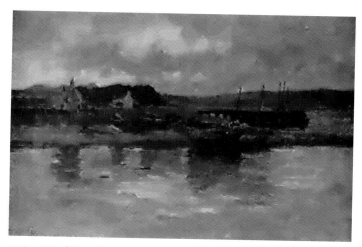

**Kyleakin (Skye)**

1899 or 1900, oil on canvas, 35.5 × 61 cm, 14" × 24"

Signed

Not sold, Sotheby's, Glasgow, 1991

Hunter's personal accounts show this was sold in 1899 to Vivian for £315 (today's value £39,000) therefore suggesting the painted date would be 1899 not 1900.

*Owner not traced; no image available from auctioneers*
*Low resolution image: artnet.com*

# More Hunters – no image yet found

These Hunters were listed in auction catalogues or found in other reference sources. They have probably been entitled or described by the auctioneer or vendor themselves where the original title has not been known. However, no image accompanied or was found with the listing and so it has not been possible to determine whether or not some of the listings refer in fact to other paintings, maybe some already in this book.

When vendors or auctioneers give their own titles or descriptions often duplicates are not recognised. For example, there are several Hunters given the title "Fishing harbour" or "Harbour scene" or "Coastal scene" or similar. Without the images to compare each work, it is impossible to know whether over the years at different sales, the same painting has assumed different titles or descriptions. It is timely to call for all paintings to be named verso on the canvas so the name will live with the painting forever!

1. **A coastal inlet with fishing boats**, oil on canvas, 34 × 58 cm, 13.4" × 22.8"; Shapes Auctioneers, Edinburgh 2011. (Shapes Auctions have since gone out of business and no image of this painting could be retrieved)

2. **A sunlit loch landscape**, 1871, oil on canvas, 66 × 121.9 cm, 26" × 48"; sold Christie's, London, 1998

3. **Arran**, N.B.,[101] 36.8 × 91.4 cm, 14.5" × 36"; listed in the studio sale at Christie's, 8th April 1905

4. **As they roar on the shore**, 1899, oil on canvas, 88.9 × 157.5 cm, 35" × 62"; sold after Hunter's death in his studio sale, Christie's, 8th April 1905 for £99.15s (today's value £11,500) to (surname) Mitchell

5. **Auchmithie, Forfarshire**, 35.6 × 73.7 cm, 14" × 29"; listed in the studio sale at Christie's, 8th April 1905

6. **Boats aground**, oil on board, 25.4 × 44.5 cm, 10" × 17.5"; sold David Lay, Penzance, 1996

7. **Busy coastal scene**, 1885, oil on canvas, 53.3 × 78.7 cm, 21" × 31"; sold G A Key, Aylsham, Norfolk, 1993

8. **Caller herrin'**, 1891, oil on canvas, 101.6 × 147.3 cm, 40" × 29"; sold after Hunter's death in his studio sale, Christie's, 8th April 1905 for £99.15s (today's value £11,500) to Good & ? (indistinct)

9. **Coast scene**, 1890, oil on canvas, 52.1 × 91.4 cm, 20.5" × 36"; sold, Sotheby's, London, 2002

10. **Coastline at dawn**, oil on canvas, 35.6 × 61 cm, 14" × 24"; sold, Christie's, London, 1992

11. **Cuchillin Hills, Isle of Skye**, 39.4 × 74.9 cm, 15.5" × 29.5"; listed in the studio sale at Christie's, 8th April 1905

12. **Drifting before**, 1888, oil on canvas, 61 × 38.1 cm, 24" × 15"; National Art Gallery of New South Wales, where it was described as "a sketch" in the gallery's 1888 collections catalogue. Described as an oil painting in the catalogue of auctioneer W A Little, Sydney, when it was sold 26th October 1920. No image found

13. **Dumbarton Rock**, 1901, oil on canvas, 49.5 × 91.4 cm, 19.5" × 36"; sold after Hunter's death in his studio sale, Christie's, 8th April 1905 for £50 8s (today's value £5,900) to (surname) Shephard

14. **Engelsk havneparti (English port)**, 1874, oil on canvas, 38.1 × 78.7 cm, 15" × 31"; sold, Bruun Rasmussen, Copenhagen, Denmark

15. **Fishing boats**, 1886, oil on canvas, 30.5 × 57.2 cm, 12" × 22.5"; sold, Sotheby's, London, 1998

16. **Fishing boats anchoring for the night**, oil on canvas, 41.9 × 61 cm, 16.5" × 24"; sold, Christie's, New York, USA, 1991

17. **Fishing boats in port**, 1883, oil on canvas, 61 × 35.6 cm, 24" × 14"; sold, Sotheby's, London, 1997

18. **Fishing boats in stiff breeze**, 1896, oil on canvas, 73.7 × 160 cm, 29" × 63"; sold, Bonhams, Edinburgh, 2004

19. **Fishing boats**, oil on board, 20 × 14.5 cm, 7.8" × 5.7"; listed, Shapes, Edinburgh 21st May 2010. (Shapes Auctions have since gone out of business and no image of this painting could be retrieved)

20. **Fishing fleet**, oil on board, 30.5 × 45.7 cm, 12" × 18"; listed, David Lay, Penzance, 2009

21. **Fiskare I bat vid klippkant (Fishermen in boat at ... ?)**, 1867, oil on canvas, 40.6 × 61 cm, 16" × 24"; sold, Bukowski Auktioner, Malmo, Sweden, 1996

22. **Harbour view**, 1891, oil on canvas, 39.1 × 63.5 cm, 15.4" × 25"; sold, Hodgins, Calgary, Canada, 2005

23. **In the Western Isles**, 1890, oil on canvas, 40.6 × 76.2 cm, 16" × 30"; sold, Sotheby's, Edinburgh, 1993

24. **Kelp-Burning**, 30.5 × 54.6 cm, 12" × 21.5"; listed in the studio sale at Christie's, 8th April 1905

25. **Landing the catch (2)**, oil on canvas, 45 × 65 cm, 17.7" × 25.6", signed; sold, Ramsay Cornish Auctioneers, Edinburgh 2 April 2011, Lot 93. No image found and no 2011 archives retained or accessible

---

101  North Britain

26. **Mending the lobster pot**, 1875, oil on canvas, 22.9 × 33 cm, 9" × 13"; sold, Christie's, London, 2000

27. **Mountainous landscape**, 1871, oil on canvas, 64.8 × 117.1 cm, 25.5" × 46.1"; sold, Bruun Rasmussen, Copenhagen, Denmark, 1995

28. **Nature's (or Natural) arch**, 1874, oil on canvas, 20.3 × 30.5 cm, 8" × 12" (?); sold, David Lay, Penzance, 1992 & 2006

29. **Portrait of a girl**, oil on canvas, 15.2 × 12.7 cm, 6" × 5"; sold, Leslie Hindman, Chicago, USA

30. **Pushing away from the riverbank**, 1880, oil on panel, 31.8 × 45.7 cm, 12.5" × 18"; lot not sold, Pinneys,[102] Montreal, Canada, 2001

31. **Ragamuffin, chesnut hunter/Bantam**, oil on canvas, 129.5 × 193.7 cm, 51" × 76.3"; sold, Christie's, 24 Oct 1991

32. **Seascape**, oil on canvas, 64.8 × 64.8 cm, 25.5" × 25.5"; listed, Cobbs Auctioneers, Peterborough, North Hampshire, USA, 2002

33. **Tending the boats**, 1864, oil on canvas, 55.9 × 101.6 cm, 22" × 40"; sold, Sotheby's, London, 1998

34. **The seashore**, 1873, oil on canvas, 55.9 × 91.4 cm, 22" × 36"; listed, Phillips, London, 1991

35. **The Thames**, 57.2 × 45.7 cm, 22.5" × 18"; listed in the studio sale at Christie's, 8th April 1905

36. **Waves breaking on a beach**, 1879, oil on canvas, 30 × 55 cm, 12" × 22"; sold, Lyon & Turnbull, Edinburgh, 21 July 2006

37. **West harbour Greenock**, 1880, oil on canvas, 61 × 35.6 cm, 24" × 14"; sold, Sotheby's, Edinburgh, 1996

---

102 Pinneys has since gone out of business and no records or image of this work available.

*Chapter 7*

# A family affair

**1896**

From 1896–1903 the Royal Academy exhibitions became a family affair, with father (Colin), son (John Young Hunter) and (from 1900) daughter-in-law (Mary Y Hunter), exhibiting their work together.

This chapter shows paintings by other members of the family that hung with Colin's.

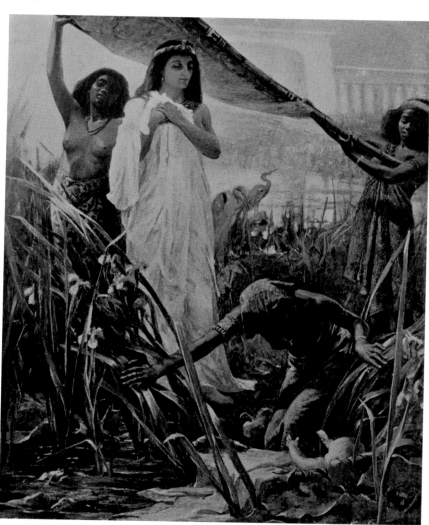

John Young Hunter "The finding of Moses"

NB: In 1896 John was still calling himself John Hunter, not "Young Hunter"

**1897**

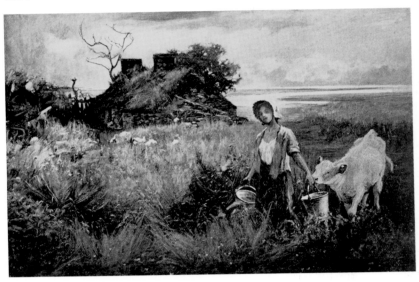

John Young Hunter "The crofter's home"

NB This year John had started calling himself Young Hunter

**1898**

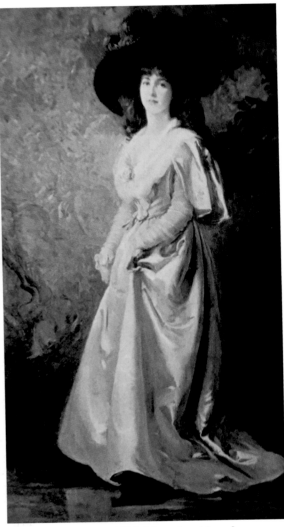

John Young Hunter, "Edith Mary daughter of
N Macmichael Esq"

**1899**

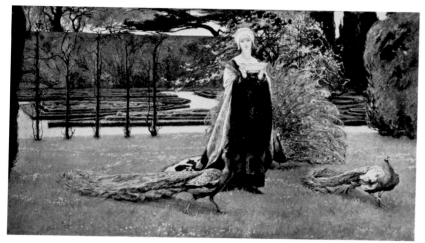

John Young Hunter, "My Lady's Garden"

This picture is painted in Holland Park, Kensington, right across the road from where John lived with his parents at 14 Melbury Road. It was in 1899 that John married Mary Towgood.

Tate Britain. Reproduced by courtesy of the Trustees of the Tate Gallery, London

**1900**

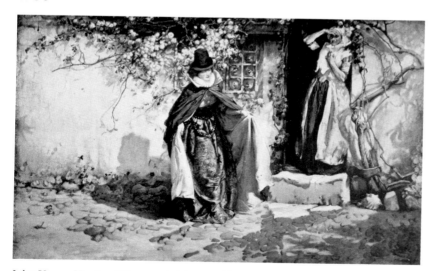

John Young Hunter, "Rings and things and fine array"

**1900**

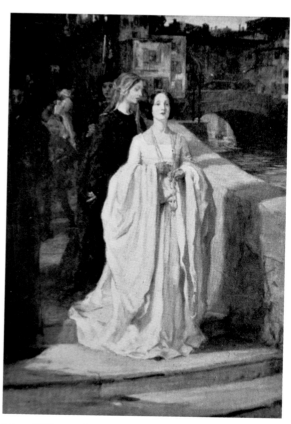

Mary Y Hunter,[103] "The Denial"

(the first year Mary had exhibited in the RA having married John the year before)

---

103  Mary Yerberry Hunter (née Towgood)

**1901**

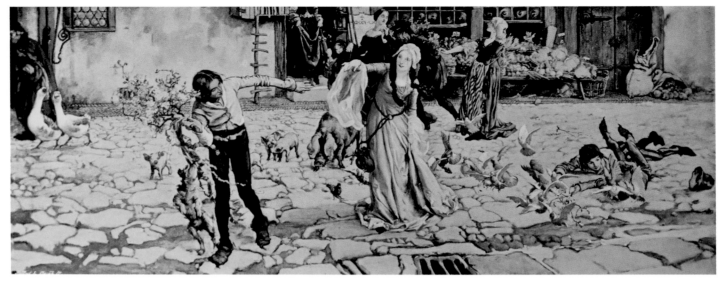

John Young Hunter, "Come lasses and lads"

**1901**

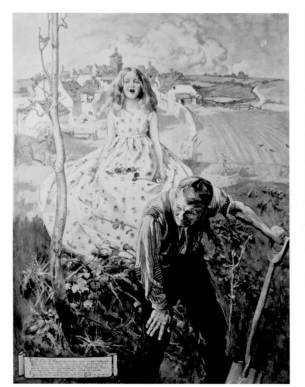

Mary Y Hunter, "Joy and the labourer"

**1902**

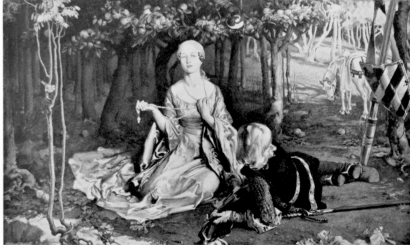

John Young Hunter, "Forest lovers"

**1902**

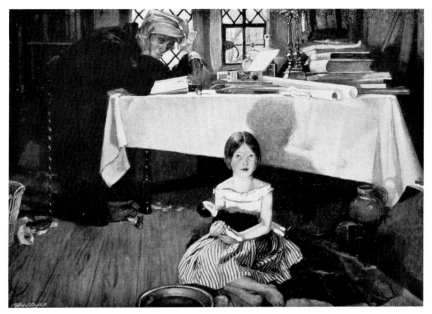

Mary Y Hunter, "Where shall wisdom be found?"

**1903** (the last year father Colin also exhibited)

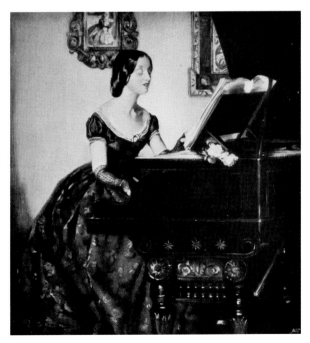

John Young Hunter, "The Nightingale"

**1903**

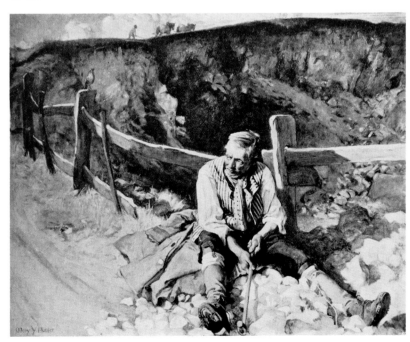

Mary Y Hunter, "The Road Mender"

*Chapter 8*

# Colin Hunter's signatures

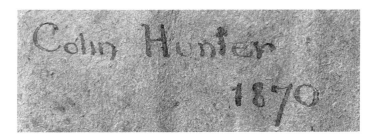

**Rocky coastal landscape**, 1870 (verso)

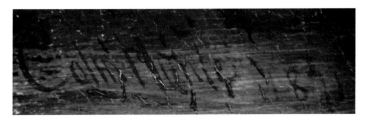

**Emptying nets**, 1871 (taken under a UV lamp)

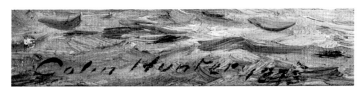

**Off the west coast**, 1873

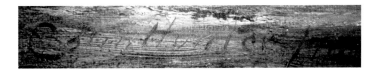

**Carradale Pier (Harbour)**, 1874

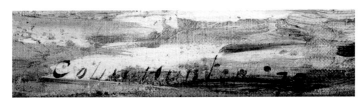

**The Clyde Coast**, 1878

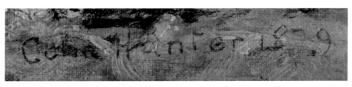

**The Dover Cliffs**, 1879 (Beer, Devon?)

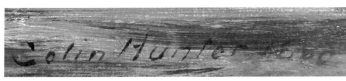

**A Scottish fishing harbour**, 1880

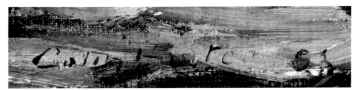

**Fishing boats off the coast of Cornwall**, 1883

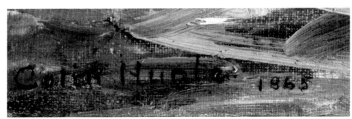

**A fishing harbour**, 1885 (1865? "8" may have been damaged in cleaning?)

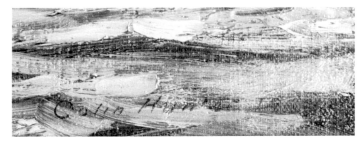

**Fishing boats moored on the shore**, 1885 or 1889

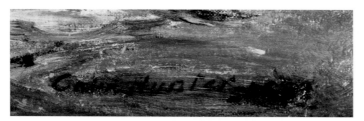

**Crab fishers**, 1887

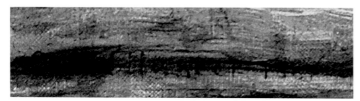

**Harbour scene**, 1887 (possibly Coldingham)

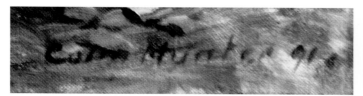

**Fishing boats unloading at a quay**, 1891

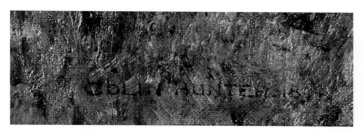

**The coast of Devon**, 1891 or 1894

This is an unusual signature for Colin Hunter as it appears in block capitals so perfectly formed that it looks as if the name could have been stencilled. But there is no other reason to question the painting's authenticity.

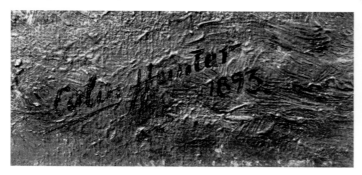

**The young explorer**, 1893. Unusually, signature on an angle

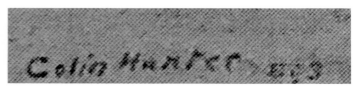

**Reflections**, 1893

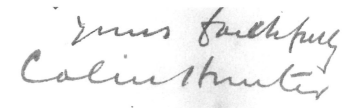

**Personal handwritten letter signature**, 1895

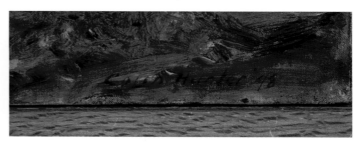

**The hills of Skye from Loch Duich**, 1898

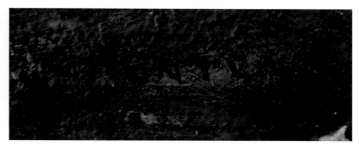

**Loch Achray at sunset with lone figure and beached sailing vessel**, undated

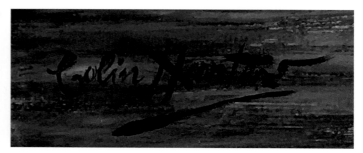

**River scene Norfolk wherry**, undated

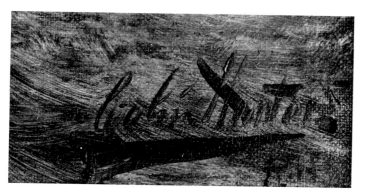

**America's Cup 1876,** painting undated but presumed shortly after 1876

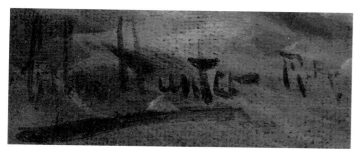

**Rocky seascape,** courtesy Heritage Auctions HA.com

Notice the similarity of this signature with that of the America's Cup painting above. Was Rocky seascape also painted circa 1876 and possibly in the USA?

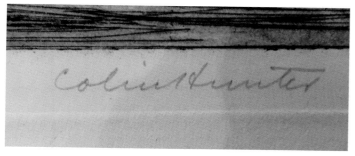

**The Gareloch,** undated, etching, on mount

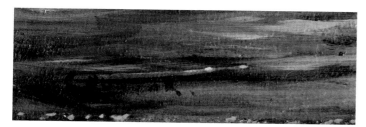

**Fishing boats at dusk,** undated

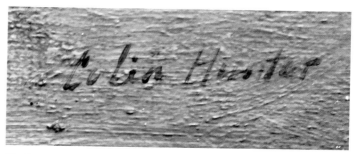

**Harbour scene with blue boat,** undated

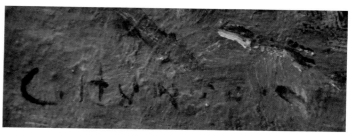

**A coastal walk,** undated

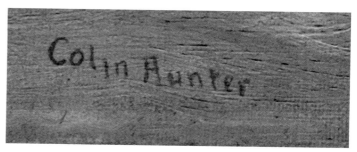

**On the coast of Scotland,** undated

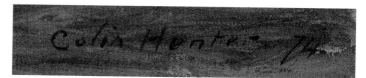

**Fishermen,** 1874

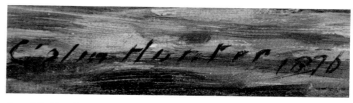

**Seaside fire (Kelp burning),** 1876

# Chapter 9

# The jury is out

# AUTHENTICITY QUESTIONED, UNKNOWN COLIN HUNTERS AND OTHER PUZZLES

## Authenticity issues

In September 2016, the saleroom manager of an auction house informed the author:

*... it came to our attention just as the sale was starting that the authenticity of the Hunter could not be guaranteed. As it turns out, a few have been popping up around the country and being offered as works by Hunter. That is why it was withdrawn from the sale at the last minute ...*

The extent to which works have been "popping up" as Hunters when they are not, has proved difficult to establish, but a warning like this from a reputable auctioneer highlights the need for *caveat emptor.*

## Is this our Hunter?

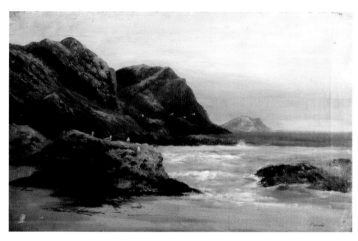

### Meereskuste "Seashore"
Oil on canvas, 41 × 61 cm, 16" × 24"

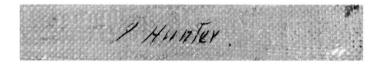

**Meereskuste**, signature LR undated

This painting was sold as a Colin Hunter in 2009 by Martin Wendl auction house in Rudolstadt, Germany to a private collector in England. Provenance: from a trader in Berlin.

The signature is not typical and the initial is more like an "I" or a "J" than a "C". Maybe this could stand for Isabella Hunter or John Hunter? However, family descendants do not believe Colin's wife, Isabella, painted. And if it is Colin's son, John Hunter, he typically signed his works with a "Y" as in "J Y Hunter" or "J Young Hunter".

As to where this scene is, the painting bears a resemblance to Lion Rock on the Island of Cumbrae. This island is in the lower Firth of Clyde in western Scotland – in Colin Hunter's stomping ground. If this location proved to be correct it could add some substance to the painting being our Colin Hunter.

On balance, the author doubts this is a genuine Colin Hunter. But the case remains open.

# Is this our Hunter?

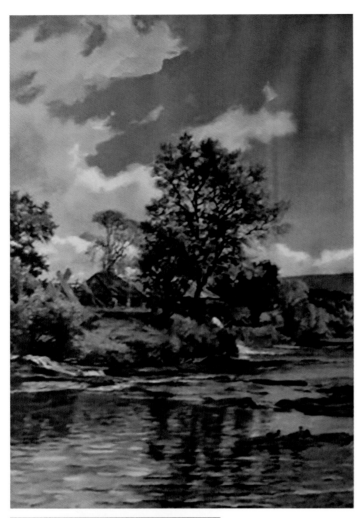

## A Saw Mill on the River Snake

Lithograph print of original painting – possibly **The Mill 1889**

*Low resolution image of lithograph only available, courtesy EBTH.com (USA)*

## The Mill

1889, oil on canvas, 111 × 86 cm, 44" × 34"

Sold or exhibited at Old Hall Gallery, Iden, Rye, Sussex[104]
Signature below left believed to be on the original **The Mill**, 1889.

The title of this lithograph is puzzling, if it is indeed of Colin Hunter's original work. The only River Snake found is in Idaho, USA. Other than the title of this picture, there is no other suggestion that Hunter visited Idaho.

The only known Hunter with "saw mill" in the title, appears in Hunter's own accounts of 1881–82 when he sold a picture called **The Saw Mill** (no mention of the River Snake) for £100 (today's value £8,500). Unfortunately, no image of that painting has been found to compare it with **Saw Mill on the River Snake**.

Another Hunter called simply **The Mill** was exhibited in The New Gallery in 1889. But again, unfortunately, no image of that painting has been found to compare with this scene. But the date 1889 is the same, so maybe **The Mill** was indeed the original painting of which this is a lithograph print and given a misleading American title.

---

104  Since gone out of business.

## Is this our Hunter?

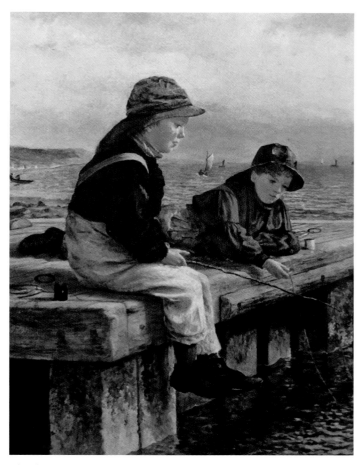

### Fishing

1864

Photograph of a lithograph

This picture is a complete mystery. It is displayed on the internet and owned by Mary Gilmartin[105] who found it discarded in a rain-soaked frame about 2013. But no other reference to this painting has been found despite a search through many sources. Initially, Gilmartin thought it was by an Arthur Hunter (unknown artist), but on closer inspection, the signature is seen to read Colin Hunter 1864 (see right). If this is an authentic Colin Hunter, Colin would have been twenty-three years old when he painted it and was probably living in Helensburgh.

There is a work with the title **Boys Fishing** which was exhibited in 1872 at the Royal Scottish Academy but there is no photographic record of it.[106] It was sold to a Mr John A Brown of Sunnyside

House, Paisley.[107] Regrettably, without an image of the work to compare with this scene it cannot help to authenticate **Fishing 1864**.

The signature of **Fishing** below is arguably consistent with other Colin Hunter signatures, but no provenance has been established for the painting. So the jury must remain out.

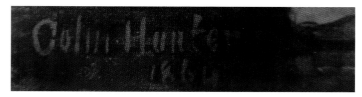

The signature on **Fishing**, 1864

105 Attempts to get in touch with Mary Gilmartin have been unsuccessful.

106 Acknowledgement: Robin Rodger, Collections Department, RSA

107 Acknowledgement: Agnes Wood, RSA Collections Volunteer

## Another Colin Hunter on the art market?

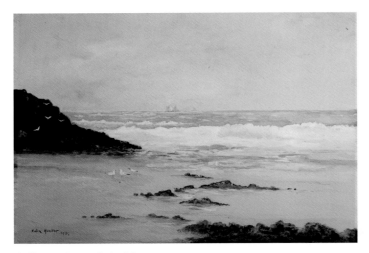

### Off the Berwickshire coast

1931, water colour, 24 × 34 cm, 9.3" × 13.3"

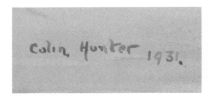

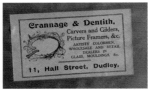

Signed LL

Original framer's label on back of watercolour

Sold by Swan & Turner Auctioneers, Jedburgh, Scottish Borders, 2015

This painting is of course definitely not our Colin Hunter with a date of 1931. However, it is intriguing that the name is the same and there are Scottish connections.

Firstly, the painting was sold in Scotland. Secondly, it came from a private collection in Scotland. Thirdly, the location Scotland's east coast (our Colin Hunter frequently painted on the east coast – e.g. Coldingham is in Berwickshire in the Scottish Borders). This may suggest that the Colin Hunter of 1931 was local to that region, but an attempt to track him down there has not been successful.

Finding the "1931 Colin Hunter" was only of interest in case he turned out to be related to the Victorian Colin Hunter family. After all, here was another Scottish Hunter painting Scottish coast lines. But further family tree research did not find him.

The picture was at one time framed by a company in Dudley, near Wolverhampton in the West Midlands. However, it seems that the business Crannage & Dentith, no longer trades and any attempt to get a better provenance through the framing company, also failed.

Another Colin Hunter water colour (see **The Lizard Cornwall** below) was listed with auctioneers Ewbank's, Surrey. There was no known provenance and this water colour is undated. However, the signature is similar to the painting (left) as are the colours. This may provide further evidence that there are definitely two Colin Hunters in the art market.

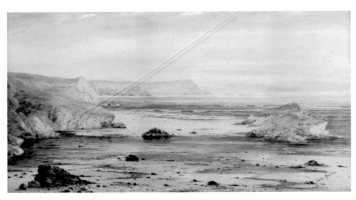

### The Lizard, Cornwall

Water colour, 25.4 × 45.7 cm, 10" × 18"

Signed Colin Hunter undated

Image courtesy Ewbank's Antiques & Fine Art Auctioneers and Valuers, Surrey

Listed but not sold, Ewbank's, 2014

NB The mark that may be seen across the painting is not damage to the work, but rather a crack in the glazing.

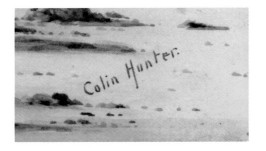

## Attributed to our Colin Hunter incorrectly

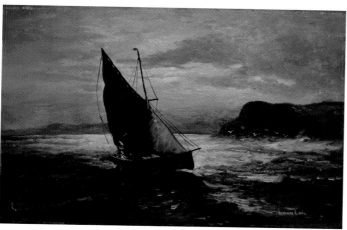

### Loch Goil

Oil on board, 30.5 × 45.7 cm, 12" × 18"

Signed LL C H Hunter and title LR Loch Goil, undated

Description: a lugger on Loch Goil

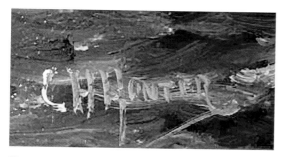

Signature on **Loch Goil**

This painting was sold as a Colin Hunter by Sloan's Auctioneers, Bethesda, Maryland, USA in May 2001 to the Hands of Time Art Gallery in Savage, Maryland, USA. It was then sold to a private collector in New Mexico, USA. Hands of Time dated it as 1894 although the current owner says there is no date on the painting.

It is not accepted that it is our Colin Hunter. Firstly, Colin did not have a middle initial "H". Secondly, Colin Hunter did not typically paint the title of his work on the canvas (or board).

The argument for believing it is a Colin Hunter is supported by the fact that Loch Goil is certainly within Colin's stomping ground. It is a small sea loch located in the Loch Lomond and Trossachs National Park where Colin often painted. However, different sources were consulted on the authenticity of it being our Colin Hunter. Not one believed it was so.and none found "C H Hunter" listed in any of the more well-known reference sources. It may have been an amateur painter using a pseudonym or copying a Colin Hunter work.

# APPENDIX 1

## Hunter's buyers

*Transcribed from Hunter's handwritten notes, records and accounts. Some errors may be due to illegibility.*
*Where known the first and last years of purchase are provided.*

Adelaide Government (1884–85)

Adler (1896–97)

Aerid, J, Hyde Park Terrace, London

Agnew & Sons (1883–1901)

Aitken, John (1880–81)

Anderson (1886–87)

Andrews, A, 25 Bedford Square, London W.C.

Armstrong, Lord

Barnett, G R, 160 Cromwell Road, South Kensington

Bell, Henry (1899)

Black, Wm

Brown, Dyce

Brown, John A. (1872, Sunnyside House, Paisley, bought *Boys Fishing* from RSA)

Campbell, Duncan (1895–96)

Cassell (190–01)

Connell (1896–97; 1900–01)

Council Connemara

Currie, Donald MP (1881–1901) *Silver of the sea* lent to RSA exhibition 1881

Davies H E M (1896–97)

Dennistoun, Alex, Golfhil, Glasgow; *In the gloaming* lent to RSA exhibition 1882, *The Gare Loch* 1881

Dennistoun, Mrs

Donaldson, Wm A

Dowdeswall & Son

Dowell, Mr, Edinburgh, *On the shore at Balintrae* 1881 £42

Drew, Mrs (1896–97)

Dumfries Council (1899)

Dundee Exhibition (1890)

Ellis, Col J, 51 Portland Place

Farfield (1886–87)

Fletcher, James (1878–1901)

Forbes, J S, Garden Terrace, London

Gill, Dr David

Glasgow Corporation (1895–96)

Goldsmid, Sir Julian

Graves (1900–01)

Hall, Stuart (1891–92)

Harris (1885–86)

Heath, Louis, 28 Hertford St, Mayfair, London

Hoare, J R , 29 Cadogan Square, London

Holliton (1887–88)

Hopkinson, Geo, 78 Holland Park, London

Hull (1886–87)

Inules (?), Dr

Jarvis, Lewis (1883) at the RI

Johnson, Shewlis (1890–91)

Joshua, S, 18 Westbourne Terrace, Hyde Park, London

Keeller, John (1891–92)

Kilnwick, H

Knight (1891–92)

Knowles, James, Queen Anne's Lodge, St James's Park, London

Laing, James (1884–85)

Langridge, Dr

McCulloch, J

McKeiller, John (1891–92)

McKinnon, Australia

McLean (1890–91)

Michael, W H, 2C, 54 Cornwall Gardens, South Kensington

Miller, Miss

Mirten J S (1888–89)

Moncrieff, G G

Moncrieff, Gent

Moore, Dr (1883–88)

Murray (1890–91)

Ness, Gordon (1889–90) (portrait)

Ness, P (1889–1901)

Nettlefold, F, Streatham Common, London

Orrock, W, 48 Bedford Square, London

Oyston (1894)

Powell, Frank

Redcliffe, Miss

Reid, James (1885–86)

Renton, J B, London Stock Exchange

Rhodes, Fairfax (1885–86)

Sanderman, J Glas, 24 Cambridge Sq W., London

Schwabe, Mr G C (1880–81)

Scott Moncrieff, W D

Seton, Lady (1887–88)

Smiles, Dr

Stop, F C (Surrey)

Tate, W, Park Hill, Streatham Common

Templeton (1883–84)

The Royal Academy

Thompson, James (1894)

Thompson, S E, Belfast, loaned *Lobster Fishers* to RSA Exhibition 1926

Thompson, C E Mrs (or S E ?) (sold *Lobster Fishers*, Sotheby's)

Thwaites, Addison Road, London

Tooth (1898) (this may be Arthur Tooth & Son Gallery)

Turner, H T, Stockleigh House, North Gate, Regents Park

Vaughan, H, 28 Cumberland Terrace, London

Vivian

Wallace, Sir R, Hertford House, Manchester Square, London

Wark, J. (died 1905)

Watson, J (1888–91)

Weir, James (1894–95)

White, E F

Whyte, J G

Wyllie, C C

Wyllie, W J (1888–89)

# APPENDIX 2

## Sales of etchings, prints, engravings from Hunter's own accounts

(Hunter added notes in the last column.)

| Title | Mount size (inches) | Sold to | |
|---|---|---|---|
| **A western shore** | 14.75 × 8.25 | Miss Miller | |
| | | David Gill | |
| | | Duncan Campbell | |
| | | Dowdeswell & Son | special vellum |
| | | Gent (?) Moncrieff | |
| **Friendly Aid Towing** | 14 × 8.25 | Mrs Dennistoun | |
| **Mussel Gatherers** | 10.75 × 6.75 | David Gill | published in july Art Magazine |
| | | Miss Miller | |
| | | Mrs Drew | |
| **Lowering sail** | 22.5 × 13.5 | Wm Black[108] | |
| | | Mrs Drew | |
| | | David Gill | |
| | | Mr G G Moncrieff | |
| | | Haliwell | |
| | | J G Whyte | |
| **Tarbert wet day** | 9 × 5.5 | Mr D Scott Moncrieff | |
| | | Wm Black | |
| | | J G Whyte | |
| **Shaking the nets** | 11 × 8 | Miss Miler | published in the portfolio |
| | | Mrs Drew | |
| **Etching of the Gareloch** | 23.75 × 13 | Mrs Drew | |
| | | C C Wylie | |
| | | Wm Black | |
| | | Moncrieff | |
| | | Dr David Gill | |
| | | Frank Powell | |
| | | Mrs Dennistoun | |
| | | Dr Inules (?) | |

---

108 William Black, novelist, Glasgow 1841–1898 Brighton. He bequeathed his Hunter pictures to his sister Mrs Morton. Also see **Black's Tower**, page 35

# BIBLIOGRAPHY

*Artists at Home*, The Holland Park Circle 1850–1900, Caroline Dakers, Exhibition Catalogue Leighton House Museum 29 November 1999 – 26 February 2000

*Benezit Dictionary of British Graphic Artists and Illustrators*, Oxford University Press USA 2012

Database of National Biographies

*Dictionary of Scottish Painters 1600–1960*, Harris & Halsby, pub Canongate Books 1990

*Edwardian Pre-Raphaelites, The Art of John and Mary Young Hunter*, Pyms Gallery 2000

*G F Watts in Kensington*, Barbara Bryant, Watts Gallery 2009

*Kensington Past*, Barbara Denny & Carolyn Starren, Historical Publications Ltd, 1998

*Painting Labour in Scotland and Europe 1850–1900*, John Morrison, Ashgate Publishing 2014

Royal Academy Pictures

*Reviewing the Years*, John Young-Hunter, Crown Publishers Inc, New York, 1963

*The British Seas*, W Clark Russell, pub Seeley, London 1892

*The Holland Estate Since 1874*, Survey of London: Vol 37

The Album of the Scottish Artists Club 1892

*The Art of Colin Hunter ARA*, R C Trafford, The Windsor Magazine, 1912 No. 214

*The Kensington Book*, Carolyn Starren, Historical Publications Ltd, 2006

*The Notting Hill & Holland Park Book*, Richard Tames, Historical Publications Ltd, 2004

Numerous internet search sources

# INDEX OF ART WORKS

## Hunter's pictures: a lifetime of art works

Most of these pictures are as named by Hunter himself, but some are variations on his names or are titles given by others (e.g. auctioneers, galleries, individual owners) in later years.

Many pictures have not been found and have been referenced only once somewhere in Hunter's records or in exhibition catalogues.

Where years are provided these may refer to the date painted, or sold, or exhibited. Multiple dates may suggest the sale of an etching of an earlier original painting.

---

109  North Britain

---

110 *Glasgow Herald*, Monday 4 April 1881

111 *The Art Journal*, April 1885

112 Royal Scottish Academy of Art & Architecture

# GENERAL INDEX